Designs of Darkness

Designs of Darkness

Interviews with Detective Novelists

Diana Cooper-Clark

Bowling Green State University Popular Press
Bowling Green, Ohio 43403

Acknowledgements

Four of the interviews in this book were previously published and are being reprinted with the permission of *The Armchair Detective* and *Clues*.

"Ruth Rendell," *The Armchair Detective,* Vol. 14, No. 2, 1981.
"Peter Lovesey," *The Armchair Detective,* Vol. 14, No. 3, 1981.
"Patricia Highsmith," *The Amrchair Detective,* Vol. 14, No. 4, 1981.
"Anne Perry," *Clues,* Vol. 3, No. 2, 1982.

All photographs by *Trevor Clark*

... All the plays that have
ever been written, from ancient
Greece to the present day,
have never really been anything
but thrillers.
Drama's always been realistic
and there's always been a
detective about. Every
play's an investigation brought
to a successful conclusion.
There's a riddle, and it's
solved in the final scene.
Sometimes
earlier. Might as well give the
game away at the
start.

Ionesco: Choubert, *Victims of Duty*

And any explanation will satisfy:
We only ask to be reassured
About the noises in the cellar
And the window that should not have
been open.
Why do we all behave as if the door
might suddenly open, the
curtain be drawn,
The cellar make some dreadful
disclosure, the roof disappear,
And we should cease to be sure of
what is real or unreal?
Hold tight, hold tight, we must insist
that the world is what we have
always taken it to be....

Eliot: Chorus, *The Family Reunion*

"Do violence to no man"—**St. Luke 3.14.**

Contents

Dedication

To my husband, Trevor, and to my mother and father, with love.

Acknowledgements

I would like to thank the secretarial services at York University for the excellent job they did in transcribing the interviews from the tapes and then typing the book. My sincere thanks to the writers in the book for their many kindnesses, hospitality and marvelous interviews.

And finally my thanks to my husband Trevor for all his patience, support and love in addition to his superb photographs of the writers.

Introduction

There was a time when I was a snob. I do not mean in the sense that I was fastidious in my search for excellence. No! I was a snob in the smallest sense. My snobbery was based on ignorance. Until a few years ago, I hadn't read any detective or crime literature with the exceptions of Ross Macdonald and Patricia Highsmith, both of whom I greatly admired. Since I have always disliked those people who reject something even though they remain uninformed about it, I decided to leave this objectionable company. I did not want to be like the character in one of Wilfrid Sheed's novels: "Betty went away to college where, like everyone else, she majored in condescension." This, in conjunction with my own personal discovery of the pervasive power of both overt and subliminal negative cultural attitudes toward detective fiction, and my recognition that this was the one major gap in my literary education, was the first step leading to my acquaintance with the world of detective and crime fiction.

Some writers of detective fiction, such as Nicolas Freeling, conspire in this attitude of condescension. A few years ago, he discussed why he had written his novels about Inspector Van der Valk of the Amsterdam police: "His beginning... sprang from my boredom with existing crime writers' platitudes.... Was not the answer to present a crime tale that introduced people one could care about, with problems that were ours?" Robert Fulford, the editor of *Saturday Night*, in Canada, rightly objected that Freeling "had to label himself an explorer even though the territory was already well mapped." If detective fiction is indeed the "bastard baby" of literature, consigned to that position by the literary nabobs, I will not insult the fine writers in this book by defending or analysing their work in those terms. After all, who wants to be the tallest pygmy?

The prejudice against the detective novel is seen in many ways. For one, most reviews of detective novels are relegated to what the critic Anthony Boucher called the "ghetto page." Or, we can see the

1

prejudice in more insidious ways. William Goldman is an example of the "divide and conquer" strategy. He undoubtedly thought he was paying Ross Macdonald a compliment when he wrote that Macdonald had transcended the genre in which he writes. Macdonald has refused to play that game and be elevated to "serious" literature. In other words, to be legitimized. He has repeatedly stated that he writes detective novels. He has worked to extend the possibilities of the genre as have many of the other writers represented in this book.

As I started to read these novels, Jacques Barzun reassured me that detective stories have always been written for and by highbrows. Phillip Guedalla considered them "the normal recreation of noble minds." Q.D. Leavis also soothed that detective fiction was a "highbrow cult." But at this point in my emancipating education, snobbery was still in my blood, to use George Eliot's phrase. I was pulled further into my reading because of my awareness that great writers and critics took the genre seriously. A few years ago, I was asked to do a book review article on J.I.M. Stewart's critical biography of Thomas Hardy. It was while I was writing this article that I discovered that he was Michael Innes. I was impressed that a scholar such as this wrote detective stories. What could I be missing if writers as diverse and as good as T.S. Eliot, William Faulkner, Jorges Luis Borges, William Burroughs, Donald Barthelme, W.H. Auden, W.B. Yeats, George Bernard Shaw, Heinrich Böll, Ellen Glasgow, Edith Wharton, Arthur Miller and even Bertrand Russell, not only were interested but also used and/or extended the form of the genre or wrote critical articles about it? What did great critics such as Joseph Wood Krutch, Northrop Frye, Geoffrey Hartman and Jacques Barzun know that I didn't?

As I started to read more and more, I found that there was little written about the writers I admired and almost nothing of any depth. Therefore the seed for this book was planted there. Margaret Atwood, the Canadian novelist, has said that Canadian books are like "snails" on a gourmet shelf in the bookstores in that they are *not* treated as books but as a Canadian gourmet specialty. For me, the novels of the writers in this book and other fine detective novels were novels, not snails. In addition to the genuine pleasure these writers gave me, my reading of detective fiction forced me to re-evaluate my perception of literature and my aesthetics of the novel. It was helpful to me to pursue Jorge Luis Borges's hint in *Other Inquisitions, 1937-*

1952 that G.K. Chesterton's Father Brown stories influenced his own writing. For instance, both employ mirrors and masks to explore their interest in good and evil, identity, and the artist's sense of self. As Father Brown clarifies: "For the enjoyment of the artist the mask must be to some extent moulded on the face. What he makes outside him must correspond to something inside him; he can only make his effects out of some of the materials of his soul... an artist will betray himself by some sort of sincerity" ("The Dagger With Wings").[1]

Mostly, my reading raised many questions. My introduction can only hope to reflect part of the motion of my mind rather than produce the book length answers the questions surely deserve. What has the term "greatness" come to mean in our time? Why is our certifiably great literature inaccessible to many contemporary readers? Can great literature be read by most people or is it by definition exclusive? How is it that illiterate (in both the connotative and denotative sense) people in the past were fully conversant with the House of Atreus yet university students today can sometimes hardly pronouce their names, much less remember them? The compartmentalization of art into "high" and "low" prevents the connections that would make our aesthetic awareness fuller, richer, more profound. Perhaps the Ife tribe in Africa is on to something. They have no word for art. Their word for art is life. These questions must always be before us. They are not tired; they are necessary. In its time, Spenser's *The Faerie Queene* was considered to be pandering to a middlebrow appetite for tales of dragons, courageous knights and beautiful maidens. Today, this epic is thought to be "high" art. Is it that his allusions and allegories are unobtainable to most and therefore flatters those readers who can enter his inner *sanctum sanctorum* of knowledge? Is the inaccessible the "best" to which only a select few are privy? There are writers who do not care whether or not they communicate with the community as a whole. The English poet Swinburne wanted to communicate only with people like himself—educated, erudite and with like sensibility. However, there are writers such as the novelist Toni Morrison (*Song of Solomon* and *Tar-Baby*), who wish to have a wider readership: "I could make a book to which one has a visceral response and is exciting to non-readers, and at the same time has a lot of food for people of fastidious intellect. That's what I'd like to do, to do both."[2] This is certainly an attractive ideal but difficult to do. Toni Morrison does it and so do a significant number of detective and crime writers. In a time when, as Roland Barthes has said, "reading is a form of work," detective literature is interested in communicating with readers. In a time of structuralism, post-structuralism, deconstruction, semiotic analyses of Agatha Christie and Arthur Conan Doyle, what is wrong in saying that a book is lucid?

Why does Borges in his introduction to his *Ficciones* describe "The Garden of the Forking Paths" as a detective story? Why don't writers such as Thomas Hardy, Dostoevski, Robertson Davies, Shakespeare, Euripedes, Robert Browning, Camus, James Dickey, Walker Percy and John Cheever, who all use murder as an organic part of specific works, suffer the opprobrium that detective writers do? (I do not agree with those who argue that murder in "great" literature is peripheral to what the particular novel, poem, short story, or play is really about. Would Faulkner's "A Rose for Emily" be possible, both structurally and contextually, without the murder of Homer? Doesn't the murder in Camus's *The Stranger* serve as the nucleus for much of what he wants to say?) What is it *exactly* that makes these writers greater than the best writers in detective and crime fiction? If the considerable bibliography on the relationship between the nouveau roman and the detective novel (in both form and content) is at all pertinent, then should not major writers of detective fiction stand beside Alain Robbe-Grillet, Nathalie Sarraute, Michel Butor and Marguerite Duras?

How and why are *Oedipus Rex, The Aeneid*, The Arabian Nights and the tales of Chaucer antecedents of the detective story? Why did Cleanth Brooks consider Faulkner's novel *Absalom, Absalom* "a wonderful detective story"? When Cynthia Grenier asked Faulkner if he read detective stories, he replied, "Well, I like a good one like *Brothers Karamazov*." Of course Faulkner is known for his playfulness but he was obviously drawn to the detective story.[3] What was it that drew him? How is it reflected in _is work? What does he see in Dostoevski that reminds him of detective fiction? Is the world of mystery stories too tidy? Wouldn't it be possible to do what Doris Lessing did in *The Golden Notebook* in her effort to write a "messy" book that would be commensurate to the messiness of life?

One of the answers that several have offered to the question of "why" the detective novel is inferior to its mainstream counterpart is that the plot or story is the focus. Andrew Lang reflected this in his response to Dickens: "Dickens was not, in Francis Meres's phrase, 'our best plotter.' In the mechanical construction of a puzzle plot (a low branch of the art of fiction) he could not shine." Hillary Waugh, the novelist and a past president of the Mystery Writers of America, has expanded this idea: "There is, . . . a whole universe beyond the tightly fenced realm of the mystery, a universe wherein only the straight novelist roams. In this vast otherworld lie challenges not available to the mystery author, and demands of craft that are not imposed upon him. Herein resides the fact that the great names in literature belong to the novel, not to the mystery!.... The mystery novel does not contain the equipment to carry messages. It is too frail a box to hold the human spirit. It allows an author to speak, but not to explore and instruct. The credo can be expressed as follows: "If you want to write and have nothing to say, write a mystery. If you have other ambitions, the mystery form had best be eschewed.... In the mystery novel, the story is the core, the be-all, the end-all, the Heart of the Matter. This is its glory, and its liability. This is what sets it apart from the straight novel. This is why it doesn't serve the purposes of the straight novelist. The author of a straight novel has other fish to fry. His aim is not to puzzle the reader or tell him stories. His basic aim isn't even to entertain. He writes for all the other reasons: to save himself, to objectify his life, to express his preoccupations and concerns with the human condition. He writes, more often than not, because he has to write, to get the monkey off his back. Sometimes he is consciously trying to send messages, to argue a cause, put forth a concept, or present a viewpoint, but for the most part his statements are not consciously expressed. The insights he puts forth, for however much or little they are worth, lie hidden in the depths of his prose. They are sought for and argued over by critics, if the ore that is found is deemed worth the mining."[4] Nobel Prize winner, Isaac Bashevis Singer, is one who would disagree. Story-telling is the focus of his intent. In response to Mr. Waugh's list of reasons why authors write, I would add this one. When asked why she wrote Flannery O'Connor replied, "Because I write well." On behalf of the writers in this book, I would apply O'Connor's answer to them.

Is the form of detective fiction too closed to move from the guiding hand of the authorial narrative to the possibilities of reader participation? Leading contemporary novelists, most notably the Latin Americans, often invite the reader to participate in the composition and creation of the novel. There is an interest in having both reader and author observe the author in the act of creating fiction. I suppose we have to ask whether this is a valuable experience for the reader. Or is it possible for all people to reach the level of the author's imagination? Jean Stubbs admits that the detective novel does dish up the entire meal to the reader who only has to eat it. But so does much of nineteenth century literature and that hasn't hurt the reputations of Thackeray, Carlyle, Eliot, Meredith, Stendhal, Tolstoy or Mark Twain, to name a few. On the other hand, a writer like Julio Cortázar finds nineteenth-century writing extremely limited. Obviously, aesthetic swordsmen must declare their bias before they begin to parry. Perhaps we should accept the conventions of the detective story just as we accept the conventions of other forms—the sonnet, the dramatic monologue, masques, the epic poem, Horatian or Juvenalian satire, Aristotelian or Elizabethan tragedy. Northrop Frye has written: "Now if we do find wit, lively plotting, vivid characterization, or cogent social comment in detective stories—and it is not so difficult to find such things—we should appreciate the author's ingenuity in getting good writing into so ritualistic a form. The right next step for criticism, it seems to me, is not to assume that there is a difference in value between detective fiction and other types of fiction, but to realize that all fiction is conventionalized, and that it is equally a *tour de force* of ingenuity to get good characterization and social insight into a story as complicated as *Tom Jones* or *Emma*, both of which also contain mysteries impelling us to continue reading until we reach the solution."[5] Is it possible to respond to detective fiction at the same level that we respond to traditional romances and epics of the past? Our pleasure could derive from the same sources as these, in the artful variation of the familiar as Zahava K. Dorinson has suggested. What is valuable is not the unique creativity of the artist, the creation of new meanings, new forms, new events, but his inventiveness in expressing traditional meanings, manipulating traditional forms, recounting familiar kinds of events so that they remain fresh and intriguing.

Does detective fiction have a function that expands the boundaries of literature? At the beginning of *Shikasta*, Doris Lessing has written in defense of another bastard baby, science fiction: "These dazzlers... have played the indispensable and (at least at the start) thankless role of the despised illegitimate son who can afford to tell truths the respectable siblings either do not dare, or, more likely, do not notice because of their respectability." Similarly, Ross Macdonald agrees in his discussion of detective fiction in A Preface to *The Galton Case*: "...the literary detective has provided writers since Poe with a disguise, a kind of welder's mask enabling us to handle dangerously hot material." Joyce Carol Oates has written that "art is built around violence, around death; at its base is fear. The absolute dream, if dreamed, must deal with death, and the only way toward death we understand is the way of violence."[6] If she is right, why hasn't the best of detective fiction taken an honorable place in the hallowed halls of the literary establishment?

How have writers such as John Fowles in "The Enigma," Julio Cortázar in *The Blow-Up and Other Stories* and Heinrich Böll in *The Lost Honour of Katherina Blum* used the established form of the detective story to pursue their own complex literary purposes? I wish David Madden had explained why Saul Bellow's *Mr. Sammler's Planet*, Norman Mailer's *An American Dream*, Thomas Pynchon's *V.* and *The Crying of Lot 49*, and John Hawkes' *The Lime Twig* are contemporary ironic detective fictions.[7] I would love to know.

Why doesn't Canada have a tradition of detective fiction when countries like Japan do? Where are the fountains from which a Canadian writer such as Howard Engel must drink? What is it like to be writing your first detective novel in a country with no detective genre? Why has Canada never developed this genre, given that violence, murder and death are at the heart of its mainstream fiction? What will be the indigenous characteristics of the Canadian detective novel?

I will not attempt here to explore the connections between mainstream literature and detective or crime fiction. Although Bernard A. Schopen has written that "no serious student of prose fiction has ever suggested that the detective story manifests the qualities and characteristics which constitute the generic requirements of the novel,"[8] a number of authors and scholars would disagree. Also, I would suggest that the generic requirements of the novel would be as virulently open to debate as would be the arguments concerning the worth of detective fiction. Nor will I attempt to explore who reads detective fiction or why they do. I don't know whether or not people read detective stories to sublimate their aggressions or to feel less impotent in a chaotic world or to find their identity or to escape to an ordered world or to experience vicarious thrills or to re-enact mythic rituals or to recreate their childhood apprehension of the "primal scene." I will leave that to psychologists, sociologists, theologians, philosophers, ethologists and literary critics.

As detective literature has become more "respectable," university courses on detective fiction have proliferated. There is now an extensive bibliography of scholarly books and articles and a growing number of specialty stores devoted to mystery fiction. "Respectability" has its price, however. Absurd comparisons are sometimes the result. Did you know that Agatha Christie's plots are Aristotelian or that Mickey Spillane is a twentieth century Jacobean? In their desperation to find a generic foundation, a category, in which to put detective fiction, the critics often wear the face of Polonius. Raymond Chandler was probably right when he wrote in 1950 that "the average critic never recognizes an achievement when it happens. He explains it after it has become respectable." The categories are provided not only by the critics but also by the writers as well and they have several touchstones: Stanley Ellin is regarded in Germany as an expressionistic writer in the Germanic mode; if we so choose, we can look at the hermeneutic aspect of the crime novel; Dick Allen and David Chacko refer to Henry James's "psychological" mystery story, "The Tree of Knowledge"; the detective story can also be read as a twentieth century fairy tale or folktale, a fiction closely allied to myth.[9] G.K. Chesterton remarked that, "No one can have failed to notice that in these stories the hero crosses cities with something of the loneliness and liberty of a prince in a tale of elfland, that in the course of that incalculable journey the casual automobile assumes the primal colours of a fairy ship." Northrop Frye puts detective stories in the convention of the romance: "The reading of an individual romance, say a detective story... may be in itself a trivial enough imaginative experience. But a study of the whole convention of... detective stories would tell us a great deal about the shape of stories as a whole, and that, in its turn, would begin to give us some glimpse of still larger verbal structures, eventually of the mythological universe itself."[10]

The modern sensibility has been trained by Dostoevski and Freud, by Nietzche and Kierkegaard, by Eliot and Yeats, to see the ambiguous, the ambivalent, and the amorphous as the most profound and appropriate vision of human existence. We have moved from man's rage for order to man's rage for chaos. Given this persuasion, clarity, conclusions and communally shared communication, therefore, seem to be simplistic and one-dimensional as a response to modern life. I think that this is one reason why detective fiction has been considered trivial. Although its world is dark, it is a designed darkness. The darkness has a structured quality that moves toward the light of order. This is a reason why the composer John Cage never "got into mystery books:"

> mY notion
> iS
> that mystery's What
> lIfe is:
> we Need
> Not to know.

But several contemporary detective novels, such as P.D. James's *Death of an Expert Witness*, concludes with an order that doesn't quite compensate for the shattered remnants that remain of the victims' lives. Although social and cosmic order is restored in Shakespeare's tragedies, his plays nevertheless refer us back to Lear's "unaccommodated man" and Macbeth's "tomorrow, and tomorrow, and tomorrow" soliloquy.

The contemporary reader has also been trained to see the non-plot novel as more profound, more complex. Jacques Barzun has said that the "plot" is no longer felt to be necessary because it has been transferred to the psyche—and that's where things tangle and either resolve or don't resolve themselves. Of course, this also provides some writers greater license to be sloppy and disguise their lack of craft. Plot is essential to the detective story but plot melds with psyche, atmosphere and meaning in the work of most of the writers in this book. In her appraisal of Ruth Rendell's novels, Jane Bakerman says that the emphasis falls as much upon the "who" as upon the "done it."

Criticism in the twentieth century, most particularly the New Criticism, was basically a revolt against the Aristotelian and the Western humanistic traditions. This critical spirit found an analogue in the influence of the East. We were exposed to a new way of seeing. We were urged to move beyond our formulas for exegetics, our rational modes of thought, our linear perception of the world, into a world that redefined and even rejected coherence. The revolt took its form in a rejection of "prose" in favor of "poetry," a rejection of linear plots and chronological time in favor of time that is telescoped, simultaneous and circular, a rejection of the closed ending, the resolution, in favor of an open or on-going non-conclusion, a rejection of books and even sentences with beginnings, middles and ends, a rejection of the well-made play or novel (*la pièce bien faite*), and a rejection of the conscious, rational world in favor of the subconscious, the irrational. Within this critical sensibility, the detective novel would seem archaic and hopelessly minor.

It has been suggested that the roots of the crime or detective story are to be found in such different places as the Bible and, according to Régis Messac, in the account of Archimedes' discovery of the principle of liquid displacement, while investigating a possible crime. But contemporary detective fiction has evolved considerably from its roots. The interviews in this book focus on some of these changes. The detective story has often been accused of being no more than a mind tease of the most trivial kind. Throughout the twentieth century there has been a movement away from the puzzle to more complex characterization and a greater emphasis on human values. Respected critics such as Northrop Frye, Richard Chase and David Lodge agree that developed characterization is a salient characteristic of the novel. Sheldon Sacks, in *Fiction and the Shape of Belief*, has stated that the novel requires "characters about whose fates we are made to care." Joseph T. Shaw, the editor of the magazine *Black Mask*, printed stories like this. He said that "... in this new pattern, character conflict is the main theme; the ensuing crime, or its threat, is incidental." As early as 1930 Anthony Berkeley Cox, author of *Panic Party*, wrote that the detective novel was gradually "holding its readers less by mathematical than by psychological ties." In 1937 Michael Innes' Appleby declared that detective stories "always have a psychological drift now." Contemporary novels explore the genuinely mysterious and irreconcilable more fully. Life is the mystery story as well as "who-done-it." Reason does not triumph so cleanly or clearly. The mystery is not so much "who-done-it" but "why-done-it."

Detectives have also changed considerably. They are not such fantasy figures nor are they omnipotent. Adam Dalgleish is tragic and Robert B. Parker's tough, wise-cracking Spenser cries when he has taken a life. They reflect the ambivalence of the world they live in while retaining personal and not necessarily socially sanctioned codes of honor. Evil is not so cut-and-dried. The detective may well have the seeds of corruption within himself. Contemporary detective fiction can and does depart from narrowly relevant details that lead to the inevitable solution. We can learn as much about photography in Dick Francis' *Reflex*, Victorian sports in Peter Lovesey's novels, and nuclear devices in Nicolas Freeling's *Gadget*, as we can learn about quantitative history or creative computer mathematics in the novels of Marge Piercy (*The High Cost of Living* and *Small Changes* respectively) or the physical sciences in Thomas Pynchon's *Gravity's Rainbow*. The details are intrinsic to the meaning of all of these novels.

In addition to those notions already touched upon in this introduction, the interviews look at these ideas: the mirror image of the criminal and the policeman/detective (in "Inspector Maigret Pursues," Georges Simenon writes "a curious intimacy has sprung up between follower and followed...." The similarity of the criminal and the policeman can sometimes generate satire such as in John Gay's *The Beggar's Opera* but the writers in this book are looking at something deeper—the possibility of evil in all of us); the presence of women as characters and as authors (Michele Slung has written that women are more lethal because of their historical camouflage and look at how well Laura in Jean Stubbs's *Dear Laura* uses this to her advantage); murder as a perversion of the creative instinct (the narrator in Graham Greene's short story "The Destructors" says "destruction... is a form of creation," Valentin in G.K. Chesterton's "The Blue Cross" says, "the criminal is the creative artist; the detective only the critic," and W.H. Auden considered murder to be "negative creation"); the writer's response to the growing critical response to detective fiction; the limits and the possibilities of the genre; and, needless to say, the writers' work.

I started as an uninformed snob. Where am I now? I must confess that I am not a "buff." But I am firmly committed to the excellence of the writers in this book. Among the past masters I particularly enjoy G.K. Chesterton, Raymond Chandler, Josephine Tey and Robert van Gulik. I find books that are not strictly within the genre, such as J.B. Priestley's *The Shapes of Sleep*, C.P. Snow's *A Coat of Varnish* and the writing of Friedrich Dürrenmatt, utterly intriguing. There are others that I have read and doubtlessly many meritorious that I have not read or perhaps have read but do not particularly like. But the point is that I have learned much and enjoyed fully. Dorothy Salisbury Davis, mystery writer and a longtime mystery editor of the late *New York Herald Tribune*, sums it up very well in her introduction to the 1958 *Anthology of Stories by the Mystery Writers of America*, which she edited: "I have a feeling that so long as contemplative man walks the city streets, the country roads, musing on the ways and wonders of his fellows, seeking the predicate in that which was unpredictable but happened nonetheless, so long as there is surprise in love, joy in discovery, fear in the unknown, honor in courage, and humor in the ironic, so long will the detective story discover for man."

Diana Cooper-Clark
Toronto

Notes

[1] For a more detailed discussion see Robert Gillespie, "Detections: Borges and Father Brown," *Novel*, 7, Spring 1974.

[2] My interview with Toni Morrison, Oct. 25, 1980.

[3] For greater discussions, see the following: Peter J. Rabinowitz, "The Click of the Spring: The Detective Story as Parallel Structure in Dostoyevsky and Faulkner,"*Modern Philology*, 76, no. 4, 1979: 355-369; Mark Gidley, "Elements of the Detective Story in William Faulkner's Fiction," *Journal of Popular Culture*, 7, no. 1, 1973: 97-123; and Warren French, "William Faulkner and the Art of the Detective Story," in *The Thirties: Fiction, Poetry, Drama*, ed. Warren French (Deland, Fl. 1967), pp. 55-62.

[4] Hillary Waugh, "The Mystery Versus The Novel," in *The Mystery Story*, ed. John Ball (Middlesex, 1978), pp. 74-76.

[5] Northrop Frye, *The Secular Scripture: A Study of the Structure of Romance* (Cambridge, Mass., 1976), pp. 44-45.

[6] Joyce Carol Oates, *The Edge of Impossibility: Tragic Forms in Literature* (London, 1976), p. 7.

[7] David Madden, "Thomas Berger's Comic-Absurd Vision in Who is Teddy Villanova?", *The Armchair Detective*, 14, no. 1, 1981, p. 37.

[8] Bernard A. Schopen, "From Puzzles to People: The Development of the American Detective Novel," *Studies in American Fiction*, 7, 1979, p. 175.

[9] For a good detailed study, see Nadya Aisenberg, *A Common Spring: Crime Novel and Classic* (Bowling Green, Oh.: Popular Press, 1979).

[10] Frye, *The Secular Scripture*, p. 60.

Interview with P.D. James

Diana Cooper-Clark

DCC: You have said that one of the reasons that you started writing detective fiction was that it would be a useful apprenticeship for someone who wanted to be a serious novelist. This may be a tired question, but are you suggesting that even the best detective novel is inferior to the best novels written outside the genre?

PDJ: No, I don't think so. I have been writing for over twenty years and at the time I made this decision I certainly thought that the formula, though interesting, would be too restrictive really for a serious novelist. Then, after I had done three or four novels, I realized that in fact the restriction of a form could almost help, in a sense, by imposing a discipline and that you could be a serious novelist within it. When I began, I think I would have said, not that detective mysteries were necessarily worse written, (I thought in many cases they were a great deal better written than many more pretentious novels) but simply that if you set out to be a serious novelist, you wouldn't probably wish to restrict yourself to what was basically formula writing.

DCC: Would you say that formula writing is limited in a way that other writing isn't, and for the worse?

PDJ: Well, I think for the worse.

DCC: Of course, because the detective novel had a plot, a beginning, a middle and an end, the writer was not allowed to indulge himself or herself in the same way that other writers may, and still be acclaimed nevertheless.

PDJ: The self-indulgence of so many novels is artistically bad and makes them worse novels. As I said, the very fact that there are constraints can, in fact, be helpful to a certain kind of novelist and that's why I don't think that the detective novel is an inferior genre, although the books may be inferior. But when I began, I thought that anyone setting out to be a serious novelist wouldn't set out specifically to restrict herself to the conventions of the orthodox mystery, certainly not throughout her writing career.

DCC: Which you haven't done.

PDJ: No.

DCC: Should we re-examine the critical standards and the critical methodologies that we use to interpret and evaluate detective fiction?

PDJ: Many people are doing just this, really. I suppose that because there are very many detective books written which can't lay claim to being a novel in any real sense of the word and which are just intended to be a popular entertainment and no more, quite a number of people do categorize the whole genre and say, well, there are novels and there are mysteries. I think there is quite a substantial body of critical opinion by some academics and certainly quite a number of reviewers who have long since stopped doing that. It probably is not helpful but nevertheless, mysteries tend to be reviewed together as if they are total categories. It is generally accepted now that it is a very interesting form and, in a sense, a modern morality play and that very good work is done within the restriction. After all, it is just as silly to say that you can't write a novel within these conventions as it is to say you can't write a good play if it has three acts. How on earth can you say something is not true about human beings just because you use the orthodox stage and you have a first, second and third act or that you can't write a great poem if you use the sonnet form? There are people who prefer to use the sonnet form because they find it an absolute challenge to write a poem within the strict rhyming sequence, fourteen lines. There are writers who find it a challenge to use the mystery as a vehicle for saying something true about human beings or about society.

DCC: Do you think that critical perception as a discipline is helpful either to the writer or the reader? Or does it obfuscate the novel?

PDJ: Most people will read sensitive popular critics, that is, the reviewers one has confidence in and who say what they think about the book (and sometimes having to say it within a very short compass) and perhaps make a decision as to whether they want to buy the book or get it from the library. The in-depth criticism probably doesn't reach a large number of, as it were, common readers. The reader is going to depend really on the general literary section of his paper. Perhaps it's difficult for me to judge because I have been so very lucky in my reviews. It seems to me that in most of the articles I have read, the writers have understood what I have been trying to do and certainly haven't grossly misrepresented the work. To that degree, I may be fortunate. But this may be because I write within the genre and don't get so much in-depth critical attention as I would do if I was regarded as a mainstream novelist. With the shorter reviews, I think that the mystery often does get a bit neglected. The reviewer tends to have perhaps ten, fifteen more books to do and very short, very pat reviews that perhaps take half an inch. I don't think one could say very much about a novel in that way and that perhaps is a mistake. On the other hand, one of the virtues of this kind of popular reviewing is that you do get different opinions on a large number of books. Whereas I am sure it must be awful to be a playwright when there are certain highly acclaimed, reputable reviewers, and what they say is going to determine whether that play stays on. I think this must be terrifying. I don't know what the answer to this is. At least with a novel, it has been produced, it will be there in the shops. These reviews may decide whether it is going to be very popular and a success, financial and otherwise, but people are going to be able to gain access to it even if the reviews are bad.

DCC: Your novels are much written about but, as you have said, no one has done an in-depth critical analysis of your writing. Would you like to see someone produce an intensive critical response to your work?

PDJ: I don't think I would particularly like it; I don't think I would dislike it; I don't think I would get obsessed by this sort of thing really. I write books basically because I need to write them. I write them to please myself and I do the very best I can with them. If I am going to be fortunate with a particular book and the critics like it, and the readers like it, and it sells well, this is, of course, immensely gratifying. I suppose when people have come, usually from America, to interview me because they want to do articles which are going to look at me in depth, this is also gratifying. Nobody, I suppose, welcomes neglect but I don't think that I would be awake worrying what they were going to say about the books.

DCC: Nathaniel Hawthorne said that he wanted to write about the mystery of the human heart. You do this in all of your work. What is that mystery?

PDJ: Any novelist is concerned with human beings; any novelist is concerned with the mysteries of the human heart. I don't think that one can give an easy or glib answer to this because every single human being is an individual. I suppose what I am interested in really is the compulsions and the expediences which people devise to enable them to face reality.

DCC: It has been suggested that a crucial element in detective fiction is that the reader identifies both with the detective and the criminal; that the detective and the criminal are opposite sides of the same figure; that, as Julian Symons has said, the detective and the murderer are the light and dark sides of the reader's nature. Do you agree with that?

PDJ: I do to one extent. I think this is what we mean when we say that detective fiction may be a substitute for the old morality plays. Certainly in detective fiction, right does triumph and wrong is punished, if not in this world, in the next, as it were. The problem is solved and this is the difference perhaps between crime fiction and detective fiction; and the detective who is a kind of avenging, judgmental figure is always successful. I can't think of any novels in which the whole of the investigation is a total fiasco. This wouldn't, I think, then fall within the genre. But on a fairly low level, the detective is the light and the murderer is the dark. In modern mysteries, it is less simple because the detectives are becoming much more complicated and more psychologically interesting so that within the detective you get the dark and the light. He is no longer just a figure representing the good part of man's nature. He may have within his personality the seeds of corruption which he undoubtedly does have. He may do things that he knows himself are immoral, unethical, wrong, he may deceive and trap and betray. He may in his relationships with other people, particularly his subordinates, be less than fair. Because the detective is increasingly becoming a human being, that part of his personality which is evil has to be shown. So, to an extent, this destroys the old idea that you have the good and evil, the dark and the light.

DCC: I do see that moral ambiguity in modern literature. You have said that in your writing you would like to release the reader from the anxieties of the modern world. I feel sometimes that the detective novel eases the reader's sense of impotence in a modern world full of uncontrollable forces and violence. Do you feel that a prime function of detective fiction, in fact all fiction, is a cathartic one?

PDJ: No, I don't think it is. I am surprised I said that actually because I don't think that is what I am trying to do. That is what happens with a great deal of detective fiction because it does release us from the anxieties of the modern world. But I don't think I set out to do that. There are books which are essentially tragic and some of the characters are tragic. The genre as a whole can serve that function, in fact, I think it does serve it. Paradoxically, the less well written the novel is, the more it relates to the strict formula, the more it is able to do this. It does it, first of all, because (and this is true also of my books) the philosophical basis of the novel is that murder is a unique crime which is uniquely wrong and that however unpleasant a character may be, however evil he may be, however disagreeable he may be, he still has the right to live his life to the last natural moment. If someone bludgeons him to death, then the forces of order, the forces of morality, in the figures of either the professional police force or the private eye, will come to bear on the crime to solve it and this is reassuring in an age which chooses violence. Then, of course, the books do provide a puzzle, and this is related to what you were saying, which is solved by human ingenuity and by logical deduction, in other words, by the human brain. I am sure that this is part of their appeal in a world in which we are increasingly coming to believe that so many of our social problems are literally beyond our capacity to solve and that we are at the mercy of vast impersonal forces, social and economic, against which we are absolutely powerless. Here is a genre in which the problem is solved and solved by human beings; order and justice and morality are then restored. I think as writers use the genre to write more realistic books, this kind of reassurance will be less effective. Even in *Death of an Expert Witness*, the problems are solved, Dalgleish is successful, but you leave behind a ruined family, two extremely vulnerable children, including a young child, now fatherless, probably going to be at the mercy of a neurotic mother; you have a young girl whose life has been, to an extent, contaminated by murder. Things are not the same afterwards. It isn't as simple as that to solve the problem; the problem may be solved but other problems are left unsolved, because these are problems of the human heart and problems about which perhaps nothing effective can be done.

DCC: This is certainly true. In Shakespeare's tragedies, order is always restored; murder affects not only the individual, the society, but also the balance of the whole cosmos. You have suggested this in *Death of an Expert Witness* when one of the characters says that murder is a "crime which contaminated everyone who it touched, innocent and guilty alike." You have both a sense of irrationality and reason in your writing. Very often, even though reason does triumph, because Adam Dalgleish is a man of reason, I find that irrationality always leads to dire consequences. It always leads to something destructive and chaotic. Do you put more faith in reason even though the whole shift of modern art has been to put more faith in the irrational, the absurd, the chaotic, both thematically and structurally? In our time, reason is often seen as stultifying, non-creative, arid, illusory.

PDJ: Oh, yes! I put my faith, such faith as I have, in rationality and in order, that is probably why Jane Austen is my favorite novelist.

DCC: There have been many suggestions about the history of the detective novel. Where do you think that its roots lie?

PDJ: I think there is a distinction really between the crime novel and the detective novel. Crime stories certainly go back before the Bible. It is rather interesting, isn't it, that you get Cain and Abel in the first stories in the Bible and this is the story of a murder. As far as the detective novel is concerned, it may have been Dorothy L. Sayers who thought it couldn't begin until you had got an ordered police force. I don't think the detective story as such could go back much beyond a time before society was reasonably ordered and there were accepted forces of law and order in that society. It can't go back much before early Victorian England.

DCC: How would you define the detective novel? How is it different from crime novels like *In Cold Blood* or *Compulsion*, aside from the fact that the murderer is known in the latter and they tend not to be known until the end in detective fiction?

PDJ: The detective novel has a death at the heart of it, a death which is mysterious. At the end of the book, we know what we didn't know to begin with, that is, who committed the murder, whereas in the crime novel we may know from the very beginning either who has done it or who is going to do it. Therefore, one of the prime interests in detective fiction is the solution of the mystery and why it happened. The prime interest in the crime novel may be the effect of this crime on the characters who come in touch with it or the effect of the crime on the murderer himself. In detective fiction you certainly do have justice personified or at least represented by a detective. You obviously couldn't have a detective novel which didn't have a detective. He doesn't have to be a member of an organized professional police force; he can be a private eye or in fact he can be an absolute amateur who has come in touch with the crime fortuitously and is able to solve it. In the crime novel, there may be no police from beginning to end or the police may play a very subservient role. I think the detective novel has a more ordered form, simply because the crime is solved. Inevitably there is a last chapter or a conclusion to the book in which there has to be an explanation that gives intellectual and one would hope emotional satisfaction. This comes from the tying up of loose ends and the resolution of the mystery. This certainly wouldn't be so in the crime novel. I think these are the main differences really.

DCC: What is the role of the detective now? Do you agree with Willard Huntington Wright that the detective should stand outside the action like a Greek chorus or do you agree with G.K. Chesterton that he or she should be regarded as a romantic hero, the protector of civilization? Or do you think that today the detective has a totally different function in the novel?

PDJ: To an extent the detective should stand outside the action. I can only talk about the books I write really. I wouldn't wish him to be a romantic figure, a sort of Sir Galahad in shining armour rescuing damsels and the innocent. I made my detective a very private and detached man who uses his job to save himself from involvement with other human beings because of tragedies in his own life. Now this seems to be quite logical for the detective because his job is to observe and to deduce. He is concerned not only with physical facts, material clues, but also with human nature. I think that this idea that he comes into the action from outside appeals to me for this reason really. You very seldom get the body on the very first page. I like to build up the situation in a usually closed society where the victim, the suspects, and obviously the murderer are together. You get the attentions, and resentments, and dislikes, the jealousies that can boil up. Then when the murder takes place, the detective comes in from the outside with his army of experts to solve it.

DCC: There is a strong tendency in Western civilization to romanticize and even admire the villain's bravado and quick-witted avoidance of capture, from picaresque novels like *Gil Blas* to the outlaws of the American West, and more recently Jacques Mesrine in France. Detective fiction reverses this and the reader's sympathy tends to be with the detective. How do you account for this dichotomy in our culture?

PDJ: I don't think I can account for it, I agree it is there. Most people's lives are fairly humdrum. This must be true of the great majority of human beings who inevitably have to spend their lives earning livings, seeing that they and their families have a roof over their heads and have to do it in jobs that are not always very interesting to them, perhaps for some forty years of their lives. It is inevitable that they must feel how wonderful if one could step outside these constraints and do something daring and antisocial. Therefore, they admire, to an extent, and identify with characters who do just that, who say, 'well, these are the rules and you are all living by them. I don't live by them, I live by my own. I do what I want to do and not only that, you see, but I get away with it.' He isn't going to get away but if he didn't then you couldn't romanticize or identify with him. He doesn't end up standing in a dock. A dock is a very symbolic thing; there the one figure stands with the rails around him, uniquely set off, where everybody is in judgment of him and this is what happens if you get caught. But these heroes don't get caught and they must be splendid identity figures. That probably is one kind of fantasy. The other is the fantasy that, 'yes the world is wicked and evil but there is a benevolent deity and there is a benevolent civil power looking after us,' and this is the fantasy that looks for the detective as a personification of order and reassurance and goodness. I suppose these are the two main fantasies and people choose which one really most suits their particular psychological needs.

DCC: Morality is a central part of classical British literature in general. The detective novel is a part of this British tradition. In your work, one aspect of this mainstream is the emphasis on upright moral behavior. E.M.W. Tillyard, in *The Elizabethan World Picture*, has said that English literature as a whole has spoken an idiom permeated with Christian dogma. In this respect the detective can perhaps be seen as the archetypal Moses or Joshua who instructs or guides a bewildered people and brings them to justice. Dalgleish in *Death of an Expert Witness* does not come down from a mountain but he does come down from a helicopter. The question of "justice" is debated beautifully in that book between Dr. Kerrison's daughter, Eleanor, and Dalgleish, when she questions him as to the validity of imprisoning the murderer when he cannot alter the crime, and then wonders whether the murderer who kills an old and dying man who has only one week to live should go to jail. Do you see this aspect of morality as an extension of concerns that are central to the British novel?

PDJ: The concern with public and private morality has always been central to the British novel in general. Certainly this applies to all the major English novelists in my judgment. With some writers, Graham Greene and Evelyn Waugh for example, the preoccupation is primarily religious and I think this is true, too, of such very different novelists as Jane Austen and Anthony Trollope who examined private and public morality in the light of generally accepted tenets of organized Christianity. One of the most interesting problems for the modern writer is that there is no longer any accepted philosophical or religious standard against which to judge private morality; we now make our own rules. But surely all major novelists are concerned with the values by which men and women perceive and live their private lives and the dichotomy between our desires and the rights and needs of others. They are concerned too with the way in which society attempts to reconcile private freedom with public order and with the precarious bridges of law which society erects over the underlying chaos of human nature.

DCC: One of the things that I have noticed in your novels is that sometimes you make the first murdered person eminently 'murderable' but the second victim is not. It is much harder for the reader to emotionally accept the reasons for this. I am thinking of *Unnatural Causes* and *Death of an Expert Witness* where the second victim is not as clearly marked as a "rotter."

PDJ: The main victim is one that the murderer feels he has to get rid of, then usually in my book he has to get rid of another one because in fact he is now on this path. If he is going to save himself from being discovered, someone else has to die. I think this is understandable because in murder, it must be the first murder that is the difficult murder. Once you have taken a human life, I think you would probably feel that you had stepped outside morality, and once you had done it by running someone over with a car, you persuade yourself that it was not meant. But once you had deliberately planned it and done it successfully, it would become very much easier to kill a second person if that second person stood in your way. In fact, it would become almost essential if the second person was going to lead to your discovery. Perhaps that is the intellectual justification to the second crime but because of this it probably does seem to the reader that the motive for the second crime was less strong and undoubtedly it is less strong.

DCC: Thomas de Quincey has pointed out that the writer turns crime stories into high literature by throwing "the interest on the murderer: our sympathy must be with him, our sympathy of comprehension, not approbation." Do you agree with that?

PDJ: I do to an extent certainly because I think even putting it at its lowest level, the reader must understand why the murderer did it. The reader is not going to be satisfied at the end if he feels, 'well, that was such a stupid way out of his problems.' For example to have a book in which the murderer murders his wife when there is easy and swift divorce, and he obviously has grounds for it, or when he is murdering for money for which he has no great or particular need, or he is murdering a blackmailer when what he was being blackmailed about wasn't all that dreadful really and any intelligent man would have gone to the police, is artistically wrong. It offends reason and whatever faults a mystery has, it should never offend reason. You must have a motive that seems to the reader a valid motive, and when you have got that of course you must have sympathy because the reader is beginning to think, 'well, given those circumstances, I can almost see myself doing that.' If he identifies, then he feels that, 'well if I were in that corner, how else could I get out?' If it is because the murderer has really had his life ruined or the life of someone else ruined by the person he murders, you want the reader to feel, 'yes, he deserved it and I would have done that you know. I don't think I could murder many people but by God if I were him I would have done it.' So that kind of feeling is an identification.

DCC: You inject several interesting paradoxes into your novels. One example is in *Death of an Expert Witness*. Lorrimer is the 'victim,' if we look upon it as a classic detective novel but the murderer, is also a victim. He is both hero since he kills Lorrimer, clearly a rotten man, and yet he is the typical victim in the ironic mode. He is a victim of life. He is unhappy with his job, (if he could wipe the "smell of his job from his body, he could cleanse it from his mind"). He has no respect for himself, (if he had been less accommodating, "he would have respected himself more," and so would others). He feels that his life is "anxiety-ridden." He is also a victim of circumstances. Because Stella, and not the police, or somebody else found the letter, she signed both their death warrants. Are you consciously trying to develop these paradoxes in the book?

PDJ: Yes, I see paradox as inevitably there in human lives and human nature and I do consciously try to include it in the books. Perhaps the paradox is best summed up by Robert Browning in "Bishop Blougram's Apology:"

"Our interest's on the dangerous edge of things.
The honest thief, the tender murderer,
The superstitious atheist..."

The centre of the paradox is not that good comes out of evil but that evil can come out of good.

DCC: Yes, that's true. There are theories in criminology that murdered people often have 'victim' personalities. Again, in *Death of an Expert Witness,* we read that the "victim was central to the mystery of his own death. He died because of what he was." These ideas put some of the responsibility on the victim, just as the criminal by his own action in the Greek world precipitates a process of retribution that he is powerless to escape.

PDJ: But, of course, the victim isn't responsible very largely for what he was and for what he is. This is another paradox. One can talk of the victim being responsible for his own murder in the sense that he behaves in such a way that he is more or less overtly asking for it. He behaves in a particular way because that is what his inheritance and his childhood and his environment and his personality have together made him and the result of this is that he is a man or she is a woman who represents a threat to some other person and sufficient of a threat to them to murder. So I think to that extent, yes, the victim is partly responsbile for his own murder because of what he is and the murderer murders because of what he is; the secret lies in the personality of the essential person.

DCC: You once said that your characters are waiting somewhere and through some mysterious process used 'you' to come into life. That would, of course, include the murderers. Do you think that all people are capable of murder or is there a particular homicidal mentality?

PDJ: There are particular homicidal mentalities. We are all capable of murder in one circumstance and we are all capable of murder in self-defense and this is almost an animal instinct. It would seem to me that if we had, for example, a very sharp knife and someone was coming toward us, someone has broken in with a weapon, we are going to kill him before he kills us. Even if we aren't really convinced that he is going to, but nevertheless if we are frightened enough, we are probably not going to think out very clearly whether we are really convinced that he is going to kill us; we are not going to give him a chance to make up his mind on that. If we had with us at the time young children or old people, we would be the more likely in their defense to kill another human being. I am sure that we could do it in intense anger. But the deliberate planning of the destruction of another human being is something that a very great majority of people would not and could not do. This is what makes the murder so interesting because it has always been regarded as the unique crime and indeed it is the unique crime because it is one for which we can't make reparation. I mean, if you or I knew a wealthy relative had left us a large fortune in her will, we would not be capable of thinking, "Well I am not waiting perhaps another ten or twenty years for that money, I need it now, now, how on earth can I kill her without being found out? How can I plan it?" I don't think we could bring ourselves to do that. It is a good thing we can't possibly, for society.

DCC: But isn't the question one of a fear of punishment? What if punishment were removed?

PDJ: I still feel that the great majority of people couldn't bring themselves to do it. This may be almost an atavistic horror of murder bred in us through generations. Certainly bred in every single civilized society and in societies which we like to regard as less civilized. It is there. Indeed, we couldn't exist in society unless we lived really by the rule. It is bred in us perhaps as strongly as things like incest. I can't see myself doing that, certainly. It is not really, you see, the taking of life that bothers us so much because we wouldn't have the slaughter we do on the roads if we worried very much about taking human lives. We persuade ourselves that it's nobody's fault, particularly, if we have to have our automobile as our God. Presumably we need this blood sacrificing.

DCC: You have been described as a realistic moralist and so has Adam Dalgleish. He notes that occasionally there are some cases better left unsolved, that there are some parts of most lives that are better left unexamined. Would you agree with that description of yourself?

PDJ: There are some thoughts better left unexamined. Are we talking about examination in literature or examination, as it were, in real life? I suppose in real life there may well be situations, I think there are, in which people have contrived lives for themselves, a way of living that is reasonably satisfactory but which does depend on not facing reality and not examining motives or not looking at the truth of their relationships with their families or lovers or employers or jobs or anything else. To that extent, an absolute determination to seek after honesty could be very destructive of the amount of happiness which they have managed to devise for themselves.

DCC: In what way does a book start to take shape in your mind? Does the plot come first, a character, a mood, a situation?

PDJ: Well, it differs with the books. Something certainly sparks-off creative imagination, sometimes it is a place or a feeling that I would like to describe this place, that I would like to write a book about this place. This was certainly so with *The Black Tower*, set in Dorset. I felt that I would like to set a book here. It was also true, of course, with the closed community ones, in effect, all of them really. I am not sure that setting hasn't been the first idea. I wanted to write a novel set in Cambridge. The next idea might follow very closely such as in the Cambridge novel, *An Unsuitable Job for a Woman*; almost immediately I thought of the girl detective and the failed agency which she took over. They came very closely together. There nearly always is a 'place' first, and to an extent, that dictates what one is writing about. If it is going to be a forensic science laboratory, the attraction here is that you have got your closed community which is also a secure community so you have the 'locked door' device. You have the interest of a community which is diverse with people with different disciplines and all the problems of hierarchy and the tensions, and resentments, petty or otherwise, and jealousies which can arise. You also get the added interest in the fact that their disciplines are scientific but they are spending their lives investigating murder and murder comes into the laboratory and the idea develops from there. Characters come very quickly afterwards. Who is going to be murdered? How? And why? 'Why' is often the most difficult question simply because in real life and particularly in modern life there are few problems which can't be solved to some extent. They either can't be solved at all or they could be solved without recourse to murder, because murder really doesn't solve anything and in all my books it doesn't, of course. It merely makes things worse for the person who does it. In the old detective stories, perhaps in the 1920s or early 30s, people might be more liable to murder and you could have a plot in which someone wanted to get ride of a wife. Nowadays, divorce is so much easier that it doesn't become a motive really. Blackmail was always a potent motive, it still can be, but nevertheless, in our private lives today we are quite entitled to say that it is my private life, make of it what you will. A politician is not now likely to be put out of office because an adultery is discovered, as we all know. So these are no longer motives. Money probably does remain a fairly important motive especially if the money is wanted for someone else. This long-term hatred and this opinion that "I can't live my life, I can't live it happily while he is walking there," is still powerful but that is the difficult part. One should decide who is going to be killed, and why, and in what way. If you are very lucky, I think there is a coming together of an original setting, a different setting which no one has used before (and most settings have been used before), a new method of death which hasn't been over-used and the motive which the readers will feel is credible. If you can get all those elements together, then at least you have got the making of a good mystery.

DCC: How did you create the character of Adam Dalgleish? What attracted you to his personality, the avant-garde poetry, the essentially tragic and solitary man?

PDJ: One of the first decisions you have to make if you are going to write mysteries and if you think you may be carrying on with mysteries, at least for a time, is whether you are going to have the amateur or professional detective. The amateur certainly has advantages because he can have a job outside his detection and that can be an interesting job, and, of course, you can have a man or woman, or you could have someone young or old, you can make him totally original, the sort of person who obviously wouldn't fit into a professional police force anyway. But, on the other hand, if you are aiming for realism, it's probably better to have a member of the professional police force. Then your question is "How am I going to make him a rounded human being, how am I going to make him someone different, how am I going to interest readers in him, how am I going to interest myself in him so that he is the sort of man I want to go on writing about?" Assuming that once you have got him, you are going to carry him through and most of us do, I gave Adam Dalgleish many of the qualities that I admire myself in men. I wanted him to be very professional, I didn't want to overromanticize him, I didn't want him to be too much the upper crust, splendidly mannered, rather snobbish detective very much in the English tradition. I made him the son of a parson, so he was very out-of-date. He probably could be described as a gentleman and he is educated. I didn't think it would be much fun to write about someone who wasn't, and making him a poet really was a device, in a sense, both to emphasize his sensitivity and to mark him from the ordinary, non-corrupt British detective.

DCC: What differences do you see in the writing of female authors of detective novels as opposed to your male colleagues?

PDJ: Yes, there are differences really. There is the obvious one that the men, and particularly the Americans, are much, much better at dealing with the private eye or with the strictly police procedural novel. Some of the English writers do this very well too. Men are good at more violent crimes, physically as opposed to emotionally. Women on the whole have more gentle crimes, I don't mean the crime itself is necessarily gentle, some are quite horrific, but nevertheless they are set against ordinary, everyday life, and fairly gentle, ordinary, everyday life. The crime is the more shocking because it takes place on the library floor or the rectory or in the small village where very little happens or in the respectable town. This contrast is felt very strongly by women. Women are more interested in motives and in characters, in these strong emotions which can boil up and erupt into murder. Women, and this is a great strength, have a very good eye for detail and these are so important in a mystery. The arrangement of detail is almost like a literary flower arrangement and women are good here, but I think they are good at this also in the mainstream novels that they write. Elizabeth Jane Howard is excellent at this, so is Margaret Drabble, if one thinks of contemporary English novelists. So often in novels by men, even in the great novelists, one longs to know what people looked like and what their clothes were and what they had for tea and what they had for dinner and the description of the room. I find this is a strength in a novel because it is so important. In a mystery, this detail is often necessary to the solution of the problem and so this gives women a strength. Generally, women always had the lead in the classical English detective mystery.

DCC: This sense of detail is reflected in your highly developed visual sense. I am often reminded of paintings, particularly

Constable's. In one novel, you refer to the sky "as a painter's sky."

PDJ: I enjoy looking at paintings. It is useful for a writer to have a painter's eye in the sense that one responds strongly and visually to shape and colour. As I am a very English writer and all my books have so far been set in my own country it is to the English landscape that I most respond. Descriptions of places can, too, both influence and enhance the action.

DCC: In what ways have Evelyn Waugh and Jane Austen influenced your work?

PDJ: I don't think one can say specifically how one is influenced because the very fact of an influence is that it is exerted in some rather mysterious way. You don't consciously say, "Here is a stylist that I enjoy and like and admire, I will write in this way," at least I couldn't do that. I don't think any real writer does that; you write in your own way so that the influence is a fairly subconscious influence. Austen is an influence for her love of order and reason. *Emma* is a magnificent detective story, one of the best ever written, except it hasn't got a murderer at the centre of it. Waugh is an influence, particularly in his dialogue and in his prose style. I think he was one of the great English prose writers in modern years.

DCC: What do you like about the novels of Dorothy Sayers?

PDJ: Dorothy L. Sayers, and she was absolutely insistent that she had that "L " probably did more than anybody else to make the genre intellectually respectable because she had a fine intelligence. When she decided to write mysteries, (and I think she probably decided to write them because she wanted to make some money and that's not as ignoble and aimless as some purists would wish to believe) she applied this intelligence to the task at hand. That is admirable and she could write well. I know that Lord Peter was a fantasy figure but I doubt he is more of a fantasy figure for her or her readers than the sardonic, wise-cracking, sharp-shooting private eye is a fantasy. She also taught me the importance of setting; she used, as I do, settings she knew and was familiar with and she used them superbly. We know far more from *Murder Must Advertise* about what it was like to work in an office in the years of the depression in London than we could ever learn from more pretentious works.

DCC: *Innocent Blood* deviates from your other novels. It is not a murder mystery. What did you want to do in that novel that you had not done before?

PDJ: I don't think I was setting out to do something that I hadn't actually done before. I was setting out to write a novel without using the strict conventions of the mystery form certainly, and that I hadn't done before, but I don't think I was trying to do something new in the sense that I was trying to deal with human beings more realistically because I have always tried to do that. I felt that given the plot I had, and the nature of the characters and the themes, the book couldn't be written or written as well within those constraints. I suppose I wanted space to deal with a smaller number of characters. If I had used the search for the natural parents as a motive in an ordinary mystery, there would obviously have to be more suspects with motives for getting rid of the murdered person. This is one of the challenges of the genre. They all have to be made real and their motives have to seem believable and I didn't want to do that. I wanted to have a smaller number of characters and deal with them in depth and at greater length than I could do within the classical detective story.

DCC: Some reviewers have criticized Philippa as an unsympathetic, unpleasant and too cold protagonist. But obviously you created her exactly that way. What were you thinking when you sat down to create the central character of that book?

PDJ: I did intentionally create her that way. I am always surprised when critics criticize a character because she is unpleasant; if, in fact, she is unpleasant, she is unpleasant. You can criticize a writer because she means to make a character unpleasant and hasn't succeeded or because she obviously intends to make it sympathetic and hasn't succeeded. But in this case, here we have a girl, adopted at an early age with a very tragic early history. We don't learn how tragic until late in the novel. She has never known love in the years in which if we do not know love we probably won't ever learn to love, who thought she was adopted because of her intelligence, which is very considerable and has therefore developed that intelligence, relied on that intelligence, seen that as the only way in which she is going to gain approval from other people. That is not a human being who is very likable or very lovable. She is extremely arrogant and I intended that she should be like this at the beginning of the book. She is very unkind to her adoptive mother at the time when she has first learned who she is, but the shock of that is absolutely tremendous. Do we expect her to come in and throw her arms around her and say 'I understand all about it?' She can hardly touch her adoptive mother let alone throw her arms around her. There is a time when her adoptive father comes in and she wonders what would happen if he was able to come across the room to her and put his arms around her and say, "don't worry," but he can't do that either, that is the sort of people they are.

DCC: You mentioned something the other night that we didn't have a chance to expand. You said that there is a clue in that book and I didn't have a chance to find out what you were really talking about. What did you mean?

PDJ: I mean there is a piece of information which is absolutely specifically given in that book in black and white which would lead the readers to think something has gone very wrong, but nobody ever picks it up.

DCC: Do you mean in terms of her background and her relationship to her mother?

PDJ: Yes.

DCC: And you don't want to say what it is, not at this point.

PDJ: No (both laugh).

DCC: Why the title *Innocent Blood*? Is there anything else involved other than the fact that Philippa's blood comes from people who are not innocent and that the blood of the murdered child was innocent? Are there any other ramifications?

PDJ: No, the title was very difficult because it wasn't going to be called *Innocent Blood*, it was going to be called *The Blood Tie*, but someone else had used that title, and then it was going to be called *The Blood Relation* and someone else had used *The Blood Relation* or *The Blood Relative* and I couldn't use that either. It became very, very difficult and it was very late and long after the book was finished, and very shortly before publication, that I hit on *Innocent Blood*. It immediately struck me as a very good title because it had this ambiguity about it as to whether the blood she had inherited was or was not innocent. And, of course, it ties up with the section in Ecclesiastes about it being an abomination to the Lord that one should shed innocent blood.

DCC: Are we going to see the girl detective, Cordelia Gray, again?

PDJ: First, I'm going to do another very straight forward mystery, if a mystery can ever be described as very straight forward, with Cordelia Gray. I would like to write another mainstream novel and I shall plan to do so, but I think in between I may write another mystery.

Interview with Jean Stubbs

Diana Cooper-Clark

DCC: Raymond Chandler was asked too often by fans: "Oh, Mr. Chandler, you write so well. Have you ever thought of working on something serious?" Chandler admitted that he had never learned how to construct a proper story (this, is of course, highly debatable). Do you ever meet with this attitude in reference to the Inspector Lintott mysteries, either in reviews or from writers in the mainstream?

JS: Yes, I think that the attitude toward crime writing and historical writing is the attitude of someone who looks slightly askance, as though it's not literature, as though you don't have to work very hard at it. But in my opinion it is the writer and the quality of writing and thought which matters.

DCC: In other words, you think that your Inspector Lintott series is as good as any of the other books that you have written or novels in the mainstream.

JS: I didn't write the Inspector Lintott series because it was something easy to write or because I wanted to make quick money. I put as much of myself into it as I put into everything. I treat everything that I write very seriously. I give of myself, as I am at that moment, one hundred percent. In *Dear Laura*, I wanted to depict the attitudes of the Victorian middle-class. The surface of society was very light and very delicate at that time, with an emphasis on the sanctity of women in the sanctity of the home. Underneath this delicacy there was another life where eighty thousand prostitutes and four thousand brothels existed in London alone. I wanted that contrast; I wanted the contrast of the woman on a pedestal and the woman as marketable flesh.

DCC: Edgar Allan Poe, in his critique of *Barnaby Rudge*, asserted that the regular novel and the legitimate mystery will not combine. Obviously you don't agree.

JS: I disagree with this idea that if you don't write an absolutely straight novel set in modern times you haven't written anything

35

worth writing. I believe, particularly with the historical novel, that we are yesterday, we are the past, these are our roots, this is why we are as we are now. I think that until you examine history and look into the past you don't see yourself or can't see yourself as you are. Also, the further back I go in history the more I find that history is people. You can go back to the year eleven hundred; all right, they feel differently about religion, they eat different things, they are prey to a great many diseases which nowadays we can control or mitigate, but underneath you find human beings, recognizable human beings as we are now. Apart from the fact that I believe I am tackling a broader subject in my present series of novels, the Howarth Chronicles, and that hopefully my writing improves, I would say, "Yes" to the first half of your question. But when you ask if detective novels are as good as mainstream novels I would say that their subject is narrower, since the detective novel imposes certain rules and a certain structure. This can be transcended by great writers. Dare I call Dostoevsky's *Crime and Punishment* the supreme detective novel? *Barnaby Rudge* wasn't one of Dickens' best novels, but if anyone could combine every ingredient of novel-writing, it was Charles Dickens. He had an outstanding individual talent, which transformed and transcended his subject matter. Of course, he also had tremendous compassion and a deep concern with social reform, so he wrote the mystery against a broad background, as Dostoevsky did. On the other hand, I know that the limitation of the detective novel is the subject itself, which can be absolutely fascinating but is essentially no more than a riddle. You have a problem, step by step you solve it, and hey presto! At its best it stands with the mainstream novels (I'm still thinking of Dostoevsky, and everyone is going to scream that he didn't really write a detective story but I'm prepared to argue about that!), and at its usual level it's no worse than its mainstream counterpart. In the end you get back to the quality of the author and the quality of thought. And the same applies to historical re-creations. Think of George Garrett's *Death of the Fox* and Thomas Keneally's *Confederates*. Magnificent books, important books, books which use history to say something that matters and say it exceedingly well.

DCC: Your last novel, *Kit's Hill* (in Britain, *By Our Beginnings* in the United States), was a departure from the detective genre. Do you find it restricting to write within one genre all the time? Do you like to experiment with different modes?

JS: Yes I do. I can remember someone saying to me, "Are you going to stay with Inspector Lintott for the rest of your life?" and I said, "No, God forbid, much as I love him, I might go back to him, but I am certainly going away from him although I don't know where I *am* going at the moment." I reckon myself to be an old-fashioned writer, which means I can turn my hand to anything. I want to be able to explore any subject I am interested in. Fortunately, so far, I have had publishers who have encouraged me to do just that. I would hate to think I had written the same book, slightly differently, over and over again.

DCC: Exactly. History is such an important part of all your books. What are the requirements of a historical mystery?

JS: I would say that my requirement would be a scholarly one, which is to study the period that one is writing about as closely as possible.

DCC: How is that combined with the detective genre?

JS: Well, the fact that some mystery is going on at the time which has to be detected doesn't alter the historical background because people go on murdering each other and being mysterious when and wherever they live. So, therefore, you combine the two, and I certainly have studied crime because crime itself fascinates me. I would say I don't write "who done its," I write "why done its"; I want to know *why* they did it. I also want to know *how* they did it and you can study that as well. I studied poisons.

DCC: Yes, very nineteenth-century.

JS: Indeed.

DCC: Very female.

JS: The female weapon is usually poison. It was the only one the Victorian ladies could get hold of, you see!

DCC: Also in the nineteenth century they didn't have forensic medicine.

JS: That is right.

DCC: Josephine Tey's *The Daughter of Time* is the centre of a controversy mostly generated by historians who reject her portrayal of Richard III. Have you had any controversy concerning your historical portraits of the alleged murderesses Mary Blandy and Kitty Ogilvie, or Henry VII?

JS: I have had disagreements. My friend Audrey Williamson wrote a very scholarly essay on the Princes in the Tower. She is pro-

Richard III and she was convinced that Henry VII had the boys murdered, whereas I am totally convinced that it was the Duke of Buckingham. But you can find that if you hunt around in history as I did because either view can be supported.

DCC: What about your portraits of the murderesses? They tended to be sympathetic.

JS: I think I agree with my own mother, who when she had read *My Grand Enemy*, which was the case of Mary Blandy, said that even if Mary didn't kill her father, he deserved to be killed. It was almost the only thing that desperate women could do then. It is a terrible thing to say so because murder horrifies me.

DCC: In your novel *Dear Laura*, we also see a woman driven to murder by her situation, her impotence as a Victorian woman.

JS: Yes. It is a very good thing that nowadays there are lots of other ways out. Women used to be quite helpless. They belonged first of all to their fathers, and then to their husbands if they were lucky enough to get married. If they didn't get a husband they then belonged to their father until he died and afterwards, perhaps, to whichever brother would take them in. This was a cruel situation. I was very sorry for Mary Blandy because her case was, in fact, not proven. The jury, nevertheless, pronounced her guilty; and I wanted to prove her, as far as I could do, innocent. She said that she was innocent on the scaffold, and that was in the day when people truly believed that they would burn in hell-fire if their last words or indeed their actions were lies. Mary Blandy, I feel, could not have said that if she hadn't at least believed it and that is what I wanted to prove. Certainly Kitty Ogilvie was innocent, there was no question of that whatsoever. Ann Clark killed Thomas Ogilvie, Kitty Ogilvie didn't kill him.

DCC: Your books deal with the eighteenth and nineteenth centuries. What is it exactly that you find attractive about those particular centuries?

JS: Two different things. The eighteenth century was the age of elegance. They were, as far as I can see, totally incapable of producing anything, a building or a gown or a piece of furniture or a china cup which was not in exquisite taste; it was the most graceful age we have ever had. The manners didn't always go along with it, but then that made it interesting, the fact that it was rather rough and elegant simultaneously. I am beginning to admire a new thing about the Victorians which is their industry, the fact that they would tackle anything. The amount of energy they put into their work, the enterprise they had was astonishing; and there were marvellous men like Brunell who did about ten jobs in one, he was amazing. But the other thing about the Victorians that I treasured was their hypocrisy. Now this sounds dreadful, I don't like hypocrisy in itself, but it is very fascinating to observe: what they said and what they really meant. Again the contrast, as I said, between this sanctity of the home, the sanctity of wives, and then four thousand brothels, eighty thousand prostitutes!

DCC: That reminds me of something that Peter Lovesey said in his article on the historical mystery. He said that for atmosphere, the counterpoise of teacups and terror, cosiness and crime, the Victorian mystery is supreme.

JS: Oh, the Victorians were the best at murder, that is why I chose them. Before I wrote *Dear Laura*, I wanted to do a reconstruction of a Victorian murder mystery. But, as you know, there are about half-a-dozen classic crimes which have been reconstructed beautifully over and over again, so I made up my own. I wrote a mystery which was based on a typical heroine of the time: you know, fair hair, blue eyes, beautiful and all the rest of it. I wrote almost a classic blue-print of a Victorian murder case, but I made it up.

DCC: When you say that the Victorians were best at murder, what do you mean?

JS: Murder is largely a domestic affair and the Victorians had an obsession with domesticity. Queen Victoria set the example for that. Queen Victoria made the royal family respectable and everybody wanted to be like our dear Queen. So, therefore, they had those idyllic domestic set-ups. Some of them worked, of course, but others fairly seethed underneath: all heart-burnings, and misery and hatred and imprisonment and perversion, yes indeed. And all the ladies who languished on couches because that was another escape! All right, I won't say they hadn't got the guts to murder their husbands but I will say that they hadn't got that particular quality which they required to *murder* anybody. So therefore they retreated into themselves and they just lay on their couches and languished away until they died, making everybody's lives and their own a misery.

DCC: The woman's situation is acutely emphasized if you think about the Brontës, Charlotte and Emily, not telling their brother

Branwell, who was a complete waste of time, that they wrote and were published because they didn't want to hurt his feelings as he was a failed artist. You have set two novels in the Edwardian period, *The Golden Crucible* and *The Painted Face*. What is there about the Edwardian period that appeals to you?

JS: That was like a breath of fresh air. Those thirteen years between Queen Victoria dying and George V being in the first years of his reign were something of a Golden Age. There was great intellectual and social progress. The structure was becoming much more free and easy, producing and encouraging intellectual-minded women and broadminded progressive fathers, which is what matters. Because if your father didn't approve of your being educated, you weren't going to *be* educated!

DCC: The common denominator in these novels is murder and mystery. What in particular attracts you to the detective genre in order that you may incorporate your historical interest? Why not write an emblematic biography that will incorporate the historical background; why not write a history book?

JS: There wouldn't really be any point in writing a history book because I am not a professional historian, I am an amateur historian. I am interested in crime. I like the atmosphere of the thriller; you don't quite know what is going to happen next. I like the mystery of it, and Inspector Lintott never completely solves his mysteries if you have noticed. He is a very wise man and he has both his feet on the floor, he knows his job, he is a good cop, but he never solves his mysteries entirely. I like the mystery of crime, I like the mystery of human nature.

DCC: Were you first inspired to write an Inspector Lintott mystery because surrounding historical events interested you? What initiates an Inspector Lintott novel as opposed to any of your others?

JS: He was initiated first of all with *Dear Laura*. I had to have a detective because I wanted to write a Victorian murder mystery and he began as an adjunct to it and then became a central character. I am very devoted to Lintott. He combines a great many qualities which I admire, and I do relish his deviousness. I also like the fact that he leads two lives; he is a very good cop, he is a very good husband and a very good father, and he keeps those two lives quite separate and they give him his strength.

DCC: In one way you deviate from most other detective writers in that you give him a wife. Very often detectives are either celibate or if they are married, their wives are never seen or they are totally in the background.

JS: Yes, that is very true. The single detective, even if he is a bit sleazy or down-at-heel as in Raymond Chandler's novels, is essentially a romantic figure. He is the loner with a golden heart, or even something of a black heart, and he is free of family ties. So each woman reader can feel in her bones that *she* could reform him and make him happy, and each man feels that if only he didn't have a wife, family and mortgage he would have been such a tough and attractive tom-cat as this man! It's the old escape route again. Now I am unimpressed by this sort of image and therefore I gave Lintott the stability of a contented marriage. And, incidentally, the great Simenon—and *there* is a writer whose detective novels range over human nature and the human condition so marvellously well, and who is far more than a riddle-solver—the great Simenon gave his detective a lovely wife who goes to the market and prepares his soup and is a quiet strength in the centre of their life together. Madame Maigret. To me that is more real than a dozen tough guys with overblown egos.

DCC: Are you interested in writing a novel about a Victorian murderess such as Kate Webster, for example?

JS: I don't think I shall write any more Victorian murder novels but I will tell you what I have got upstairs and that is the complete set of notes for Lintott's earliest case. You see, I happened upon Lintott when he was an old man and that was my difficulty. I thought I would like to have him back at the beginning; I want to see where he starts as a young officer. I am very fascinated by the beginning of the police force. I have the complete plot written out and all the characters researched and I can sit down and write that Lintott in less than six months. It will be written sometime because I want to write it very, very much indeed. It is of his early days and includes a criminal of great style. It is a very intricate plot which I also love doing.

DCC: Does the plot have a trial? Richard D. Altick has written that "murder trials, if held to the light at the proper angle, are an almost unexcelled mirror of an epoch's mores." You, of course, have a trial in *Dear Laura* and you have written of the trials of your historical murderesses.

JS: I would certainly agree with him. I remember that in Kitty

Ogilvie's case the hangman of Edinburgh used to have a particular costume, silver lace at his cuffs, if I remember. I know that everyone knew who the hangman was, and as he walked through the streets of Edinburgh he was both revered and feared. It is like light on a prism when I look up the historical data. One of my characters in *Dear Laura*, Molly Flynn the prostitute, wore scarlet silk stockings with little swallows on them. Those were a particular fashion at the time and I love that. I have an encylopedia of costume which is fascinating.

DCC: The plight of women in the eighteenth and nineteenth centuries, which we have touched on, is a theme to which you continue to return. Sometimes murder is the only way to free a woman from the burden of her husband or her father. In *My Grand Enemy* we are told that women "were trained like circus animals to perform to man's satisfaction; and passed from a father's to a husband's house with or without their consent." In *Dear Laura* Dr. Padgett describes her house as a citadel in a state of siege or a doll's house. Both her father and husband in these books are tyrannical. Laura sacrifices herself out of habit; she exchanged her father's dominion for that of her husband just like Nora in Ibsen's play, one luxurious cage for another. In *The Painted Face*, Odette Carradine is a suffragette and continually fights for her independence because she says that she doesn't want to be in a meat market. Inspector Lintott's daughter, Lizzie, wanted to go to university, wanted so many things that her age wouldn't allow so that by *The Golden Crucible*, she has already been in jail for suffrage, has been turned out of her house by her husband and even Inspector Lintott worries that she *thinks* too much. He feels that marriage is all a woman can do. How important is this aspect of your work because you explore women to a very large extent in your books and their fight to free themselves from the restrictions of history and society?

JS: It's immensely important. I hadn't realized how important it was until I went to America in 1973 on a publicity trip connected with *Dear Laura*. I was met by people who felt I had written a woman's lib book, to which I sincerely replied, "I have done nothing of the kind. This is a Victorian mystery!" But as I travelled across to the west coast, I began to see what they were on about. I remember being told by my father that his elder sister Ethel, who would have been born in the 1880s, wanted to go to university. This was a middle-class provincial family in the north country, so what chance could she have had, although her mother had been a head mistress? She died at the age of 20-21 of TB. After her death,they were turning out all her clothes and at the bottom of the drawer they found a prospectus for Manchester University.

DCC: There is also a darker side to women. In the eighteenth and nineteenth centuries, the fashionable went as spectators to murder trials, and many were women. These genteel women were fascinated by cold blooded murder. This is reflected in the novels of the time and the trials in *Dear Laura, The Case of Kitty Ogilvie* and *My Grand Enemy*. In Julie Kavanagh's *Sybil's Second Love,* Mrs.Mush says, "I dearly like a murder. Of course, I do not wish for murders but when there is one, why I like it. It is human nature." Thomas Carlyle's sister, Jane, wrote in her journal about Palmer,the physician-poisoner, whose case was a sensation of the day: "From first to last he has preserved the most wonderful coolness, forcing a certain admiration from one, murderer tho' he be!" How do you account for this dichotomy; on the one hand, the surface gentility and on the other hand, the clear fascination with 'horrible murder.'

JS: They were living vicariously. They were experiencing an excitement which was certainly not present in their own lives. The difficulty with the Victorians was that they hadn't accepted the fact that there is a light and dark side to each of us. They weren't prepared to accept the dark side. They wanted everything to be light and lovely and bright and beautiful. Of course it wasn't, and therefore their women would love anything like murder because it was the dark side of life.

DCC: Do you think that the dark side makes each of us capable of murder?

JS: I think that each of us feels capable, emotionally, of murdering someone or other at some time in our lives. But there is a tremendous rift between the emotion and the act, just as there is a vast difference between being rather neurotic and downright mad. I think that most people, given sufficient incentive and the right circumstances, could kill on the spur of the moment. Only a few psychotics kill for fun, and deliberate calculated murder requires either deep hatred or a warped nature. But I draw upon my dark side to create my murderesses, and I'm sure many authors do. I can think and feel myself into their condition but I so loathe the idea of taking life that only the sort of desperation I have described would drive me to it, such as killing someone who was trying to kill me or someone dear to me.

DCC: Some people feel that the murderer is the dark side of us and the detective is the light side. Do you agree with this?

JS: I am not sure that the detective and the criminal are totally different people because they have so much in common that the line dividing them is very fine. The detective's business is with crime. He sees its effects, he seeks its causes, there is nothing he does not know and has not seen of the meanest and most savage side of human nature. On occasion he treats violence with violence, counters guile with guile, puts himself in the criminal's place mentally to forecast his reaction. The better the detective the closer he is to the criminal. He crosses this line between them many times in the course of his duty. So he is not "the light side" though he represents and works for the light. He is a mirror image. This is a fascinating subject which has been explored by quite a few writers; Friedrich Dürrenmatt constantly studies the idea of right and wrong, justice and injustice, and the curious ways in which they mingle and separate. It is the theme of the Lintott novel I want to write next: the one which is sitting in notes on my shelf!

DCC: What you say is true of contemporary detective fiction. P.D. James creates a more ambiguous morality and the dark is also the detective as well as the murderer. There is sympathy for both the victim and the murderer. Lintott as well feels very sympathetic to Laura.

JS: Oh, yes he does, and in fact, he is always prepared to be quite lenient if he does find an affinity with people. He has his own morality, he carries it about with him.

DCC: If you read all of the Inspector Lintott novels, it becomes clearer and clearer that given his shrewdness and his knowledge of people that he must have known that Laura committed murder. Yet he ignores the murder in a way that he simply wouldn't normally. We are told repeatedly that he is persistent, he is like a bulldog who clings to a case, he doesn't let go. Thus, we can't believe that he could have been really duped by Laura. He looks the other way as he learns more and more about her husband, even though he himself is torn about the position of women in society as well. Should Laura have escaped retribution?

JS: Laura cannot escape retribution. He leaves her, as it were, to heaven. She has only escaped the letter of the law. I believe that if retribution is not inflicted upon us by society or circumstance then we inflict it upon ourselves—I am speaking, of course, of ordinary people not of psychopaths. I regret leaving the novel where I did, though it went as far as I wanted to go at the time. I was dealing in simple justice: an eye for an eye. But that isn't good enough, and I have often thought of her life afterwards. How the weight of that murder would press upon her, how she would pay in a thousand ways for it, and carry the secret all her life. Oh, Laura didn't escape retribution.

DCC: Are bed murders, love, hate, home, peculiar to women? Are there any other female characteristics in murder?

JS: A lot of women are very fine private actresses. I thought that the way that Laura killed her husband was wholly female. Under guise of being a ministering angel she poisoned him to death, dose by dose. That, to me, is female. It takes an awful lot of hate, built up over a very long time to kill like that. I think a man would be more direct, less patient.

DCC: Also, Laura counts on her husband's assumption that she will be passive, she will be nourishing. Your mention of acting reminds me that the first fictional detectives were first rate actors: Poe's Dupin who bluffs the minister, Doyle's Holmes was a master of disguises, and also Dickens' Inspector Bucket. In *The Golden Crucible*, a novel of illusion and magic, Inspector Lintott disguises himself as a religious fanatic and shaves off his whiskers. Inspector Lintott is acting out what I think is an important part of your novels. This is the idea of appearance and reality. We cannot accept anything at face value and Inspector Lintott himself says: "Appearances mean nothing to me." What is the balance between the surface of reality and its underbelly? Do you feel that murder best illustrates this tension? Is this why you are drawn to it?

JS: Yes, I suppose it is. You are quite right. To take your first question, about the balance between appearance and reality. I think it is the tremendous imbalance which causes tension in a person, and between people. Take Laura's situation as an instance. Both she and her husband Theodore are totally different inside from the other people they are outside. This same situation with a milder-tempered man and/or a less passionate woman would still be unsatisfactory, but it wouldn't lead to murder. The tension rises in proportion to the conflict between them as a couple, and between their inner and outer selves. And when it becomes finally unbearable and the opportunity arises—slash! Murder is relief from the ultimate tension. To take a life is to take the most precious possession a person has, and the act is irreversible.

DCC: Your creation of Inspector Lintott is marvellous. He is hard, shrewd, a realist, but also tender and kind. His home is his sanctuary, he loves his wife more than anyone else, and he worries about his daughter Lizzie. He has working class values and he is certain about what is right and wrong. When you first created the character, how did you flesh him out? Did you want somebody who embodied all of these contradictions that were in some way emblematic of the period as well?

JS: No, I will tell you a fascinating thing. I was brought up first of all on Charles Dickens and by the time I was ten years old, I had read most of Dickens. I turned up one of his conversation pieces which was called "On Duty with Inspector Field" and this was when Charles Dickens was doing his research as a reporter. He went along with a very famous Inspector of the time in the 1830s, called Inspector Field, and they went around Saint Giles, the cellars and everything. I thought that this was the perfect detective, and to the picture that Charles Dickens had drawn of Inspector Field, I added some qualities and made him into a character. When I was near the end of writing *Dear Laura,* I discovered that Dickens had used Inspector Field for Mr. Bucket in *Bleak House* and Wilkie Collins had used him for his detective, Mr. Cuff, in *The Moonstone.* That is where I got Lintott from. If I had known that he had been used, I wouldn't have used him. I didn't, fortunately, until near the end of the book when it was much too late.

DCC: That is interesting. Lintott sees his detection method as an intricate jigsaw puzzle. He uses the straight-edged facts and makes a frame, then fills in what he can. At some point Lintott says in one of the books, "if those trees refuse to come together, start on the church, if the sky was difficult, put in people." This seems to contradict his instinctual side. Of course, the nineteenth century was devoted to rationality and progress in science, but underneath all of that, starting with people like Poe and the Romantics, you have a rebellion against 'I think, therefore I am.' There is distrust of rationality and reason and Lintott seems to embody that contradiction.

JS: But don't you think that he uses reason as far as it goes because it doesn't go all the way, and then uses his instincts and his intuition? That's how I work, anyway, and I have to become Lintott in order to find my way through the case. Reason is an excellent and necessary thing but it is not everything. And if the chips were down I'd rely on my intuition any time!

DCC: Were you thinking of that contradiction when you wrote the books?

JS: I don't do things as consciously as that. Ideas and characters appear and I find the reason afterwards.

DCC: Although the detective novel restores a sense of unity in the world through its resolution, form and logical deduction, is it fair to say that, generally, it does not lead the reader to self-investigation, to a means of correlating fragmentation, both internal and external, as Doris Lessing did in *The Golden Notebook?*

JS: Yes, I know exactly what you are after. We're back to the 'mere riddle' of the detective novel—always with my proviso that this form can be transcended! Yes, I would agree that the reader is dished up a complete meal and only has to eat it. The detective novel asks questions which it can answer. The mainstream novel—the good mainstream novel—deals with universal questions which can only be answered individually, which are paradoxical, which deeply concern each of us as thinking and feeling human beings. But just let me say something about the trend of modern mainstream novels. They are *less* concerned with universal questions than their predecessors were, that is in the Western world. It has taken present day Russia to produce an author like Solzhenitsin and a book like *Cancer Ward* or *The First Circle*. I think very little of the trend to psycho-analyze oneself on paper, of a narcissistic preoccupation with one's warts. And I will often read a novel which is marvellously written, and think, 'Now why bother to write that?' The Self is important, but the Self is not enough. That is almost certainly the reason why I have switched over for the time being from the detective genre. I am writing my Howarth chronicles because I am trying to equate the past with the present, or perhaps I am investigating myself, using myself as a mirror.

DCC: Do you think that it is really not so much a question of content as a question of style? *The Golden Notebook* exemplifies Doris Lessing's idea that life is commensurately messy so the style has to be messy. The novel forces the reader to question herself. The detective format, on the other hand, by its very nature, re-enforces the reader's need for resolution and order.

JS: I like order. I've read and admired *The Golden Notebook* but I don't agree with her. I agree with her that life is messy, but that's why artists must put some kind of order into it. I would never deal with it messily because art is the ordering and illuminating of chaos, isn't it? Like Mrs. Ramsey in *To The Lighthouse,* making an art out of everything. Look at the chaos she had to cope with; that demanding husband, eight children and not-too-wanted guests in their holiday house. Yet out of it all she created the art of the dinner party, that marvellous dinner party.

DCC: Lily says she is the only artist in that book.

JS: Yes, beautiful woman, and she created order out of jumble.

DCC: That is against the whole modernist drift.

JS: To hell with the modernist drift!

DCC: Is that one of the reasons why the detective novel has suffered critically? Because it hasn't gone along with the general aesthetic movement of the twentieth century?

JS: I think some critics are afraid of not being in the vanguard, aren't they? They are frightened they might miss something. It's a case of the Emperor's new clothes—he hasn't any, but only the most unselfconscious person dares say so!

DCC: They are also afraid of being omniscient. The detective narrative tends to still believe in omniscience. Lintott says that he knows what is right and wrong; he doesn't say, "I am ambiguous or ambivalent."

JS: Yes, but although he says this, I, as the author, don't say it. I show that he is not simply right or wrong and I show that he has weaknesses and I show that he doesn't solve his cases. My tongue is firmly in one cheek when Lintott pontificates.

DCC: That's true. In *The Golden Crucible* the ultimate voice is San Francisco's earthquake. Things are not neatly tied up. As an extension of all that, Inspector Lintott has an intriguing definition of justice: "Justice is more than the law, sir, though the law administers justice. There are strange ways of bringing it about, and sometimes it happens in a way you couldn't have planned. It's personal, too, sir. Each man carries his own justice with him. I've done a few things in my time, I don't mind admitting, which ain't exactly the letter of the law. But they were always a form of justice."

JS: It is a summing up of Lintott but it is also a summing up of my own philosophy. The letter of the law killeth but the spirit maketh alive! And though we must abide by laws in order to live reasonably together as a society, we are more than rule-keepers. I haven't been in Lintott's position, except in a fictional sense, so I haven't ever had to bend the *Law* to be just, but I have sometimes had to flout other rules in order to do *myself* or others justice. There come times in all our lives when we must stand up and be counted as ourselves, and our decisions may seem selfish or stupid or ridiculous to other people. But you must certainly know yourself in order to arrive at the correct solution for yourself, you can't just do something because you feel like it. Like Lintott, I am my own judge and jury, and I take full responsibility for my actions. Oh, and there's a beautiful Arab proverb which says, "The face of justice is the face of God, but the nature of justice changes." And that expresses my philosophy, too.

DCC: Hear, Hear! Murder was a distinctive part of nineteenth century fiction. The Gothic novel introduced readers to the romance of terror, murder, rape, sadism, incest, vampirism. To what extent do you think that the Gothic novel cultivated the reader's craving for sensation in literature?

JS: I think the need for sensation came first: that sensation they couldn't get any other way, like flocking to see people hanged.

DCC: Doesn't society create a contradiction in terms because you could say exactly the same thing for the twentieth century? We are living in a culture where we have to create vicarious experiences to answer that craving for sensation whether it is films of violence or porno houses. We have an impulse that society never quite answers or speaks to. Do you think that tension for both chaos and order is essential to everything that the detective genre is about?

JS: I would have said that the detective novel was an intellectual answer. It is somewhat milder, isn't it, than watching a person hanged? You know, if I had to write a sequel to *Dear Laura*, which I won't, she would carry that murder with her; she would have to cope with it, mentally and emotionally. It would influence whatever marriage or relationship she made afterwards. There is something very final and fundamental about murder, like the Cain and Abel story. What is it that the avenging Hebrew God of Justice says in the Old Testament? "The voice of thy brother's blood crieth unto me from the ground. And now cursed art thou from the ground." Because by taking life you have taken away every chance of the victim improving and fulfilling that life. And you can't give it back. It is such a final act and carries with it a supreme penalty. We believe, nowadays, that we can reason ourselves into and out of life-events. I am not mentioning these emotive issues for the sake of argument but for the sake of illustration—since I have divided feelings about abortion, test-tube babies, euthanasia and so on. But one of my friends, in the days of our youth, had to have an abortion, and I was staying with her to help her through. I remember that she woke at nights, screaming. There was good reason for the abortion but reason is not enough. Somewhere, thousands of years back and deeper down than we can delve, that ground was crying out. She came to terms with herself and the nightmare left her, but in the beginning she must have felt that she had sinned in a very fundamental sense. "And I shall be a fugitive and a wanderer in the earth." Isn't that a perfect description of unrest?

Interview with Peter Lovesey

Diana Cooper-Clark

DCC: The Victorian period is an absorbing time and you are most knowledgeable about it. The pedestrian race in *Wobble to Death* illustrates the qualities of this time—man asserting his individuality in an increasingly mass-oriented world, endurance, persistence, the will to conquer, man's challenge to mechanization and the battle for survival. Why do you write about the Victorian period as opposed to any other?

PL: I came to that period initially because I was interested in the history of sport. At this time, I didn't regard myself as an authority or expert on the Victorian period. But I had become interested in Victorian sport as a school boy because I wasn't a very good athlete and would have liked to have been. I was flat-footed and butter-fingered and couldn't really perform very well in any team game so I tried to take up the more individual sports, like high jumping. You have heard of the Fosbury Flop, well, I was a flop before Fosbury was born. One day I happened to see a photograph of a North American Indian called Deerfoot in an all sport magazine. I took an interest in him as a school boy and decided that I might try and find out a little more about him and write a history of his life. Since he was a Victorian figure, that was really how I came into the period. While researching Deerfoot and other runners for my book, I came across a description of these strange endurance contests that were featured in *Wobble to Death*. I didn't think very much about them until one day I was perusing the personal columns of *The Times* as Sherlock Holmes used to do, and suddenly noticed an advertisement for a crime novel competition. The first prize was a thousand pounds which was tremendous to a young teacher as I was then with a young family. I didn't know anything at all about crime writing, I hadn't read the crime writers very much, one Agatha Christie and most of the Sherlock Holmes short stories, which I enjoyed, but practically nothing else. I knew that Jackie, my wife, had read a great deal in the genre. So I talked to her about it and she was very

53

enthusiastic about the idea of going into the competition. I then remembered the wobbling craze. As a setting for a crime novel it was original and it won the prize. I am a cautious person and having once found something that worked, I also wrote my second book about the Victorian period and the sporting scene.

DCC: You often deal with Victorian sports in your novels— bareknuckle boxing in *The Detective Wore Silk Drawers,* hammer-throwing in *The Tick of Death*, the pedestrian races in *Wobble to Death*. What do they reveal about their society?

PL: I don't know that there is any clever answer to that one. It is simply that the sport interests me and amuses me to some degree and I like to feel that I am writing about something that I know fairly well.

DCC: Why do you use the vehicle of the detective novel to tell us about the Victorian period when you could have written history books or even mainstream novels?

PL: I enjoy the puzzle to some extent. I quite enjoy setting myself a task in bewildering the reader and solving the mystery by the end of the book. As I said, I am fairly cautious and when planning a novel I like to have it clearly worked out at the beginning and to know who did it and why and how from the outset. In writing, I will set out my chapters before I begin to write the novel, I will have it all worked out on paper, I will have talked it over very carefully with Jackie who has a pretty good idea of the clichés of detective story writing that I want to avoid. I am happy with the detective genre. I have written novels outside the genre as well but having come into crime writing almost by accident, I enjoy it. I don't know that the mystery element in my books is quite so important as it is with some other crime writers. The picture of Victorian life may be more important in some ways to me than the mystery but the genre suits my purposes.

DCC: I find it interesting that you like the 'who-done-it' and the puzzle because so many contemporary critics, writers and scholars feel that the detective novel has improved aesthetically because it has moved away from the puzzle. Patricia Highsmith, for instance, has said that the reason she doesn't write detective novels *per se* is that she doesn't like the puzzle, she doesn't like the 'who-done-it.' I think that the general movement among the best novelists today is away from the puzzle and toward more complex characterization, more complex philosophical insights, greater sociological awareness.

PL: Yes, perhaps I like setting myself difficult things to do. I am quite aware that the old 'who-done-it' is a moribund form of writing now. But that challenges me to try to keep it just a little alive and I enjoy a challenge. It is an odd thing but I don't really like reading 'who-done-its.' I admire Patricia Highsmith enormously. I would far rather read one of her novels than somebody else's 'who-done-it.' I agree with almost every word of Raymond Chandler's essay on the simple art of murder. At the same time, I feel that the form of the puzzle fits my writing to some extent. However, not all of my Sergeant Cribb stories have taken that form. *The Tick of Death* was a deliberate attempt by me to do something else and to write a Victorian James Bond. I looked at the plot of *Goldfinger* very closely and tried to see if it would work in Victorian terms. The golf match in *Goldfinger* was my hammer-throwing competition in *The Tick of Death* and there are a number of other parallels. I wouldn't press it too far but it intrigued me to see if I could manage to create a situation in which my rather staid Victorian sergeant would actually get into bed with a lady and he managed to achieve it in that book. He did it for Queen and Country, of course.

DCC: Would you like to write a nineteenth century novel in a twentieth century skin, transferring twentieth century sensibilities onto nineteenth century life, as John Fowles did in *The French Lieutenant's Woman*?

PL: Let's say that I would have loved to have written *The French Lieutenant's Woman*. I admire that book enormously and enjoyed it so much. No, I don't have any ambition in that direction.

DCC: Actually, I meant within your Sergeant Cribb's series.

PL: Yes, from some points of view Cribb can be seen as a modern man in the Victorian era. I read an essay where Ross Macdonald wrote that the contemporary American detective hero speaks for our common humanity. He listed three qualities in particular: an impatience with special privilege, a sense of interdependence among men and a certain modesty. I think I could fairly claim each of these qualities for Cribb. In that sense, he is modern.

DCC: The style of your novels, the dialogue, the syntax, the language, all beautifully capture the Victorian mode. You avoid the purple prose of the shilling shockers, the penny dreadfuls and popular crime novels of the day—foul, brutal or terrible murder, things are "horribly" smeared with blood, people's faces look "ghastly." Do you consciously and intentionally try to capture in language, in style, in tone, the Victorian background?

PL: I have a private theory that we don't really know exactly how the Victorians conversed, just what their dialogue was like. We have examples of plays, such as Oscar Wilde's, which are rather stylized in form and beautiful to listen to, but I don't know that the dialogue of the dramatist accurately represented the way people really spoke to each other. I probably have drawn on newspapers more than anything else for what I think is as close as I can get to accurate dialogue because newspapers haven't got time to look for the purple passage when they are quoting people. I read biographies, I read everything I can lay my hands on of the Victorian period, which seems to me to be useful. I would think that people were conversing in not quite such an informal style as mine do but perhaps in a more terse and practical way than you would expect from reading many of the great nineteenth century novelists.

DCC: It often sounds as though they all spoke in essay form.

PL: Yes, that's right.

DCC: In your essay "The Historian," you wrote about the historical mystery: "The world we enter is real and under control. There is a framework of fact. Even the most extravagant plots conform to historical truths." So, in other words, in *The Tick of Death*, suspense isn't the key because we know that the Prince of Wales was never assassinated by the Clan-na-Gael. Thus, the prime element in your novels as historical mysteries is to provide a historical framework that is based on fact and truth. If a plot did not conform to these criteria, you would eliminate it. Is that correct?

PL: Yes, I think that is true.

DCC: In the same essay, you wrote that "our world of social welfare and easier divorce and psychiatric care has removed many of the bad old reasons for murder." In that case, why do people murder today?

PL: I think that their reasons are sometimes more casual. The Victorian murder was usually a more insidious thing, growing gradually. The person who was trapped in a marriage because there was the stigma of divorce, because there was social ostracism, might find it easier to poison his or her partner than to get a divorce from them. Now that is the sort of decision that you would make over a long period because you were trapped by your circumstances. It might arise from an unhappy marriage, or the prospect of inheritance, or insurance. I think everything was moving at a slower pace and people couldn't move very quickly out of one social group into another, they couldn't get away, they couldn't travel very far. They were usually limited to one small town or one community, very often one family. I think that today's decisions as to whether you murder someone are rather more casual and more frightening, perhaps for that reason, but less interesting to write about. You know, the boy who decides that he will hold up a bank and has a gun with him and shoots the cashier is perhaps more terrifying than a Victorian lady poisoner but again less interesting to me.

DCC: Do you think that the Victorians committed fewer meaningless murders, what Lawrence Sanders and others call "Stranger homicides"?

PL: If I say yes, you might very well be able to produce some crime statistics that prove me wrong because I think it is quite likely that there was a lot of violence on the streets in Victorian times that led to murder. I am not just thinking of Jack the Ripper, I am thinking also of people who would attack others in the streets who appeared to have any money on them. Garrotting, for example, was a form of mugging by throttling the victim which had quite a vogue in Victorian times.

DCC: The Victorians were contradictory. They responded to murder with what on the surface seemed to have been horror but which was, in fact, something closer to celebration and festivity. During the first thirty years of Queen Victoria's reign, public hangings were the best attended of all sports of the people. The alleged female patricide Mary Blandy, who was executed after a sensational trial, dominated the newspapers in 1751 and 52. In your novel *Waxwork* ten thousand people go to Madame Tussaud's to see Miriam Cromer's likeness on the day of her execution. How do you account for their mania?

PL: The last public execution outside Newgate was, I think, in 1868 and it was attended by the usual thousands and there was street literature about the hanging and so on. After 1868, the people still wanted something and Tussaud was clever enough to see that there were possibilities in exploiting this macabre interest that the public had and started buying the clothes of the victims or the people who were executed. It was the hangman's prerogative to take the clothes of the convicted murderer. He would then sell them to Tussaud who would exhibit them on the wax model and this seemed to satisfy the ghoulish interests of the crowds who would flock to Tussaud's. It is quite true that up to ten thousand people would flock to the waxwork museum on the day of an execution to see the model exhibited there. There is still a great appetite for ghoulish entertainment and I doubt very much whether things would be different today if public executions took place. I think they would still be assured of a huge crowd, probably millions watching on television as well.

DCC: You are probably right. The lives of many writers of the time were touched by murder: Sir Walter Scott attended criminal trials whenever he could, he had a large collection of criminal narratives and printed trials and his great-aunt, Margaret Swithin, was murdered, I believe; Charles Lamb's sister Mary knifed their mother to death; Dickens, Thomas Carlyle, Elizabeth Gaskell, Charles Kingsley and many others were interested in murder. William Thackeray attended the execution of Charlie Peace. Lewis Carroll reported a conversation of Tennyson's: "Up in the smoking room the conversation turned upon murders, and Tennyson told us several horrible stories from his own experience—he seems rather to revel in such descriptions." If we look at the mainstream literature of the time we see much evidence of violence and murder from George Eliot, Thomas Hardy, Elizabeth Gaskell. Why do you think that they didn't use the newly developing detective fiction to write about what was clearly an interest for all of them but rather stayed in the mainstream novel? Do you think they found the genre too restricting?

PL: It is arguable whether *Bleak House* is a detective story or not but Dickens came very close to writing a detective story. Wilkie Collins in *The Moonstone* wrote one as far as I am concerned. I think that some Victorians were writing what for them would be as near as they could come to the detective novel. Writers such as Hardy were more interested in exploring other things. In *Tess*, which is the story of murder and an execution at the end, which he handles beautifully, he was trying to do something else which was perhaps more serious than telling a good crime story.

DCC: When you say "serious" do you object to the increasing penchant in scholarship to convert the detective novel from good entertainment to "high" and "serious" art?

PL: I don't object to anything that anybody else is doing or to any way in which the genre is moving and developing. That is all to the good. My own experiments in the detective novel have been just a little lighthearted, perhaps, because I enjoy bringing humour into the stories. I wouldn't claim to be producing anything very original or new; as you said, I am still exploiting the old "who-done-it" formula in most of my novels. Nevertheless, I am very happy to see other exciting and interesting things taking place in this form of writing.

DCC: Charlie Peace, the Victorian murderer, appears often in your novels as a reference. Why have you never written a biography or a fictionalized version of a real life murderer such as Charlie Peace?

PL: Charlie Peace was a rather grotesque character, perhaps too grotesque for me. He was a byword in Victorian times. There was a kind of joy on the part of the public that Charlie Peace actually was arrested and managed to jump out of the train and get away from the police. He had a few exciting adventures so there was a kind of glamour to him as well. But when you look at him closely, the murders that he committed were really brutal and I don't think I would want to go into his life too closely. It is a strange sort of relationship that a crime writer has with real crimes. I came closest to producing the real situation in *Waxwork*, when I tried to show the way I thought a hangman might feel. The executioner, James Barry, was a real figure. I tried to reproduce some of the atmosphere of those few days that led up to Miriam's execution which did intrigue and interest me. But I was rather horrified after I had written the book to receive a letter from a hangman saying that he would like to meet me and talk about executions. He also invited me to see the gallows that he had erected in the basement of his house. It repelled me. And I wrote him a polite letter saying no.

DCC: That was a case of fiction and life being too close. Social critics of the nineteenth century like Charles Kingsley felt that murder was the result of a society which created appalling conditions in which murderers were bred. Many of the murderers in your novels, however, are not socially oppressed people. Is or was society at fault?

PL: In the majority of cases, yes, I am sure that social conditions had much to do with it. There was an interesting book called *Murderess* by Patrick Wilson, which listed all the women who had been executed and gave a brief account of the circumstances which led to their crime over a period in the Victorian era. Most of them were executed for murdering their children or members of their family and it was pretty clear that they were desperate people. The main thing I felt from reading that book was that these were prisoners of their circumstances and you feel nothing but pity for most of these women. There were a few wicked ones who were baby farmers, who were taking in children and killing them. They killed when perhaps somebody else couldn't bring themselves to do so. I don't want to dwell too much in my books on the circumstances that produced the murderer because they are lighthearted books, most of them. I don't underrate the horror of murder in the books but at the same time I don't feel the need to talk too much about the psychology of the murderer or the circumstances that have been impinged on him or her.

DCC: Detective Sergeant Cribb embodies both the fixed qualities of his time and the restless paradoxes of his time. You have mentioned that you see him in some ways as a modern man. He is courageous, perceptive, private, his own man. He is also capable of being insensitive, callous and cruel to Thackeray and subordinates. He has a restless temperament, a sense of irony and marvellous deductive powers. How did you create the character?

PL: I was looking in *Wobble to Death* for a realistic Victorian detective. I was conscious that the great detectives were super figures, the omniscient Sherlock Holmes, the sophisticated Lord Peter Wimsey and even Hercule Poirot, with the little grey cells. These were not really for me. I wanted somebody who would have to struggle to solve a crime and have to work against the limitations of the period. For example, there was no forensic science as we understand it today. They didn't even have accurate fingerprints tests in the 1880s and they couldn't deduce anything from them. The policeman was hampered by his own superiors at Scotland Yard. If you read a little about the history of the police at that time, it is pretty obvious that some of the people at the top were inept and corrupt. For a genuine detective working hard at his job, which is what I wanted Cribb to be, it was very difficult just to carry on doing his work without people like my Chief Inspector Jowett and his boss ruining the case at some point or other and perhaps almost at every turn. That is really what I was aiming for.

DCC: Elliot L. Gilbert has written: "If, then, the detective was a metaphor for the nineteenth century's faith in man's problem-solving abilities, he was just as importantly a symbol of growing nineteenth-century disillusionment with reason as a meaningful response to the human condition." Would you agree?

PL: Yes, I think that is fairly true of my sergeant. The statement seems a fairly apt illustration of what I was saying just now.

DCC: This disillusionment with reason is something we see in more than one nineteenth century writer. We could refer to Edgar Allan Poe, who possibly as Joseph Wood Krutch has said, "invented the detective story that he might not go mad." Dickens in *Bleak House* does not allow the triumph of reason—murder can never be undone. Inspector Bucket cannot bring the victim back to life. This was not, of course, true of popular mystery fiction where the detectives were always triumphant. Even Sherlock Holmes withdraws to Sussex Downs to his bees in the story called "His Last Bow," unable to prevent World War I with his detection of the German agent, just as his creator Arthur Conan Doyle moved from the world of reason to the world of the occult. Is this disillusionment one of the reasons why Sergeant Cribb has a flair for intuition, why in *The Detective Wore Silk Drawers* he tries to innovate new methods that are not necessarily deductive?

PL: I think he has to resort to anything that he can in order to achieve his ends. He doesn't play the rules completely. He is prepared to set a trap for a witness or a suspect who may be innocent in order to arrive at the truth. For him, arriving at the truth is the ultimate goal and the rules can be sacrificed to the achieving of that goal. I would be prepared to justify that for Cribb allowing that the orthodox methods, the sort of methods that his Chief Inspector would like him to pursue were so dominated by social conventions, the way one ought to behave. Cribb, for example, couldn't possibly in a book called *A Case of Spirits* walk into somebody's house and suggest that he might go down and question the servants without speaking to the employer first. He has to resort to what might be rather dubious practices and cut across the orders, cut across the way that Chief Inspector Jowett would like him to behave in order to arrive at the truth.

DCC: Good enough. Sergeant Cribb needs to meet Miriam Cromer, the murderess, in *Waxwork* because detective work is more than clues and statements. It involves people, their ambitions, fears, innocence and guilt.

PL: Yes, that is right and this is perhaps what I was driving at just now when I was talking about Sergeant Cribb's effort to arrive at the truth. The limitations of forensic science were such that there was very little that a detective could do when he arrived at the scene of the crime. He would look for footprints and he would look to see if there was a dagger there or if there were blood stains, a few obvious things like that. But as soon as he was concerned with suspects his job was to assess them as people and to begin to try to break through, to penetrate their mask, if they had one, and to try to understand whether they could be murderers, murderesses and if so why. I think that policemen of the period had to be students of human nature, if not psychologists. That is one of the reasons why I find the period so appealing.

DCC: In *The Tick of Death* Cribb claims to have understood only seven people almost totally, and five were murderers. He probed and looked for a motive, he took the measure of their minds. What are the crucial elements in the mind of a killer?

PL: Oh dear, that is a difficult one. I don't know, I don't know. I think probably that is a question that I shall have to duck.

DCC: Cribb comments that a woman who will kill is a rare one. Why does he think this considering views like those of Arnold Madison that the female is more inherently evil than the male? Kipling also said that the female of the species is deadlier than the male.

PL: I don't think Cribb had read Arnold Madison but I think he was probably mindful of something on a much lower level, that, in fact, there were far more male murderers about than female. Cribb has a soft spot for the ladies and tends to be gentler with them than with men; he is tougher with the male suspects than the ladies. I mean he is prepared to forgive rather more in the ladies and be a little more surprised, I think, when they actually turn out to have committed the crime. Cribb and Thackeray are two different parts of my own character; in some way, every writer is writing about himself and drawing from his own experiences. I see myself sometimes as a rather put upon character like poor old Thackeray, blundering about in the world and not getting any breaks and generally being taken advantage of. When I have been feeling in one of my more depressed moods, I see myself like that.

DCC: Don't we all!

PL: When I am in a better frame of mind, I can persuade myself that I am more like Cribb, in control, "fly to everything," as he would say, and no man's fool, but gentle with the ladies.

DCC: I know it is *de rigeur* that detectives concentrate on clues, not women. Many detectives are celibate or unmarried: Sherlock Holmes, Father Brown, Poirot, Miss Marple, Dr. Thorndyke. Others are happily married but their wives are in the background; they are never really present except by reference: Simenon's Maigret, Freeling's Inspector Van der Valk, Crispin's Professor Gervase Fen, Keating's Inspector Ghote and your Sergeant Cribb. Why is Cribb's wife, Millie, kept in the background?

PL: It is mainly circumstances. It is the fact that we are concerned with his job and with the process of investigation. In my writing I like always to be moving the story along in the direction of the plot and I don't dwell too much on the thoughts of the detective. He is not the kind of man who would come home and start talking with his wife about the problems of the day. She appeared briefly in the very first book, *Wobble to Death*. She was mentioned right at the end; he had put a bet on for her and so he was interested in the outcome of the race and hadn't stopped it before. She comes into *Waxwork*. I think, too, that there are occasions when Cribb likes to be a bit of a ladies man and certainly in *The Tick of Death*, he had a soft spot for the heroine and the wife can't be too obvious. It wouldn't do for our detective to be two-timing, he really ought to behave properly like any Victorian gentleman towards his wife and so I don't like the readers to be reminded too often that he has a wife. Unless it comes fairly naturally into the story, as it seemed to fit in *Waxwork*, I don't want her to appear. I wanted also to show Jowett's meanness when he came to look around the section house where Cribb lives. It was part of the ritual that the house had to be inspected by the superior man every so often. Before, another sergeant had done it and hadn't really observed the formality, he had just come to have a cup of coffee with Cribb, but Jowett was going to do the thing in a thorough way or so Cribb suspected.

DCC: You speak of a soft spot for the ladies. This might partially answer something that confused me in *The Tick of Death*. How could Rossanna go free? She has broken several laws, not the least of which is participation in a conspiracy to kill the future King of England. Why did you let her go free?

PL: I think this probably goes back to Cribb; he is playing God in a way, I suppose. I think there are sometimes occasions when the law turns a blind eye.

DCC: But, in her case, it was not merely a conspiracy she is involved in but she is also a cold blooded killer.

PL: Yes.

DCC: She killed the man in cold blood, she is quite ruthless.

PL: That is right and she gets away with it.

DCC: You let her get away with it. What about the question of retribution and justice?

PL: You are the first reader to have mentioned any sort of worry on that score in that book. If it is a big factor and a big element I would be interested to know if other people have felt cheated in some way by the fact that Rossanna wasn't punished.

DCC: I didn't feel cheated. Rather I felt that many murderers do go free.

PL: Yes.

DCC: It is probably more realistic that retribution is not always offered. But it was such a departure because Cribb always does get his man and in *A Case of Spirits* he was also sympathetic to the killer. However, he still arrests him for murder.

PL: Yes.

DCC: I found it interesting that the male killer in *A Case of Spirits* is a very sympathetic figure but he doesn't go free. However, Rossanna who is *not* a sympathetic figure, other than the fact that she is beautiful and magnetic, who is ruthless, a cold blooded killer, does go free.

PL: Ah, you have made a very good case, I will have to rewrite the book. (Both laugh)

DCC: Why did you write *Goldengirl* under the pseudonym of Peter Lear?

PL: Simply because I was pitching for a different readership. That was the first book that I wrote after I had given up my full-time teaching job, which I did for some fourteen years, to become a full-time writer and I wanted to extend my range. I thought that I couldn't expect to earn a living writing Victorian detective stories until I retired. People knew what to expect when they picked up a Peter Lovesey book but I didn't want them to pick up *Goldengirl* and find out that it was all about the 1980 Olympic Games, a book really in quite a different style.

DCC: On the other hand, readers shouldn't pigeon hole and categorize writers; they should allow them to be free to write anything they want. If you have a fertile mind it is quite feasible that Peter Lovesey could write a romance, or *War and Peace* or *The*

French Lieutenant's Woman, anything you want.

PL: Certainly I am interested in different kinds of writing and in doing new things but it doesn't worry me too much that I gave myself a different name for *Goldengirl*. Perhaps I was glad in a way to shelter behind the pseudonym because I wasn't too sure how the book would turn out, whether it would have any success; happily, for me, it did turn out well and it was a success.

DCC: Are we going to see any more books about Sergeant Cribb; *Waxwork* was written a couple of years ago.

PL: Yes. First I want to try something else in the area of crime fiction; I think I will write a more modern book next. But there are still many other corners of the Victorian period that I would like to explore.

Interview with Margaret Millar

Diana Cooper-Clark

DCC: You were born and raised in Canada. I have always wondered why Canada has no tradition of the detective novel.

MM: In my day, when you wanted to get published, you sent your books to the United States to get published and there was a tendency to follow them. I came to the United States because I was being published there. It was my area of business and I can only assume that that is why people don't stay in Canada. A lot of writers simply emigrated to where it was possible to function as a writer. Canadians never really did respect writers until recently. They were hangers-on, like actors, and so we (her husband, Ross Macdonald) are hoping that has changed and perhaps a lot more people will live in Canada and still be able to go on with their writing.

DCC: So it really has nothing to do with the culture *per se*? It has to do with more practical reasons.

MM: I think so, yes.

DCC: In her autobiography, Agatha Christie revealed: "I still have that overlag of feeling that I am pretending to be an author." Dorothy L. Sayers also once stated that her desire was to write a book that "was less like a conventional detective story and more like a novel." What are the elements that separate mystery novels from those outside the genre?

MM: I used to think about that a great deal but I never let anything like that bother me. I have always written as well as I possibly could within the field that I had chosen. Once you're inside a form like detective fiction, you can do almost anything. You are much freer actually than you are writing a novel outside the genre, and you can say almost anything. And I like that freedom, that freedom of style, of being funny if the situation demanded it, of being able to go from comedy to tragedy and not be buttonholed as a Stephen Leacock or a writer of tragic fiction. I have always been accused by critics of continually writing new things, of originality.

In fact, Agatha Christie accused me of it in one of her books. In a nice way, she said that I was one of the most original writers she had read and I like that. Since I have been legally blind, I have managed to pull myself together and attempt to keep my sanity. I can no longer read or watch television or attempt anything like that. But I just wrote another book. I wrote it faster than any book I have written in years, just to see if I could do it under extremely difficult circumstances. It's called *Mermaid*, which doesn't have much to do with the book, but we'll see. I managed to have a lot of hysterics, but I did it, by God! The book was nearly finished before I was able, by means of a closed circuit television, which I now own, to go back and even read a single word of it. I didn't know what I had written. I touch-typed it. I fortunately went to business college at one stage in my life. I have always written in long hand but I remembered how to type. So I did all that and I had all these pages of manuscript and didn't know what was on them. So it was kind of a revelation when my closed circuit television enabled me to read the pages. It's called a 'visual tech' and it's one of the electronic marvels which enables people who are legally blind, like myself, and have only peripheral vision left, to see things that we otherwise could not see.

DCC: I take it, then, that you believe that the best writers in the detective novel tradition are equal to the best mainstream writers.

MM: Of course I do. I put everything of myself into my books. I have always. Sometimes I write a sentence ten times. Sometimes fifty times. It has got to sound right. I haven't put that same amount of attention into *Mermaid* because I wondered how it would work out if I didn't pay so much attention to style. And we'll see, won't we?

DCC: What attracted you initially to the crime novel? You even steered your husband, Ross Macdonald, toward it.

MM: My brothers. I had two older brothers and they used to bring home *Detective Fiction Weekly* and *Black Mask* and hide them under their mattresses. And so I automatically went and took them out from under their mattresses and read them. Therefore, I knew quite a bit about murder by the time I was ten and it just seemed like a normal kind of thing for me to go into when I was put in bed with a heart condition. I had nothing to do. So I decided to write a book. This is absolutely one of those ridiculous things, I mean, here was this invalid in Kitchener, Ontario of all places, suddenly deciding she could write a book. But I wrote it in fifteen days, thus proving I wasn't totally an invalid. I rewrote it a couple of times, maybe three times, but you tackle things sometimes when you're a writer that you should probably have more sense than to do. When I wrote *The Birds and the Beasts*, which is the only book on natural history that I have done, I had only been bird watching, I think, three years when I decided to write a book about birds. Now, don't ask me how I got that much nerve. It just came naturally, I researched, I studied so hard, you wouldn't believe, and it was marvellous. It is still the book that I get most letters about and requests for. And that was published more than fifteen years ago.

DCC: You are a first-rate novelist and you mentioned before that you will rewrite a sentence as many as fifty times. It reminds me of Flaubert who sometimes spent as long as a week on a sentence. Do you think that generally detective writing is sloppier than those written outside the genre?

MM: Terribly sloppy. I can't read most detective fiction. The writers don't have any pride in their work. They are not really convinced that they are writing; they don't value their work. They seem to have the same attitude that a lot of screen writers have; if they can get away with sloppiness, they will do it. This is certainly not true of everyone but it is true of too many of them.

DCC: The novelist Jessamyn West said that Hemingway affected her writing because he moved away from the prevailing style of the time—florid, embellished language. Hemingway made the simpler prose form, "he said," "she said," respectable. Who were your major influences?

MM: F. Scott Fitzgerald has always been my favorite, even when he was out of favor. I was always telling people how much better he was than Hemingway and people did not believe it. But now I think they are a little more inclined. I think once, when I was reading D.H. Lawrence, I was in the middle of a book and I had a tendency to imitate him. Ken (her husband, Ross Macdonald) caught me and I did some thinking and rereading and decided that I would not read D.H. Lawrence until I had finished my book.

DCC: You are erudite and articulate. Why haven't you ever written anything critically on mystery fiction?

MM: I'm not interested. I've never been a critic. My husband has written criticism but I don't criticise. I don't feel that I'm capable of doing it and I'm not the type. I don't think I'm catholic enough in my tastes or tolerant enough. I think you need both those qualities to be a good critic. I would be prejudiced. I might like or dislike something for reasons that are not reasonable. So I don't try to be a critic.

DCC: I wouldn't think you'd agree with Dorothy L. Sayers about the difference between detective novels and mainstream ones. She wrote: "There is the whole difficulty of allowing real human beings into a detective story. At some point or other, either their emotions make hay of the detective interest, or the detective interest gets hold of them and makes their emotions look like pasteboard." That's certainly not true of your work.

MM: Well, what is true of me is that I cannot read Dorothy L. Sayers. I have never been able to and I wish she hadn't believed that. If she had believed it she would not have written so damn much detective fiction. If she believed that she should have been in another field. While it may be too late now, it would have been something I would have recommended to her.

DCC: Your novels embody what Joseph T. Shaw, the editor of *Black Mask*, saw at the time as a new approach in the writing of mystery. He said that the new literature emphasized "character and the problems inherent in human behavior. In other words,... character conflict is the main theme, the ensuing crime, or its threat, incidental." Julian Symons has pointed out in discussing your work that while the solution in your novels always lives up to the best of what he calls "bamboozlement," by the time it's revealed, many readers will have become so much concerned with the fate of the characters, the problem itself becomes secondary. Is character more important than plot? Or are they inseparable?

MM: That's right. They're inseparable. I just start with a bunch of characters and let them kill each other off if necessary or just talk and work things out. I don't know what they are going to do. One of my books was a *tour de force* in the sense that I knew exactly what I was going to do from page one and I went ahead and did it. This was *Ask For Me Tomorrow*. I like to think of it as a *tour de force* rather than a "bamboozlement," in spite of Mr. Symons.

DCC: Julian Symons meant it as a compliment. W.H. Auden has remarked that people who read detective stories suffer from a sense of sin. They want "escape" literature which will absolve them of their unease. E.T. Guymon Jr. feels that mystery fiction is the greatest escape literature of them all—escape from the reality of problems. Dorothy L. Sayers also wrote that "the detective story is part of the literature of escape, and not expression."

MM: I don't agree. My God, just look at the crime statistics that are now available on Los Angeles where murder has increased something like 60% this year over last year. This is absolutely insane. Ken's books and mine more truly reflect what is happening than some of the stuff that Sayers wrote about. Peter Wimsey is far remote from anything, really.

DCC: In her book *The Development of the Detective Novel*, A.E. Murch has stated that in England the detective interest remains dominant, whereas in America the essential element is mystery, a return in spirit to the tradition inherited from Poe and Brockden Brown. She cited your novel *The Soft Talkers* (British title, *An Air That Kills* in the United States) as one in which the mystification intrigues and baffles but there is very little detection in the English interpretation of the term. Do you know what she means by that?

MM: Certainly. I don't go in for the actual detection part. There are detective writers who do and some who don't and I just can only assume that people who want that sort of thing should be sensible enough not to try and read my books. I write about characters. I'll give you an example. A young man in town called me one day and said, "I've got a marvellous place where I want you to set a book." I said that I wasn't interested, I never accepted ideas like that. But he said, "I'll take you up." So he took Ken and myself up this God awful winding road and just at the top of this terrible road there was this marvellous place which had been at one time a religious colony. It had been vandalized to the extent that there wasn't a pane of glass, there wasn't a piece of plumbing. We looked around for a long time and I thought about it for a number of years and eventually I wrote *How Like an Angel* and the setting was that place. Who lives next door to it now? President Reagan. So I started a religious colony there. Nobody joined. I should have charged more. If I had said this is going to cost you three thousand dollars, I would probably have made an enormous fortune. (laughs)

DCC: In talking to you, I pick up the wit and the humor present in all of your novels. It has been suggested that the mystery novel is one of the last outposts of the comedy of manners in fiction. Like the fiction of Jane Austen, George Meredith and Henry James, the detective novel presents what John Williams says is the "stable and numerous society in which the moral code can in some way be externalized in the more or less predictable details of daily life." Would you agree with that?

MM: Well, whatever the hell he was talking about, I guess I'll have to agree. That seems a bit obfuscated. I agree that the mystery novel is a comedy of manners. That is what I meant before when I said that within the form of the detective story you can get away with a great deal. If you want to have a comedy of manners, which I did in *The Murder of Miranda* (which took place right where we are sitting, practically), you're able to do it. You don't have to have things all of a piece.

DCC: Hillary Waugh said that it is "the story element" that separates the mystery story (which he feels emphasizes this) from the straight novel. He feels that the author of the straight novel has to get a monkey off his back, therefore, in the so-called straight novel, the heart of the novel is character, whereas the mystery writer is only telling stories. I don't agree.

MM: No, I don't either.

DCC: While you might be able to make a case for that idea with older detective fiction, it certainly isn't true today. You used the word "obfuscating" before. Some of the critical attention that is being paid to detective fiction tends to be obscure and arcane.

MM: *Pretentious* too!

DCC: To go back to the notion of character, the twentieth century writer generally does not exclude his or herself from his or her creation. Consciousness is almost inevitably self-consciousness. Is this true of your work?

MM: No. I think that's nonsense. Really! I reveal myself to anybody who asks me a question. (Both laugh.) I don't need that kind of thing. I wish I did because I think it might make it easier for me to write. I find writing very, very difficult. I work a long, long time on a book. In Ken's case, he has used Lew Archer. Lew Archer has gotten older as Ken as gotten older. They have mellowed together. He has talked about autobiography. I will have none of that. I have never identified with any character, except I love to write about children. I just adore it and I'm very fond of them. I have a great many friends, especially around here at the beach club. This little music box was left at the office for me just awhile ago by a young man who I always thought was a real devil, but I go for the devil.

DCC: Is he the boy in *The Murder of Miranda*?

MM: That's right. I was accused of using this young man in that book but, anyway, now that he's 18 and off to college, he just turned out to be a fine young man and he left me this gift the other day.

DCC: We have mentioned that Ross Macdonald has written that in a novel the central character, and many of the other characters are, in varying degrees, versions of the author. Flaubert said that he was Madame Bovary and William Styron said that he became Nat Turner. Ross Macdonald also wrote: "The character holding the pen has to wrestle and conspire with the one taking shape on paper, extracting a vision of the self from internal darkness—a self dying into fiction as it comes to birth."

MM: Oh, writers are a lot of bullshitters anyway! And you know they are apt to say things for the shock value, just as I used that word, however lamentably true that is. (Both laugh.)

DCC: You were talking about not needing art as a purging catalyst. Would you say that your purpose is to entertain?

MM: No. I just have this damnable feeling that I want to write. I started my first novel when I was eight. I've always been creative. When I finish a book the first thing I do is compose a song on the piano. It's just a natural thing for me to do things creatively in any field. To do it my way. After a book is finished, I have very little interest in it. It's done, I've done the best I can. If someone dies and you've really done the very best, you've loved somebody and done everything you can, I think it's easier to bear when you have no guilt, as it were, about the situation. Perhaps that's how I feel about a book. I've done the very best I could and then I want to forget it really.

DCC: Is that why you don't like writing critically or talking about writing?

MM: Yes. I just hate this kind of thing really. I never talk about my books. I have had friends here for fifteen years who don't know I write. This pinning down interview that you're doing with me is really hard for me. Usually I can control an interviewer but I can't control you. (Both laugh.) I can control an interviewer very easily by going from one anecdote to another anecdote and in that way we all have a good time. They end up with not much information except little anecdotes.

DCC: Well, you're certainly giving me a warm time! (laughs) Otto Penzler has suggested that protagonists that are not carried through a number of novels are forgettable. He lists protagonists in Fowles, Bellow, Mailer, Updike, Styron and Pynchon. I don't agree with that because I remember their characters very clearly. Does not creating a consistent hero affect critical response?

MM: I've been sorry in a way that I haven't followed through on the same detective the way Ken has. Because in the first place you have better sales. In my last two books, I've used the same Mexican, Tom Aragon. I'm very fond of Mexicans and I know so many. But I'm getting bloody well bored; next time it's going to be a Chinese or something.

DCC: Also, you deviate from a lot of other mystery writers in that you don't use detectives generally, with exceptions such as Elmer Dodd (in *The Listening Walls*) and Steve Pinata (in *A Stranger in my Grave*). You've used lawyers, of course. Eric Meecham (in *Vanish in an Instant*) was one of my favorites and Tom Aragon. There was also Inspector Sands of the Toronto Police Department.

MM: I really did like Inspector Sands. I think he is different in the fact that he never had a first name. It's a hell of a lot harder to create a new detective every time. It's much more difficult. I can remember reading some writers years ago and they would repeat themselves. And I couldn't quite square that with my conscience. I couldn't do that. I don't think you can write many books about a detective without repeating yourself *ad nauseum*.

DCC: Why are your sleuths always men?

MM: Well, I know so many detectives and policemen and none of them is a woman. One of them was, but, by God, she was a private eye and she was a character but I don't think she was the kind of character I wanted to write about. (laughs)

DCC: So it's just the way the world is.

MM: That's right. I was surely one of the early feminists and my husband was the greatest feminist. I didn't have this sense of going out and conquering the world the way so many do. I didn't have to do it. I just assumed that the world belonged to me.

DCC: Yet you portray women as victims very convincingly.

MM: Also as victimizers, I hope.

DCC: Yes, you do. I'm thinking of Amy in *The Listening Walls* and Miranda.

MM: I think that women are so devious that they lend themselves to being victims and victimizers.

DCC: Do you think that they are more devious than men?

MM: Oh, yes, yes, by all means. I think they're more manipulative and that makes them more devious.

DCC: I don't agree with that.

MM: Oh, God! Are you sure you're being honest? I really do think women are more devious. From birth they are brought up to be more manipulative because how they are going to live is through men. You're half my age so it might be different today. But I'm 65 years old, and the women I know are more devious because they have had to be. I'm not saying anything against them but against the circumstances under which they live.

DCC: Very often in your books there are older women with younger men, such as Miranda. They fear age.

MM: This I fear is just the modern disease, the fear of age. Around here (Santa Barbara) it is much worse. A little further south in Beverly Hills, every second doctor is a plastic surgeon or a shrink. I've had friends who are on the second, third, fourth face lift. I am keeping my marks.

DCC: We were talking before about your love for birds. Very often women and people are described as birds. Amy is like a "baby bird." Eyes are like birds at sea looking for a piece of kelp to rest on. You're a conservationist. Why do you use bird imagery so much as opposed to any other kind of animal?

MM: Because they are all around us. I don't see lions all the time but I do see birds. I use dogs a lot, as you must remember, because I can't get away from them in my real life. But birds are very interesting because we know so little about them. They're still mysterious even to the scientists. So far most of the studying has been on dead birds. That is why I don't want an Audubon book in my house because his paintings, to me, look as if they were painted from dead birds. He is my least favorite of the bird artists. In fact, I was sent a book of his to review and I returned the book, as I said I didn't think I could do the book justice because I am prejudiced against Audubon. So they sent the book back and said, "Please accept it as a gift anyway." And you know I can't get rid of that damn thing. It's my albatross. (laughs)

DCC: You're highly visual in your books. For instance, the sky at twilight is the color of bruised flesh; swollen eyes look like twin blisters raised by fire; cypresses fight the wind, bent and convulsed in fury like mad boneless dancers; teeth are like dwarf tombstones. These are wonderful images.

MM: I rather like them too. I'd forgotten all about them.

DCC: How did they come to you?

MM: I haven't the slightest idea. In fact, I couldn't have remembered any of them. But I'm glad you reminded me of them.

(Both laugh.) I get that feeling when I reread one of my books or when I *used* to reread one of them—"Gee, that's good!" I'm always terribly surprised that I wrote that well.

DCC: Sea imagery is everywhere in your books. The sea is sometimes negative, alienating. In *Vanish in an Instant*, two women look at each other as if through the periscopes of enemy submarines across a fathomless and crawling sea; in *Do Evil in Return* Violet's face is lathered with death-foam from the sea. There is a parallel in the same book when Charley sees the mollie giving birth and she has this thought of "a human baby, itself a fish, but helpless, boneless, blind and deaf and fed through a cord, its growth slow, its birth cruel."

MM: The sea is my life. I'm seeing the sea in all moods. Of course, it's hostile. I always feel I can't breathe when I get more than a mile from the sea. There are certain plants, for instance, which must have sea air to survive and that's how I feel, though I never saw it until I was married.

DCC: Monsters are also repeated in your writing. You have the word 'monster' in a couple of your titles. Houses are like monsters. And the sun is a monster in *Ask For Me Tomorrow*.

MM: It's a word that simply crops up even in conversation, especially nowadays. I had to spend one summer watching movies at night on television with my grandson and so help me God, I think these Japanese movies we were watching were really the pits, with all the firecrackers going off all the time.

DCC: I seem to be committing all the critical sins. At the risk of overreaching, I would like to pursue the world of shadows in your writing. In *Vanish in an Instant*, Mrs. Loftus fumbles in a twilit world of darkness. We are told that Hearst's days were "some days": "There was no definite tomorrow or week after next, just a shady avenue of some days." Marco, in *Ask For Me Tomorrow* and also the father of Violet's child in *Do Evil in Return*, are shadowy figures.

MM: The world of shadows is just another catch-word. Since we all have shadows around us every day and night, it's a normal, natural way to describe things. Some of us have more shadows than others. I simply create a somewhat larger one than most people but I don't think it is any more profound than that.

DCC: I'm interested in shadows because I'm interested in the double, doppelgängers.

MM: I am too. To me, shadows are important right now because that's how I *see* since I am legally blind. On grey days I have much more difficulty than I have on sunny days like this where there is a good deal of contrast.

DCC: You used some wonderful lines from Yeats in *Vanish in an Instant*: "That this pragmatical, preposterous pig of a world, its farrow that so solid seem, Must vanish on the instant if the mind but change its theme." I feel that your novels are variations on those lines.

MM: Well, you spoke for me that time, I'm afraid. We all have our versions of the truth. It's not something I think about very much. I just don't sit around thinking in a philosophical manner. I sit around thinking about people in whom I'm enormously interested. I can sit in a restaurant and listen to the people at the next table discuss anything on God's green earth. Everything they say seems to characterize them. The elderly seem to spend so much time talking about their diseases, it cuts down on my eavesdropping. Because after the first few symptoms I've got it down pat, I can certainly save them a little money.

DCC: You were just saying that you really don't think philosophically. Some writers of mystery fiction have a more metaphysical approach to evil.

MM: I know what's evil and what isn't, and there it is. It's black and white. So I don't think about it. I naturally think about it in everyday terms. How can you help it when you live in southern California. You read the *L.A. Times* and at the present time the situation in Los Angeles is extremely bad. People are mindlessly buying guns and thinking that's what's going to protect them and usually or very frequently the gun is used against them.

DCC: In *Do Evil in Return*, you talked about conscience that is made of scar tissue, "little strips and pieces of remorse sewn together year by year until they formed a distinctive pattern, a design for living."

MM: That's good. (laughs)

DCC: You really are a good writer. No wonder Truman Capote asks the publisher for your novels as soon as they come out. Publish instantly! (Both laugh.) Now this is certainly true of Charlotte but what of Amy in *The Listening Walls* and Van Eyck in *The Murder of Miranda*? Clearly conscience doesn't have that function at all. Any thoughts on that?

MM: No.

DCC: No? That's like the fast ending of both those novels. Bam, that's it, no explanation, nothing, over, done with. There it is. "Amy? Well, I killed her, end of it." You don't explain, you just leave it. (Both laugh.)

MM: I try to work it all in ahead of time so I'm not boring the reader at the end—"and the reason is thus and the reason is thus." The reasons exist and if I have a good reader, which is all I write for really, then they know the reasons. Once in a while I get an indignant letter from somebody who can't figure out the ending of my book. And I don't answer that any more than I answer any of the other mail I get.

DCC: Do you ever get any mail about your sense of justice? Miranda (the innocent) is framed and Amy (the guilty) goes free. In *Do Evil in Return*, the police department was made of cold, hard material that symbolized the cold, hard quality of impersonal justice. Easter says in that book that there is no justice. We don't live in a world where retribution is a consistent thing.

MM: No. That's why I think that the people I write about are so remote from myself. I have never had to make any decisions about evil and good. It was a part of my life that it was good to work hard, to be on time. All the old clichés I was brought up with have held. I'm not a Christian of any kind, in fact, I'm an atheist which always causes people to light candles for me which absolutely annoys the hell out of me. The other day a friend of mine came down to the club here and she said that she had just gone to church and lit a candle for me. I simply blew up, "You have no right to go around spending money on candles for me." It seems like the wrong thing to do. The tactless thing to do. I'll tell you about the day I found out that I had lung cancer. I had quit smoking thirteen years before that but I knew when I was smoking heavily that I was taking a chance. So when the doctor told me that I had lung cancer, I said, "all right. I asked for it and I got it." And that was my reaction, I didn't break down and scream and cry. I went immediately to the hospital and had a lobe of my right lung removed. And I feel great, that was nearly four years ago by the way. But I really felt that I had been wrong and I really expected to pay.

DCC: There's not much I can say to that.... We were talking before about "character" in your books and I find that very often they focus and clarify the broader concerns of the novel. At the beginning of *The Murder of Miranda*, you sketch just a few lines of Van Eyck.

These touch the broader concerns of the book. Is that a fair estimation?

MM: Yes.

DCC: I know that your early ambition was to be an analyst and that interest shows in some of your novels, such as *The Iron Gates, Wall of Eyes* and *Beast in View*. You've just said that you find people fascinating.

MM: I just find them endlessly interesting. I can explore them more fully in literature than on the analyst's couch.

DCC: You have an ability to create situations that repel and attract a sensitive reader, such as in *Beast in View*. The detective novel or any novel that deals with murder creates some conflict because the reader may identify with the murderer.

MM: If you had attended as many criminal trials as I have, you really get a view of life which you don't, if you have never been to trials. I never would serve on a jury, for instance. I have managed to get out of it so far and will continue to do so now that this has happened to me (her illness). It's interesting how you feel, "God, this man did it," and then you go to the trial and you find that maybe you're not so sure. It's pretty fascinating. Some people have a hobby of it in this town. They are called the court-watchers. They go to all the murder trials and they become very erudite about the law. I can remember so many of the murders. The last one that was so profoundly affecting was the trial of a young man who had been extremely fat in his youth. He was working on a job in Texas in a meat packing plant and he fell and hurt his back and he was put on a pain killer and became addicted to it. And then he went on to other drugs, anything he could get his hands on because he was still in a great deal of pain with this broken back which hadn't healed properly. He went on a crime spree and killed somebody with this girl and came out here to California where he killed on another high. They got high and they committed another murder. When the drugs were removed, he was brought back to reality. It was the only time I've ever really seen a person in court truly remorseful. He made no attempt to defend himself. He took the stand and he practically asked, "Please punish me because I did something and I don't know why. I don't understand why." He was even in correspondence with the victim's grandfather. They had exchanged letters. How did this happen? God, everybody in the courtroom was practically crying as he was. And that night he killed himself. He had been saving up his pain pills all the time he was on trial here. He took them all at once and before the jury even brought in a verdict. Of course the verdict was guilty but it was one of the times that I was really convinced that a criminal was truly repentant and would never do such a thing again. He had had diminished capacity. You hear this diminished capacity stuff all the time and, "was the person drunk, was he on drugs, etc.?" Is this really a defense at all?

DCC: Often enough in literature the man or woman who is killed is more evil than the person who does it. In a sense the murderer becomes a victim as well.

MM: That's often true in detective stories but in real life I find it not to be true. People may ask to be murdered, they may be almost born victims but it is usually out of stupidity or dependence of some kind; it's not evil really.

DCC: Meecham, in *Vanish in an Instant*, said that the victim, like the murderer, had a certain choice of fate, a selection of circumstances.

MM: In a sense, I must keep with that. I've been to a great many trials since I wrote that. I would still think that there is a large element of truth in that.

DCC: Your mysteries often have roots deeply hidden in the past, *Vanish in an Instant, Beast in View, Beyond This Point Are Monsters, Ask For Me Tomorrow*, etc. Is it anything more complex than simply that all human beings move through history and time and that the past always has to be connected to your life now? Or is it another case of a critic seeing something that isn't really there?

MM: Nothing is really there but they have to write something. Critics are like economists and scientists, they get a new idea and they rush into print. Then the next day another economist comes out and says, "well, we are not really in a recession," and a scientist comes in to say, "No, the trouble is that Canada doesn't have strong enough rats." So we have a lot of conflicting opinions.

DCC: Your family relationships are often touching, especially the relationship of children to their mother. I love the two girls in *The Murder of Miranda*.

MM: Yes, I do too. They were based not on two sisters by the way but on a mother and a daughter here. I *mean*, not here, but some other place. They weren't as interesting but they did create scenes, to the extent that there was at one time a price on their heads. The manager had offered a $50 reward to any member of the staff who would push either of them in the pool. (laughs) The family relationships are not a reflection of my own family, certainly.

DCC: That's true, because the marriages in your books are very often terrible marriages which doesn't reflect your personal experience.

MM: God, no! My marriage is going on forty-three years now.

DCC: I can understand why people would expound on the Oedipal element in your books. In *Vanish in an Instant* there is an older woman and a younger man. On the last page in the book we are told that Birdie will always look for a son, somebody she can mother. There are other older women-younger men relationships such as in *The Murder of Miranda* and *Beyond This Point Are Monsters*. In *Vanish in an Instant* Meecham wonders if Loftus attacked Margolies because he was the father-rival-invader.

MM: After all, I reflect my times too. At that time everything was father-fixations, so I guess I was into them too. I'm a tremendous newspaper buff, or used to be, which is what I miss most, and I think I have always reflected what is going on around me. And so when people were into father-fixations, by God, I was in the middle of it.

DCC: Meecham said something that I loved. He said, "Another equation to be solved and each new equation led to still another and on and on into the infinity of the human mind." He felt stunted and inadequate, an engineer without a slide rule, a chemist without a formula.

MM: Here's another one. How about a writer without a plot!

Interview with Ross Macdonald

Diana Cooper-Clark

DCC: You lived in Canada for approximately twenty years. The Canadian historian, William Kilbourn, has written that we in Canada can best explore our identity by comparing it to that of the United States. When Hugh Kenner asked you where you'd learned so much about Americans you replied, "In Ontario." What did you mean?

RM: I meant that the situation in the United States is not wholly different from the one in Canada. You can learn a great deal about American life by observing Canadian life. Naturally, it also works the other way around. That's where it all began.

DCC: What are some of the reasons why there has not been a tradition of the detective novel in Canada as there has been in America?

RM: Canada is a culture that doesn't seem to regard itself as a free culture but is still in the learning process. Of course that's true of all cultures up to a certain point. But I think Ontario, which I'm using emblematically, has (for reasons that I haven't examined lately since I haven't been in Canada recently) a definite fear. This is the kind of fear that children nurture toward adults. Ontario is like a child that has perhaps once or twice made an attempt to become free and then has become frightened and retreated into its shell and its own history. There is a powerful life going on inside that unbroken egg. And we learn about it through the writers who do *not* tell all. Ontario writers are very much given to hiding themselves and Canadians teach the lesson and the mystery of self-hiding.

DCC: It's the lesson of Calvinism.

RM: Yes. It's simply a different tradition and it's occurred over a long period of time. It's only got worse as a result. I think that is one reason why the limited tradition of the mystery novel has transplanted itself successfully into Ontario and other Canadian

provinces, but it's done behind a mirror.
DCC: Do you mean that the Canadian writers who are now writing in the detective tradition are still behind a mirror?
RM: Yes.
DCC: Who are you thinking about?
RM: I'm thinking about a number of people who have roots in both Canada and the United States and I give myself as an example. I write on both sides of the mirror. I do this simply because that seems to be what my work needs. It expresses what I want to get over.
DCC: One of your first publishers was the Canadian magazine *Saturday Night*. In it you wrote this epitaph for a quiet man:

> His mortal bond was sundered
> And he was lodged on high
> Three days before they wondered
> If he was going to die.

You mentioned that you were thinking of yourself.
RM: Yes. Usually when you write an epitaph you are thinking of yourself; you don't write them for other people.
DCC: Previously you have discussed the relationship between your life and your fiction. You have written that in *The Barbarous Coast* you were learning "to get rid of the protective wall between my mind and the perilous stuff of my own life." Thus, there has been a consistent effort on the part of critics to penetrate the biography of your life. Writers such as Willa Cather called those biographers who try to reduce great artists to psychological cripples, explaining away their gifts and visions in neuroses and childhood traumas, "tomb breakers." Since you have been very open about the connection, I wouldn't think that you would be adverse to this kind of study.
RM: I'm very interested in it. Two books have been written about myself and my work, and many articles. I enjoyed both books. For one thing, they told the truth for the most part, as far as they were aware of it and as far as I was aware of it. I don't see any objection to a writer openly discussing himself because it's what we're doing anyway. We might as well admit it and learn from it and help other people to learn from it. As a persistent high school teacher, I feel that that is the sort of thing that should be going on in the schools. The art of self-discussion, self-understanding is the

route by which we are going to get somewhere. If we do get somewhere. I don't mean as individuals but as a culture. There's so much richness and detailed matters of interest in the Ontario tradition. It is still being hidden, not deliberately hidden, but it's kept out of sight. And we need to have it up in sight so that we can know what the odds are.

DCC: I couldn't agree with you more. You wrote that: "We writers as we work our way deeper into our craft, learn to drop more and more personal clues. Like burglars who secretly wish to be caught, we leave our fingerprints on the broken locks, our voiceprints in the bugged rooms, our footprints in the wet concrete and the blowing sand." Why does the writer secretly wish to be caught?

RM: He's holding in his own hands and in his own mind and imagination the things that he is hiding but doesn't want to keep hidden because knowledge of ourselves and of the things in ourselves that require to be corrected are the things that we're searching for.

DCC: So those clues are dropped and it actually allows other people, the readers, to join the journey and the process.

RM: Yes, it's done on behalf of other people by the writer. It's a fact because it's going on constantly, particularly in very young cultures like the Ontario culture. Although, God knows that it's been going on for two hundred years.

DCC: In his study of Latin American writers, Leon Livingstone suggested a new consideration where autobiography goes beyond historical fact to produce a fictional offspring who *is* and yet is *not* the author himself. Author and character act as mutual catalysts to produce in the artist a constant and unceasing self-revelation and self-creation. You have written that Lew Archer "tends to live through other people, as a novelist lives through his characters." Both the detective and the author then seek self-knowledge as well as the reader.

RM: I would go along with that one hundred percent.

DCC: I guess it goes back to what you were saying before about the mirror. In your novels, the past affects the living present of your characters. In *The Underground Man*, the minister's letter to Stanley tells him, "The past can do very little for us, except in the end to release us." There are deep connections between the past and the present. This reminded me of something Faulkner once said: "The past is not dead, it is not even past." How has achieving a closer unity with your own past improved your writing?

RM: All I can do is suggest what I've been trying to do. I'm trying to take a form of popular culture, at least it started out that way, and make it viable *as* popular culture. My novels are also moving backwards into the mythological as they move forward into the present. We discover ourselves again by reaching backward into the past. And we discover as we do it that almost everything is relevant to what we're doing. In other words, our current language and experience is completed by the present again and again and again. After a while we don't distinguish very readily between the present and the past. I'm going to leave that idea trailing because I couldn't conclude it satisfactorily. At the same time, it's the essence of what we're talking about.

DCC: Yes. Also, in your novels, families are our link with the past; they determine our fate. But the relationships are pained and dark in your novels. In *The Doomsters* one of the characters says, "The fathers have eaten sour grapes and children's teeth are set on edge." What does the framework of the family enable you to explore in your novels?

RM: It enables the young hero to discover the mythical and the practical, the relationships between the people who are present and not present. It is the story that immediately begins to rise when you enter into a discussion like this. The presence of people and objects and forces, which are on the other side of the silence, is opened up. It becomes necessary for the person who is telling the story or finding the meaning, to open up further into his own life. You discover, by way of the story, what the rest of the story is going to become. As you know, Proust made a life's work out of that kind of study. There's simply no limit to what can be discovered in the self and its adventures. I'm not saying that that's the only thing that contemporary fiction can or should do, far from it, it should do everything, but its central purpose is the biography of the present looking into the future. There should be a sense of continuity. Call it the past into the future.

DCC: The search for your identity into the past is not only for the lost child but also for the lost father. Our myths and fairy tales are full of stories concerning the abandonment of children, the fear of infanticide, the dark nature of family life. There is Goya's painting of Saturn devouring his young. Hansel and Gretel are abandoned by their father and stepmother. Snow White's stepmother wishes her dead. The psychoanalyst Dorothy Bloch believes that children have a built-in fear of infanticide. Her theories run counter to a central doctrine of psycho-analysis and a central concern of yours, the Oedipus complex. She believes that children are attracted to a parent not out of incestuous impulses as postulated by Freud but as a strategy to gain control over a threatening parent. I find that element of the power struggle in your novels.

RM: Yes, I think that's relevant. But it depends on what family you're looking at. You can choose your family and get any color you want really. Isn't that true? In fact, if you're going to write honestly about a family, any family, you can't leave out the darkness. But some of us put in more darkness than others. More often than not that's simply the result of early experience.

DCC: In most of the families in your novels there is only one child, at the most two, unlike the black families in *The Ivory Grin*. Why?

RM: The most obvious reason is that I was an only child. Although I had sibs, they didn't survive. I was brought up as an only child myself and experienced some of the sadness of an only child and some of the opportunities of an only child to study themselves and the other people around them. You mustn't forget that the young author begins quite early to follow his chosen study which is the study of mankind. Naturally there are conundrums that have to be solved, "Why was I born?" or "Why was I brought up as a single child, alone?" That's not the complete answer but it leads us into fuller studies of oneself and one's own experience. It forces you to zero in on yourself, on the problems and complexities of life because it's what you know, and we are all working with what we know.

DCC: Undoubtedly. It's crucial for many of the children in your novels to find their father. In *The Far Side of The Dollar*, Tom couldn't know who he was until he knew for sure who his father was. But, at the same time, children whose fathers are *not* missing in your novels almost all have poor relationships with them. Why is this? Is it that the missing parent is idealized? Or provides unknown knowledge?

RM: I think that the answer has to be yes to both those questions. That's interesting. There is the beginning there of a drama. And it is possibly a drama in which things are changed and perhaps improved. If your father and mother are missing, there's another chance to recreate your life.

DCC: As an extension of that, Lew Archer is often seen as a father figure. In *The Far Side of The Dollar*, an emotionally disturbed boy says that he wishes Lew were his father. In *The Way Some People Die*, Galatea says to Lew, "You sounded like my father." In *The Doomsters*, Carl confuses Lew with his father. In *Black Money*, Lew reflects, "I think in my nightime loneliness I'd fathered an imaginary son." But even though Lew occasionally feels the loss of a family, in *The Underground Man*, he says, "I had no children, but I had given up envying people who had."

RM: The 'father' in Lew is there but it's not the central thing about him. Of course there's a constant identification between the various father figures and son figures. One becomes the other. It works both ways. I don't think anybody misses the various stories in which that identification is brought up to the surface again and again. It's a means of getting more out of the story that one is telling and broadening the necessities that are drawn in by these various magnetic devices of reaching out. The father figure is not so much his character as the use he makes of himself. He is constantly ending off and being drawn back into the family situation.

DCC: Family relationships between husbands and wives are also troubled; they have a love-hate relationship. You twice quote the Latin poet Catullus, in *Sleeping Beauty* and *The Ferguson Affair*: "Odi et amo," "I hate you and I love you."

RM: It almost speaks for itself, this idea of a love relationship becoming rapidly, or almost immediately a love-hate relationship. It's the sort of thing that arises immediately as one of the two or three ways in which a couple can get to know each other. This is true whether their intentions are good or not. It simply is one of the main channels back into life.

DCC: The family seems to embody your tragic sense of life.

RM: This is not my adult experience. It's my childhood experience which is replete with the sort of things that we're talking about. I've spent a good many years trying to understand it.

DCC: Many of your characters are aware of tragedy. In *Black Money* a character says: "It's dangerous to get what you want, you know. It sets you up for tragedy." In *The Barbarous Coast*, a writer laments that he had to tack a happy ending on Flaubert's *Salammbo* because it is a tragedy, its theme dissolution. And why? For money. And in *The Zebra-Striped Hearse*, Lew says, "Tragedy is like a sickness, and it passes. Even the horrors in the Greek plays are long since past." There have been many different definitions of tragedy, from Aristotle to Arthur Miller. What is your understanding of tragedy?

RM: Well, I don't know whether I would have a definition. Tragedy has so many aspects and almost anything that you're likely to say about it or remember about it will be part of the explanation. I would like to settle for something short, if I can think of something short that would be appropriate. Tragedy is the discovery of meaning in one's own life.

DCC: I find that appropriate. Peter Wolfe does not think that Lew Archer is tragic. Lew doesn't suffer enough and, by withholding both moral and emotional response, doesn't share any heightened perception with the reader (the hero's "tragic farewell").

RM: I agree. He's not basically the suffering one. He's the means to it. There is always more than the one protagonist in these stories, that's the way they're told and the way that they're intended. I think, for one thing, that we're not really talking about a tragic development in which everything is rolled up into one ball and one man does all the suffering and all the experiencing. There's always at least two people on stage and if the writer or the reader tries to make too much of any one person they find themselves missing out on a good many meanings. The tragic hero has to be differentiated from other people in the story and it would certainly be too much for one man to do or for one weight to be lifted. It isn't necessary to put everything on one pair of shoulders and you don't have to limit yourself to just one kind of experience like a tragic experience or a psychological experience. It's much better, I think, to follow the story as it tells itself rather than formulating a story and then tying it up line by line with the aspect of another story. But that was terribly long. All I really had to say was that we're talking about more than one person.

DCC: In support of what you are saying, in the contemporary detective novel, the tragic lies in more than one character—the murderer, the detective, the victim, the people left behind. You are obviously familiar with Greek tragedy and the myths. What did the Greeks understand about life and art that we might not, or not in the same way?

RM: The Greeks can lead us to a binding together of the various forms of experience. They seem to have understood the connections between the physical and the mental in ways that we are only beginning to touch on now in our own culture. Everything we do has at least two meanings which can be made into one. I think that's what the Greeks were after and succeeded in touching on anyway. It's the sort of thing that a sculptor, for example, can do right out in the open without having to explain it at all. You just go ahead and do it.

DCC: I see what you mean. You explore a number of myths and legends in your books. One is the Sleeping Beauty story. A number of people in your books need to be awakened: Laurel and Tom in *Sleeping Beauty*; Stanley and Fritz in *The Underground Man*; Bret Taylor in *The Three Roads*; and in *The Zebra-Striped Hearse* Lew Archer speaks of those "who would rather die in a vaguely hopeful dream than live in the agonizing light of wakefulness." Why do certain myths such as Sleeping Beauty, Cyclops and Galatea compel your re-interpretation?

RM: There's nothing quite so pleasurable for a writer as his or her finding a story half done which needed further doing and which chimed in with what the writer already knew or half knew. I have a feeling that everything that's done in contemporary fiction is done in a half light which magnifies itself and changes itself. The stories that are half told are the really interesting ones. They are, of course, the stories that Margaret (his wife, Margaret Millar) and I have both been writing all our lives and yet everything we write, I think, is tied in with the classical tradition one way or another. I also mean the forms that this classical tradition has taken in the contemporary period. We have used the half-told tale in order to explain ourselves to ourselves, which is perfectly legitimate. That is what it is for. We not only hold onto these stories of the past, we seek them out. They seem to be necessary to our full consciousness. Isn't it interesting though that the same stories keep telling themselves and they seem to solve some of our psychic problems or lead to their solution?

DCC: That's true. It's interesting that it wasn't until the nineteenth century that the word *myth* was defined as a lie. As an extension of myth, dreams are also important to your novels. In *Sleeping Beauty*, Lew says, "Mother and son were picking up on a dialogue which had probably been going on for fifteen years and became as unreal and powerful as a dream. And I was cast a third role in this dream play." In *The Doomsters*, Lew thinks: "If they [the doomsters] didn't exist in the actual world, they rose from the depths of every man's inner sea, gentle as night dreams, with the back-breaking force of tidal waves. Perhaps they existed in the sense that men and women were their own doomsters, the secret authors of their own destruction. You had to be very careful what you dreamed." You have also written that the detective story deals with "the nightmare that can't quite be explained away and persists in the teeth of reason."

RM: To dream is a very important form of experience. We're learning to take it for granted that we should turn to the dream for understanding. A great deal of popular culture comes out of this kind of a study and this kind of a search. Popular culture has stepped around the obvious now and is writing directly about the dream vision. Popular culture can embrace it pretty well and explain it to itself. It's becoming part of the "high culture" quite rapidly, I would say. Of course, it has many various ways now of attaching itself to the main culture.

DCC: How does popular culture embrace that dream world?

RM: Young writers can just sit down at a typewriter and without any explanation at all, they can go ahead and write out of myth and into dream and nobody is in the least puzzled. The writer has this knowledge. I would claim that the writer could know these things without having been taught them or having been exposed to them.

DCC: Certain images in your novels immediately leap out. Eyes are central images. Your interest goes back to your doctoral thesis: *The Inward Eye: A Revaluation of Coleridge's Psychological Criticism*. Eyes are like birds, oysters, obsidian, the color of gin, but they are also blind. In *The Galton Case*, a man sprays Lew's face with a paintgun and for him, "the fear of blindness is the worst fear there is." In *The Moving Target*, when Lew squirted oil in his eyes, we are told, "blindness was the one thing he feared." In your short story "Gone Girl," a character says, "My eyes were my connection with everything. Blindness would be the end of me." There are one-eyed dogs, one-eyed people and the Cyclops eye appears over and over again. Even the name Oedipus comes in part from the Greek word for *eye* or *I see* (oido, oida).

RM: If I knew why I'm obsessed with eyes, I might have failed to write some of the books. It's a puzzle. I don't mean to limit it to that, but it's a puzzle to me, and yet, you can see what the puzzle is for. It opened up all these questions for the writer, for the reader, and for you. It opened up a pattern which demanded to be further opened over and over. It opened this up or just failed to do so, so it justifies itself. It's for what it's for.

DCC: Images of ears and noses don't recur, but the mouth and extensions of the mouth, like smiles or teeth, are repeated. Mouths are smeared, sensitive, brutal, clownish; smiles can bite and teeth can grin. Also, birds appear over and over.

RM: I'm a bird watcher and so is Margaret.

DCC: Yes, I know. Eyes are like birds and dead birds echo dead men; the DDT that made the pelicans sterile and cracked their eggs parallels the moral DDT of the older generation who had damaged the lives of their young. But birds can also signal hope for the future. In *The Galton Case,* the "morning birds appear there as reminders of a world which encloses and outlasts the merely human."

RM: Just think of what the bird does. The bird wakens very early in the morning ahead of everybody else and when he moves, he moves upward and generally his relationships with other creatures are comparatively friendly. His actions are not destructive except towards smaller creatures which are his prey. It seems to me that we're in a cluster of meanings which are now almost telling themselves and being told or used with not having to be told. They begin to sound to me like myths or pieces of myths which don't have to be further explained. They're simply their own shape, their own sound, their own color, but in the process of finding these relationships, we find their connections with all the other things. I was trying to give some idea of a mythical world without using any of the abstract words. That's what I've done in fiction, to an extent.

DCC: The violation of nature reflects the violation of man. There is the oilslick in *Sleeping Beauty* and in *The Underground Man* avocados "hung down from their branches like hand grenades." Much of modern American literature deals with what Leo Marx has called "the machine in the garden," the betrayal of the land. The land was the great, good place where man was spiritually nourished and enlightened, whereas the city was always evil and corrupting. You reflect this concern which is more so in the mainstream novel than in the detective novel. Do you feel a closer affiliation to the mainstream writers, in that tradition, than detective novelists?

RM: Well, yes! The mainstream is what keeps the non-mainstream alive and it works the other way too, although of course, alive in a different sense. You have to have an understanding of what we've been talking about in order to make it meaningful and viable. It doesn't just come out of the tradition, however; certainly it draws on the whole historic background. Detective novelists do draw from this background to some extent, whether they like it or not. It can't be helped. It's the relationship between these two cultures or those two aspects of culture that makes it necessary for them to be replenished, each one at the other. The whole story isn't complete unless the culture of the middle and lower class is also in some ways included and brought in. That's what is so essential. That relationship has to be expressed.

DCC: Evil is more shapeless in modern life. It is no longer clear. Your wife, Margaret Millar, told me that, for her, it's perfectly clear.

RM: Yes, but who told her? (Both laugh.)

DCC: In *The Zebra-Striped Hearse*, Archer is amazed that Manny Meyer's father had died in Buchenwald and yet he didn't believe in evil. You have said, "A deeper sense of evil (which I associate with Dickens and Wilkie Collins) has come back into the detective form in more recent decades."

RM: Both of them had a much stronger sense of evil than their immediate predecessors. There was a movement in Collins and Dickens to lead the murder story back toward the myth of murder and away from simple murder stories that didn't lead so far or so deep. I'm not a tremendous admirer of Wilkie Collins but there's no question about somebody like Dickens who is the master. Thomas Hardy is a perfect example of another writer of that period who had a deeper sense of evil.

DCC: Your idea that murder is the objective correlative of spiritual death, a metaphor for our daily lives, is fascinating. Is living on the edge thrilling and an interesting way to live?

RM: I didn't necessarily decide that I would like to live there. You can't live in a modern city without being exposed to danger. You risk your life obviously almost every day. It's well that it should be risked for some reason, some good meaning, some good outcome; it shouldn't be just a risk without a purpose.

DCC: But why is murder the objective correlative for spiritual death?

RM: I don't know. Even though I said it, I can't understand or answer that question without further study.

DCC: In *Meet Me At The Morgue* we are told that everyone walks a moral tightrope everyday. You have said that Freud "deepened our moral vision and rendered it forever ambivalent." Because values aren't there in society, as they were in traditional societies, we have to make ourselves up as we go along. That reminds me of Jay Gatsby with his platonic conception of himself. Elmer Pry feels that Lew's saving grace is his "strength as a moral agent." What is your moral vision?

RM: I think it aims at telling the truth without hurting people with it.

DCC: Do you agree that Lew is a moral agent?

RM: He certainly aims to be. Of course he doesn't succeed in being moral all the time, neither do any of us.

DCC: Morality in your books is attached to a concern for language. D.H. Lawrence had this concern. In *Lady Chatterley's Lover* it seemed to Connie that all the great words were cancelled for her generation: love, joy, happiness, home, mother, father, husband, all these great, dynamic words were half dead now, and dying from day to day. In his Nobel Prize speech William Faulkner exhorted us not to forget words like love and honor and pity and pride and compassion and sacrifice. In *The Wycherly Woman,* in an exchange with Bobby Doncaster, Lew also shows the same concern. We have to believe that words like "courage" and "loyalty" are not mere abstractions, that the eternal verities do exist, or else we descend into murder and meaninglessness.

RM: This is the form that the writer's concern has to take because that's what he is. If he doesn't handle language adequately or truthfully he's failing in his functions. I feel very strongly about this. The study of language, and this is for Margaret too, is absolutely essential. It's interesting too that Margaret is a student of the classics.

DCC: You once explained to a student: "I think my later novels are constructed to represent the workings of divine justice, that immensely complex causality that governs our lives and is influenced by our lives in turn." In your novels *The Three Roads* and *The Goodbye Look*, we are told it is mercy, not justice, that is needed. Lew says: "I have a secret passion for mercy.... But justice is what keeps happening to people." Is mercy a higher value than justice?

RM: Yes, of course. But it includes it. I think I wrote this shortly after I had an experience talking to a young priest, a Los Angeles priest. The priest without doing so openly answered me with a question, either we should aim at justice or mercy. I think we have to go for mercy everytime, that's my feeling, but it also is sort of backed up by the results.

DCC: Leslie Fiedler, in *Love and Death in the American Novel,* has written that "the private eye... is the cowboy adapted to city life on the city streets, the embodiment of innocence moving untouched through universal guilt." Lew Archer is a departure from this tradition.

RM: Fiedler is talking about another generation of detective writers. I don't think there has to be an argument between that and what I stand for. It's just that his statement is not as relevant as it should be for what we're doing today.

DCC: Your intention has been to bring the detective novel closer to the purpose and range of the mainstream novel. But mystery writers like Ruth Rendell or Julian Symons don't feel that detective fiction at its best can equal the greatest novels outside the genre. Would you agree or not?

RM: I have to agree, as of now. I really have to agree. We're comparing an enormous achievement up against something that's still very much in the "becoming" stage. I don't think it would be very useful or helpful to try to make comparisons between the small and the large. The detective novel is extraordinarily varied and remarkable, but it isn't a great novelistic form, at least not yet.

DCC: Why has the detective genre been considered inferior? What are the problems in the ways people respond critically or esthetically?

RM: I think any form of the novel should be taken for what it offers in itself.

DCC: You've written critically about the detective novel. What are the valid critical approaches to detective novels?

RM: I haven't read much in that line so I'm really not competent to judge. I did my work rather early in this field and I'm not up, I don't pretend to be up. I think the form is expanding in all directions and it's very interesting. The critical form also has to expand appropriately, and they will have to find a new language, new ways of seeing. Of course, any good writer is capable of curing these ills just by sitting down and writing a darn good book. But it's not something that has to take another century. It's something that can be done by one good writer now.

DCC: You have said that "the writer of popular literature generally doesn't invent too much. He deals with received forms which are familiar to his audience." Greek, medieval and Elizabethan audiences were familiar with these forms. Art was not "high" but communally shared; it was not in museums but in the culture.

RM: The intention has something to do with the author's willingness and desire to say things that are worth saying and that are memorable. I think a piece of writing doesn't have to be written on a very high, serious level in order to be valid, or in order to support the culture. I would simply go on from that and examine the many, different ways in which culture can be spread and fed in the presence of an already existent culture which has its values, but which has to be continually fed, refed and taught and assisted in all the different ways that we pay tribute to art. I really didn't say enough in that sentence, but I said enough so that you will understand that my feeling about the "feeling" concerning culture and art is very broad indeed. There's no limit to what we can do for culture or what it has done for us.

DCC: That is close to your dislike of élitism in literature. You feel that communication breaks down in a community if there are Mandarin novels written for Mandarins and lowbrow novels written for lowbrows. Your aim is "to write novels that can be read by all kinds of people." But how can we bridge the gap? Do you believe that the people who read William Faulkner also read Harold Robbins?

RM: Yes. I have a tendency to think that the reading public is wider than you imagine. There's more good things being read than we imagine.

DCC: Perhaps. But I still think there are two buying audiences. I think that the people who have made Solzhenitsyn a best seller are not the people who have made Harold Robbins a best seller. I think there was less of a gap before. Virginia Woolf, for instance, knew exactly who her audience was.

RM: The main thing, apart from the writing itself, that interested me all through my life, is how are you going to get people reading, and keep them reading? Well, you do it every way you can think of. (Both laugh.) I started, you know, as a high school teacher. I'm still a high school teacher. I want to see the writing on the wall again.

DCC: You have said that detective fiction serves as a model for life and action. Why do you think the detective novel more than any other kind serves as a model for life and action?

RM: I don't know whether it goes beyond all the other forms of the novel. It's a very fine teaching instrument for all the obvious reasons. It forces the reader to expand. He uses his mind in many directions. One way in which this can be true is that detective fiction (as I have written) can remind us that we are all underground men making a brief transit from darkness to darkness, that the central vice of the underground man is moral and social sloth.

DCC: You have also written about how the literary detective has provided writers like Edgar Allan Poe with a disguise, a kind of welder's mask enabling them to handle dangerously hot material. This disguise is the imaginative device which permits the work to be both private and public, to half-divulge the writer's crucial secrets while deepening the whole community's sense of its own mysterious life. You have acknowledged that Lew Archer enables you to dredge up material that you wouldn't be able to dredge up if you were writing in the first person as yourself. What is the intrinsic nature of detective fiction that allows you to do this?

RM: You see, you can present yourself as yourself, and at the same time back away from an overcommitment of yourself. It simply is an obvious way of assuming a role which frees you temporarily and then enables you to step back into your role.

DCC: Do you think it's more difficult to do that in a book like *The Great Gatsby* or *Huckleberry Finn*?

RM: It's not possible to write a book like *The Great Gatsby* in those terms. You would be jangling the elements that you were working in. You can't just put together one thing after another and assume that it will be all right. You have to obey the consequences of the form you use, you just can't say, "Now I'm going to use this form." That immediately forces you into a more difficult position as a writer than you would have been in, if you'd have gone in in the first place, on those terms.

DCC: Norman Kiell wrote a psychological analysis of your work. He feels that your consistent use of the "eye" is an effort on your part to remove the curse of the Evil Eye; it is an illustration of the primal scene, whether factual or psychical for you. He cites the beaten child as one response to the primal scene in *The Galton Case, The Doomsters, Black Money* and *The Far Side of the Dollar*. He discusses parallels in your life and Poe's and he says that Poe's concern with the Evil Eye in "The Tell-Tale Heart" displays a special form of castration anxiety as it is related to the primal scene. In like manner, he cites the characters in two of your novels, Pedro Domingo and Tom Russo (*Black Money* and *Sleeping Beauty* respectively). Do you find this kind of critical analysis of your writing valuable?

RM: Sure. I think it has a certain value; it shows that that form and its consequences can be applied and reapplied to changing forms. I've never yet found myself quite in touch with the primal scene, however. I think he has made a fair statement but I don't see that it constitutes a whole philosophy. That kind of study can be revealing. I don't mean to limit what we're talking about to the purely psychic, or whatever. What we are looking for really is something that can be experienced in a person's mind, without having to borrow necessarily from anybody else's mind.

DCC: Graham Greene once said that an unhappy childhood is a writer's gold mine. Hemingway agreed. This is Edmund Wilson's wound and the bow theory. You seem to agree when you said, "What makes the verbal artist is some kind of shock or crippling injury which puts the world at one remove from him, so that he writes about it to take possession of it."

RM: I don't resent anybody who makes any connection between my work and my psychic life. I don't see it as a reduction of my writing but a further connection.

DCC: You are one of the few writers of the detective genre who has had in-depth analyses of their work. Do you think that the approaches that have been taken to your work have been valid and revealing?

RM: Interesting and revealing, not necessarily valid. I wouldn't attempt to say what's valid and what isn't.

DCC: You grew up intellectually in the period of the New Criticism.

RM: Yes, I really took my doctorate in that specific field.

DCC: Have you published your thesis?

RM: No. Maybe some day I'll get the time to do something with it.

DCC: Peter Wolfe feels that your plots often profit from the kind of hermetic reading stressed by Brooks and Warren. Would you agree with that?

RM: Sure. But it's difficult to explain how I might profit from something that I read twenty or twenty-five years ago. The same would apply to the critic. It would be difficult for the critic to reach that far back into my experience and apply it to more current work. The New Criticism is worth reading and studying but it certainly could not be universally applied to my work.

DCC: In his essay on *Crime and Punishment* R.P. Blackmur wrote that "The act of life itself is the Crime." The nouveau roman novelists, who are thought to have deep ties with the detective novel, declare that reality is a mystery story. Some critics have spoken of "the crime of existence" in looking at the roots of the detective novel. Do you find that kind of critical response to the detective novel far-fetched?

RM: I don't think it's far-fetched but I think its usefulness is fairly narrow. Nevertheless, it's one of the useful tools in criticism.

DCC: So you are open critically to whatever works, exploring new paths, new perceptions and methodologies.

RM: I came through a period which was just breaking open this whole situation, but as soon as it had broken up I was ready to step back into my chosen role which is that of being a fiction writer. Actually a doctorate in this particular branch of English was all I needed if I was going to become a writer with a capital W. In other words, you can't make everything out of your life at the same time. I decided to become a mystery writer.

DCC: I admire your critical writing.

RM: That's nice, but I didn't waste much time on it either.

DCC: Eudora Welty has said that criticism is also an art even though other novelists would disagree.

RM: You can do both at the same time, you almost have to. One thing leads easily to the other. It just depends on what you mean by an art. A critical art, yes, but everybody knows the difference between criticism and art. I don't have to spell it out.

DCC: Jacques Barzun thinks that the great mistake in criticism of detective stories "is a failure to recognize that these are tales, not novels. They are not intended to go deep into character or to study social problems or expound philosophical or religious revelations. The interest is purely narrative." I wouldn't think that you'd agree as you have said that you are really trying to write about contemporary life and that you have found the detective form useful for this exploration.

RM: It depends on just what angle the detective novel takes. It's right if it just hits the eye as is necessary, if you're going to make it at the same time realistic and imaginatively creative. It's hard to do that in criticism.

DCC: You regard yourself as a critic—"a critic in the sense of being a custodian of the whole of literature."

RM: It doesn't mean that I assume responsibility for every book I've ever read. It just means that I know it's there and something should be done about it. But it's a pleasure rather than a curse to have that responsibility. There isn't so much difference between being a critic and some other kind of writer. It could be that the critics have had a very full day and will continue to have. We have some very fine critical writing being done now.

DCC; You have said that the writer can lie in wait in his room and keep open his imagination and the bowels of his compassion against the day when another book will haunt him like a ghost riding out of both the past and the future. Your last novel, *The Blue Hammer*, was published in 1976. Are you working on another book that has come like a ghost out of the past and the future?

RM: I'll write another book, if I can.

Interview with Howard Engel

Diana Cooper-Clark

DCC: I have often wondered why Canada has no tradition of detective fiction whereas our neighbors to the South do. Is it perhaps cultural? Canadians have faith in authority and order, Americans have a suspicion of it. America has a higher crime rate than Canada, yet Canada has one third more per capita of policemen. Americans value self-assertion, the individual above the collective whole whereas Canadians seem to understand the individual to be subordinate to the commonality. We might say that Canada is a "community of obedience;" the United States is a "community of will." Just look at the different self-images of both countries. In Canada, it is the beaver; in the United States it is the eagle. The symbol of the Canadian frontier is the Royal Canadian Mounted Police; he represents law and order, he always gets his man by moderate persistence. The symbol of the American frontier, however, is the Wild West desperado, outside society and external law. Very often the law is represented by vigilante or lynch mobs.

HE: Well, I certainly agree with what you've said. The American image has always been that of free enterprise and the private eye is, of course, the epitome of individual free enterprise on a small scale. Canada tends to be more corporate and that is why the best known policeman in the world, the Mountie, is a symbol of our country. Perhaps the British Bobby is well known. But you think of the Bobby not as someone who gets his man but as someone who can tell you how to get to the British Museum. We are a law abiding community in Canada generally, at least that is the picture. Marshall McLuhan always says we see our immediate past in the rear view mirror and so what I am talking about is what appears to be our present but is really probably our immediate past. We may have changed without noticing it. We are a colony in a way that the States isn't a colony, or it doesn't perceive itself as a colony in the way we do. Look at the difference between the old school readers of the Americans and of the Canadians. We were brought up on verses that helped us remain colonists and have an attitude toward authority that was basically subservient. I guess that is why we have so many civil servants. Maybe that is the natural end of the old Ryersonian education.* Those who don't go into the church, go into government work.

DCC: The paradox of all this is that mainstream Canadian literature is full of lives on the edge, full of violence, death and even murder. To name just a few, there are the novels of Robertson Davies, Adele Wiseman, Marie-Claire Blais, Morley Callaghan, Hubert Acquin. The central question of all of Robertson Davies's novels is "Who Kills?" Hubert Aquin's books *Prochain Episode,* *Blackout* and *The Antiphonary* all make use of the forms of classic crime fiction. For example, in *Blackout* there is a discussion of Holbein's painting, "Mystery of the Two Ambassadors": "the Holbein picture seems to me to be composed... in accordance with the laws of the detective story.... It is a painting in the form of a murder story." Another character reflects that the figures of the detective and the criminal, the murderer and the victim, so often seem to merge one with another. So, perhaps, the lack of detective fiction is not merely cultural. What is there about the nature and form of the genre that has eluded us?

HE: First of all the form is older than Chandler, is older than Conan Doyle. It goes back before "Childe Roland, to the Dark Tower Came." A lot of mystery fiction is a search and that is traditional material. The old Sagas tell stories of, "And then he did this and then he did that and then he did the other thing and then something came out at him out of the dark or something moved in the pile of bones in the Moot Hall." I think it has something to do with "story"; there is a great appeal in the story elements of what is going to happen, that you are walking on the edge as a reader. Now, because detective fiction is so basically a story, it has tended to be cheapened or debased as literature. People don't take Chandler as seriously as they take Mark Twain or Steinbeck. But Chandler was using the elements that he read in ordinary fiction and other writers, respectable writers, have used elements of mystery fiction. A lot of writers that we know, including Balzac and many others, have used

---

* Egerton Ryerson established the public school system in Ontario.

the techniques of mystery fiction to tell their stories. In Canada, we are more aware of a class structure in literature; one thing is respectable and invited to Government House and one thing had best come around the back door. I think it is a shame that things get divided that way, that the one is commercial hackery, suitable to be read on subways, and the other is real literature that you can leave on the coffee table. We accept the notion that mystery fiction is something that great people, great minds read to relax. Lord Chief Justices in England admit that they read mystery stories before dropping off to sleep, Presidents of the United States made the same claim and I am sure that we have leaders who say the same sort of things.

DCC: But other cultures such as England or the United States have had the same problem of this dichotomy between the notion of great literature versus the detective genre as inferior, yet they have nevertheless created a tradition and a genre, but we haven't.

HE: When you consider how young our literature is and how thin, and that until fairly recently Canada was known as a country of a lot of one book novelists, there wasn't very much chance that we were going to develop a side stream of detective writers. I think we are avid readers of mysteries. A quarter of the books that are bought in the English speaking world are detective fiction. In this country where people still give up novels for Lent, you would give up a Chandler or John Reeves before you give up Robertson Davies or Marie-Claire Blais.

DCC: A long time ago the American writer O. Henry wrote: "East is East and West is San Francisco." He knew that to American readers certain places were more *visible* than others, whereas other places as far as literature was concerned were *invisible*. Could you explain how that attitude has affected "place" in Canadian literature and the detective novel in particular?

HE: That is a big question.

DCC: I'm sure. (Both laugh.)

HE: Considering the size of Canadian literature as a whole, we have got a healthy regional literature. One would never expect a Jack Hodgins to write about Newfoundland or the Annapolis Valley any more than we would expect someone like Ernest Buckler to give us a novel of the prairies. "Place" is something that Canadian writers have been very conscious of. In commercial literature they have tried to stay away from differentiation, tried to make Canada appear as if it might be Montana. A story set in Saskatchewan could be really south of the border. When they made a film of Margaret Lawrence's *A Jest of God*, it came out as *Rachel, Rachel.* The setting was assumed to be in the United States and the license plates showed that that was so. There is a tendency on the part of those who are marketing books to try to keep Canada a secret. I sometimes think that someone doesn't really exist in Technicolor in this country until he has been in *Time* magazine. As soon as *Time* magazine does a story on him, suddenly he bursts into living color and he is written about in Canadian magazines. He begins a new life as a person, in a sense, because he didn't exist before. I think that in the same way a place doesn't exist until it has been written about someplace else. We have no idea how to write about Toronto until we have seen how Toronto has been written about. New York, Los Angeles are all very clear to us through the pages of Rex Stout and Chandler, but Chandler found out how to write about Los Angeles as Hammett found out how to write about San Francisco. How do you write about a Canadian small town and make it different from a town on the other side of the Niagara River? It is difficult. How do you do it without using a vocabulary that is specialized, that alienates readers, and I guess it doesn't happen until it has happened. People say "yes," that is the way it is. "Yes," it is just like that and it is not just the look of the street or the way the houses curl along the main streets of a city, but the way a man will hoist his trousers slightly when he comes back into a room or the way a girl might look shyly after a rather uninhibited yawn. We recognize these things when we see them, when the writer has shown us our own experience again.

DCC: William French wrote that Benny Cooperman in your novel *The Suicide Murders* is the perfect Canadian private investigator. He's a nonentity who retches when he looks at the body, not a tough-guy hero. He is a small-town klutz who is intimidated by waitresses and is uneasy in his relationship with his Jewish mother who regards him as a loser. French of course later qualifies this "klutziness" as a tactical expedient to throw the opposition off guard. But this seems to reflect Margaret Atwood's idea that Canadians are as obsessed by failure as Americans are by success. Do you agree that this portrait of Benny is a prototype of the Canadian identity? And what does it mean for us as we begin to develop our own detective genre?

HE: Well, if I think too deeply about that I may effectively stop writing about Benny Cooperman. I see Benny Cooperman fairly clearly. But if I start thinking of him as a prototype he is going to need oil in all his joints to get him moving again. So, I am going to tread softly. Benny is Canadian, I am Canadian, I think his klutziness is something that he has learned to live with and he has learned to use it. People open up and are more frank with him when he has just spilled coffee all over his desk blotter. If he has just put a lot of ash on his tie and has swept it on to his papers, the person speaking next to him is likely to say a little more. His Canadianess is not intended to be symbolic. I have to leave a lot of that to the critics, let them tell people what Benny Cooperman is and I will just try to keep him on the track as best I can.

DCC: Your writing seems closer to the American tradition of detective literature than to the British. For example, you have a private-eye, not a policeman. Also your writing style has the same terse, laconic style of the Americans. You have said that you were fascinated by Raymond Chandler's use of language, his invention of slang that wouldn't go stale, the vigor of his language, the mixture of American and British in his language.

HE: I do have my favorites among the British writers. I like P.D. James, Ruth Rendell, Jean Stubbs, Freeling, I like a lot of them, but there are those that are rather bloodless. The corpse found in the library with the antique stiletto in his back and the neat footprint in the soft mud outside the French windows just doesn't seem to have quite enough vigor in it for me. For me, the mystery novel is more than a puzzle, an extension of a cryptogram or the crossword puzzle in the weekend paper. The element of mystery is very important just as the element of puzzle is very important; there has to be a really mysterious situation, you have to feel that your detective is vulnerable, that none of the people in the story are safe. That is, you don't feel that anybody is going to get out of it safely. You have got to feel that the protagonist is vulnerable even though you know that he or she has to go on to another series. It is important that you are talking about a real world and that the community being discussed is the whole of the community and not a special weekend party at some country estate or a group of people on a private island or a specialized community in some way, so that the murder has to come from a group of select people not from the community at large. So the world of the American mystery is more chaotic than the British where someone may nurture a grudge for a dozen years and finally spring into action, as in the case of Christie or Allingham. There are some writers working in England who use the American tradition. I am thinking of Freeling's detective; old Van der Valk treats the whole community, it is not an English puzzle, it is not neat, it is not the murder of Sir Harry at a shooting weekend. And Gavin Lyall, although his books are more adventure stories there is always a good deal of detecting in them and he writes in a way that I think shows his admiration for what the Americans have achieved.

DCC: Up to this point, Canadian literature has been derivative. I know it is difficult to predict the literary future but as Canadian detective fiction evolves, most notably yours, such as in *The Ransom Game* and *Murder on Location* how do you think it will differ from those of other countries in style, form, content, characterization, philosophy, values?

HE: I think the wonderful thing about any book is that it takes you someplace else. It moves you from the railway car you are travelling in or from the chair you are sitting in and in that way it is going to show Canadian backgrounds, and it filters them through a mind or through a consciousness that is mine and Benny Cooperman's, and in those ways we get Canadian echoes. As far as the kinds of crime that are committed, I have certainly been on the watch for stories that seemed to be particularly Canadian. *The Ransom Game* tells a story that was in its roughest, raw outlines suggested by a real case. In *Murder on Location* I have brought into play certain memories I have of being an extra in a movie that was shot here. Although movie making has changed a great deal in the intervening years, I am still able to use some of the feelings and observations I made then and during the writing I have tried to bring them up-to-date as far as the changing technology and administering of film making today. And, of course, what could be more Canadian than Niagara Falls?

DCC: Very true. What is it that attracts you to murder, especially for a first novel? Is it what Dickens speaks of in *Barnaby Rudge:* "that appetite for the marvelous and love of the terrible" which is eternal in man's nature? Or is it Gertrude Stein's belief that "mystery and detective fiction... metaphorically stated the mystery behind creation and life itself"? Or is it none of those very profound psychological statements?

HE: They both have something to say. I didn't know I was going to write a mystery novel. I don't feel that all my reading has led up to this. I am a bit surprised that my first book is a murder mystery. I tried to be fair to the genre and I tried to obey its rules and be fair to the characters and to the readers and not pull punches. I have sifted the story through Benny Cooperman's first person narration and Benny hasn't been around perhaps as much as I have, and so he is not likely to say going into Notre Dame, if he ever walks into Notre Dame in Paris, that it is a typical example of twelfth century gothic, but that it is kind of dim and cool. And perhaps the second conveys more to more readers than the former.

DCC: Cyril Connolly made an interesting statement once. He wrote that "... in a hundred years our thrillers will have become text books... the most authentic chronicles of how we lived. For the detective story is the only kind of book now written in which every detail must be right; nobody cares in fiction, even in biography, what make of car the hero uses, or where he gets his clothes, but in the compression of the detective story where every touch must add something to our knowledge of the characters, their walk in life, their propensities for crime, such incidents become of extreme importance, they must render an accurate delineation of the business of living." Do you agree that the crime novel reflects social history and the *zeitgeist*?

HE: Oh, I certainly do, and also too because a lot of writers like Monseignor Ronald Knox took up the writing of detective novels as a hobby. Chesterton and a lot of writers who felt that they were slumming to a degree in their detective writing were able to write about things that they wouldn't put in their other books. Our prejudices and received notions about our society tend to find their way into respectable literature. We open up the stops a bit more when we are slumming. Think of the energy that you get in the old *Black Mask* pulp magazines and compare them with the kind of things being written in the acceptable magazines at the same time. A nineteenth century prose in a debased form was still being used in the respectable magazines and in the popular novels of the nineteen twenties. Magazines like *Black Mask* featured people who were influenced by Chandler and Hammett as well as introducing Hammett and Chandler themselves, and it was a format that was very much in a prose what the sonnet is to the poet. It was a tight jacket that had to be fitted to the circumstances; you had a very short space, you had to tell a lot, you had to create a world in a few choice sentences.

There was no time for fine writing and so each sentence had to pay its way, and in each sentence the thing had to actually happen in the sentence. You didn't have a chance to simply reflect on things.

DCC: You have said that you're not a specialist in talking about the novel, the detective novel, the Jewish detective novel or the Jewish detective novel in Canada. What is it that gave you the confidence to write a detective novel if you feel somewhat hesitant to discuss it critically?

HE: Before *The Suicide Murders* my longest piece of work in print ran to eleven pages and it was a poem, so I find myself a little bewildered facing you across the microphone. It is one thing to do it, but to explain how you did it is almost enough to make you trip up and not be able to do it again. I know a lot about making movies, I know a lot about the stage, but I have never directed a movie, I have never written a movie, and the plays that I have written are not very good. So I write out of ignorance. I write to try to find what it is I think, and to see what comes of it.

DCC: Why did you create a private-eye and not someone connected with the police department?

HE: There has never been, as far as I can remember, a Canadian private-eye and I thought it was time we had one. I looked up in the Yellow Pages of the telephone book and found out that there are private-eyes. Now to a large degree, as Chandler would agree, the private-eye in fiction is quite different from the fellow who peeks through hotel transoms in real life. He is a fictive being, and so my private-eye is somebody who is in the literary tradition of the private-eye. He is involved in the crime that we all consider to be the worse, murder. It's awfully difficult to write about someone who just sits in a room and to whom nothing happens. But at the same time my private-eye is a guy who does the things that Philip Marlowe wouldn't touch. Philip Marlowe would have told these clients to get lost because Marlowe had certain standards. He didn't do divorce work and frowned on peepers who did. Well, Benny Cooperman is such a peeper.

DCC: In *The Suicide Murders*, Sergeant Savas tells Benny that he's a good peeper but he'd make a lousy cop because he makes imaginative connections without hard evidence. Is that the only difference between a private-eye and a policeman?

HE: Benny isn't schooled in police work. He knows a bit about it but in normal police work they have a book of rules and a book of procedures and there are certain things that have to be done and you do your best given the length of time you have got, because you have got to get on to other things. A detailed investigation has to be done while you are on the scene and there is not very much opportunity for detailed follow-up work. Someone working like Benny can spend as much time on a case as he likes. He says that when a client comes in that he is going to push all the files off his desk and concentrate on this one. Now the reader knows or suspects that there aren't very many other cases on his desk at the time and that he is leading the client on a little. But he does have the time to give it individual attention. I guess that is why people hire private detectives because they do things that the cops won't do. There have been detectives in Canadian writing who were amateurs like John Norman Harris. His detective, Sidney Grant (in *The Weird World of Wes Beatty*), is a very attractive and likeable lawyer and he acts as a private detective in his story but he isn't really a private-eye. The John Reeves hero, the inspector and sergeant in *Murder by Microphone* are also very attractive characters and I would be glad to see more of them, but they work for the police department and are involved in the procedural routine work there, although in this case a bit unusual because they are unusual people.

DCC: How did you become so familiar with detective and police procedures?

HE: I started by phoning one of the coroners working in the Toronto area before I got to page fifty, to find out about the first crime described. Then as I needed expert advice all along, I talked to a friend who is a former police reporter who told me you don't talk about guns. A gun is a "piece" and that would be the professional way policemen would talk about a weapon: it's a "piece." Also I spoke to policemen about the registration of firearms. I found out from a policeman that a private-eye in Ontario doesn't carry a gun. I found how he is licensed. I spoke to a private detective who works in Toronto over a very agreeable lunch, and he told me about how he is licensed, the kinds of cases he will do in a year, and the kinds of reference books he would have. I tried to get a picture of how it would be. I must say that I was fairly far into the book by that time so it helped to confirm my guesses.

DCC: Benny is quite different also from other detectives in fiction. You have said, for one thing, that he doesn't go through the logical deduction process like Ellery Queen or Sherlock Holmes but Benny is a good judge of people. What are some of the other differences?

HE: He is intuitive. He has an itch behind his knee that seems to help him out of difficulties. He works hunches in a way that a cop can't justify. I mean all cops will have to work hunches because that is the way you form a theory. A theory in the beginning is a hunch, but since Benny doesn't have to justify his hunches, he doesn't have to have the hard evidence up front, so he is able to see something through in that way. Benny is naturally curious and he is a tidier by nature, his own life is pretty chaotic and I think he likes the idea of bringing neatness to other people's lives. It is more than just a professional interest in finding out who-done-it.

DCC: We often have a very clear picture of the detective in other people's novels, such as Nero Wolfe. Over the corpus of Ross Macdonald's work, we get a full picture of Lew Archer, but not in any one book. Ross Macdonald does this because he wants the other characters to be as important as Archer. Is there a particular reason why you do not describe Benny more fully?

HE: I thought that Benny might grow on people a little more if he is not described all that much. I will throw in the color of his eyes in one book as I mentioned the fact that he is losing his hair in the first, and those details can be added as they appear to become important. It is like a comedian leaving people wanting more, to not answer all the questions before they are asked.

DCC: You continue the tradition in the detective novel wherein the detective is either celibate or unmarried. However, Benny's parents appear often in the first novel and I presume they will continue to do so in the rest of the series. Why parents and not a wife or a girlfriend?

HE: The attempts to show married policemen have not been all that successful, as far as I have seen. There was an experiment to marry off Lord Peter Wimsey, wasn't there? And I don't think that was a great success. Holmes' faithful friend and companion, Dr. Watson, has a role because he tells the story. Someone who is going to be part of the stories could easily be a boy friend or girl friend or something like that. But to open up a special chapter to show the detective going home to feed the dog and have a fight with his wife interrupts the action. It becomes a side trip away from the story and I don't think that readers want to hear about things that are side trips. I am just thinking of a scene in a Hitchcock film where he does send his detective home for terrible meals prepared by Vivian Merchant in *Frenzy*. I thought that worked particularly well, but it was for its comic relief so it enhanced the story, and I think that perhaps Benny's parents do offer a bit of comic relief. They show something about him by reflection because they are his starting point in life, and I think they do get involved in the story. There is a scene in *The Ransom Game* that takes place in the family condominium and in the third book, *Murder on Location*, it is through the parents that a vital clue comes to Benny. But I am not going to say Benny isn't ever going to find a girlfriend.

DCC: Good. (laughs) You have stated that there haven't been many Jewish detectives and a few that I thought of were Janwillem van de Wetering's detective Cardozo, Henry Kemelman's Rabbi David Small and also in the nineteenth century there was a writer by the name of Wilheim Hauff who wrote the first tale of detection in German literature. It is called *Abner the Jew Who Has Seen Nothing*. *Abner the Jew* is a satire about a Jew, an amateur detective who is much too intelligent for his own good. The same thing happens to Abner which has happened to Voltaire's Zadig and Hauff converts Zadig into a Jew. Are there any brief reasons why there haven't been more Jewish detectives? There are a lot of Jewish writers.

HE: I don't know the statistics but I suppose there are about as many Jewish policemen and detectives as there are representatives from other groups. The Jew as a Jew doesn't bring anything particular to a police problem.

DCC: Harry Kemelman's Rabbi Small does. Kemelman has said that his original impulse in his novels was to explain—via a fictional setting—the Jewish religion. Rabbi David Small, his detective, uses the subtle reasoning of Talmudic logic which allows him to see the third side of every question. Also his use of Talmudic logic allows him to explicate the world of Judaism: topics such as traditional Judaism versus its role in a Christian culture, the problem of Jewish assimilation, the relevance of Jewish principles of ethics and justice as an ideal philosophy for modern man within a secular civilization.

HE: I am not an educator basically. I am speaking of my environment and my upbringing but I am doing it in a way that comes naturally, I do it as easily as I breathe. I have not tried to talk about all these questions. Benny Cooperman is brought up in a largely secular city by parents who have rudimentary fragments left of an earlier tradition and although they don't feel quite part of the larger community, they don't not feel part of it. Benny has gone to a normal Canadian public school and high school. He has read the same books that most of his friends have so he is assimilated to a different degree, and yet he too feels on occasion his separateness and uses that to see the society from the side line a bit.

DCC: You have just referred to Benny's feeling of separateness and you saw him as a man who was both inside and outside his society. It clearly goes beyond his Jewishness in a WASP culture. I find him lonely, sad and vulnerable, a man who is measured always by his brother's success, who lives outside the expectations of society and his family of how he should be living his life. He is a man in his thirties with a very erratic income, who lives in a hotel, who is not married with children, etc. You seem to be talking about his psyche more so than making sociological observations.

HE: Yes, I think so. It is difficult to stand up and say who you are today, in a way, and I think that Benny reflects this. He is working through the problems of his life and a lot of the things are put on the back burner. He has a lot of his life on hold. He knows that he is not fulfilling his parent's expectations either by becoming a father of a family or having a decent job or a job that they would think of as decent. But he's not certain he doesn't want these things either, so these problems are being suspended at the moment.

DCC: You have mentioned the importance of plot, the puzzle, but you equally have talked about the importance of characterization. As you know, there is a constant debate about the emphasis of plot versus character in the detective novel. Many people believe that the detective genre is inferior because it has stressed plot instead of more complex characterization. However, a number of contemporary detective novelists seem to agree with William Faulkner that the only thing worth the sweat and blood and anguish of writing is "the study of the human heart in conflict with itself." Where do you stand in relation to the debate?

HE: I agree with Faulkner. Agatha Christie used to say that she invented her plots in the bath, and I am sure that Faulkner never did that. (laughs) I do enjoy trying to invent people and trying to see what makes them tick in a way that doesn't dissect them, to show them operating. Certainly I do feel the constraints of plot and the necessity of playing the game according to the rules in a murder mystery, but at the same time I am interested in trying to make people real, someone the reader can recognize. If I can do that I will be very happy.

DCC: Randall Toye wrote that Benny has no particular moral code as do his fictional predecessors like Lew Archer, Philip Marlowe and the Continental Op. He seems awash in a world that he not only cannot understand but a world with which he can barely cope. Morality in contemporary detective fiction is no longer rigidly black and white as it was in earlier detective fiction but rather it has become much broader, much more ironic. Do you agree with Toye's assessment of Benny?

HE: I don't think so. I remember writing a scene in which Benny was in a position where he could use a bit of pressure, a bit of blackmail to get somebody to talk and decided not to. Now, that is in one of the books still to be published, I don't know whether it is going to survive the editing. It seems to me that Benny isn't somebody who would bend the rules in order to make something happen. He is not likely to bend somebody's arm behind his back to get him to talk. He has his tricks that I mentioned before about getting people to talk to him frankly and he knows that he has an open face and people do tend to confide in him, and he is lazy enough so that he gets the cops to do a lot of his leg work for him. They are friendly and they have got labs. So that is part of Benny. I have often wondered what would have happened to Sam Spade if the black bird had really been solid gold. Would he have split? His character seems to stand very close to the line of being on the side of law and order, or not. In *The Glass Key*, our hero was certainly treading a very fine line between which side of the law he is on. Marlowe is, I think, always the knight in shining armor. Only he is wearing a fedora and a trench coat. Marlowe is a moral person in a nasty place. He is the person who goes down those mean streets who is not himself mean. And I think Benny is a bit like that. He is not out for money or he wouldn't be in the detective game. He is not out for glory.

DCC: T.S. Eliot wrote that: "What we have written is not a story of detection of crime and punishment, but of sin and expiation." Which of these interests you?

HE: They both interest me (the mind of the murderer) but I haven't got to the place yet where the main part of the book is a discussion of ethics as Freeling has done. I don't know that Benny is particularly interested in the dark night of the soul. I don't think he is driven by a feeling of absolute morality the way the sheriff in an American western believes that the law must be obeyed, that the rule book must somehow prevail, that on the frontier somehow the moral order which has been upset has to be righted. I don't think that Benny has any kind of grand notion like that. When a dirty deed has been done, Benny feels some sympathy for the murderer in *The Suicide Murders*, and I think it is real, it is certainly not feigned. That is not an easy question for him. There are some people for whom the crime is a crime and then let us get on with it. Benny pauses and gets on with it after a time.

DCC: That idea of justice is interesting because the murderer in *The Suicide Murders* is sympathetically portrayed. She is allowed to commit suicide by Benny. Does Benny feel that her murders are justifiable because the victims are far less sympathetic than the murderer?

HE: Benny is aware of the context, he is aware of how her mind works, and that is why it is not a simple case for him. It is not a matter of black and white and he is aware of all the variations. Her sister who was so beloved was corrupt in her way. Most of the other people who came to a bad end were imperfect. It is as Hilda Black says in the book, when you watch the wife of the accused in a trial, you can tell by her face that there is no question of guilt or innocence involved here. It is a matter of loyalty and blood and something that transcends the normal text book rules about right and wrong and guilty and not guilty.

DCC: Would it be fair then to say that the law is not justice but that real justice is poetic justice?

HE: I think so, yes.

DCC: If the downfall of the murderer is an outcome unequivocally to be desired (as it is in the detective novel but not in *King Lear*, *Macbeth* or *Oedipus* for whose heroes we mourn the lost potential for greatness), then this downfall of the murderer makes the detective novel "a tragedy with a happy ending," as Raymond Chandler said. But the murderess in *The Suicide Murders* is a very sympathetic figure. She is a sadly disturbed, intelligent girl, of considerable potential. Is the novel closer to the tragic elements in classical tragedy or those in the detective novel?

HE: According to the rules of the detective novel, and one of the ones that Chandler kept to, the murderer can't be a looney, and so I came as close as you would want to come to breaking that rule. And so Hilda Black is shown to be a person of qualities in spite of her need to expiate the crime that caused her sister's death. It is a wart on her face that has to be removed and she can't really get on with her life until that is gone. But in removing this wart her life has to be sacrificed and she is willing to play the game according to those rules, so there is that feeling of loss and of lost potential.

DCC: Peter Lovesey wants to entertain primarily, Ross Macdonald wishes to explore the human psyche, Julian Symons tries to dissect the society that he lives in. Do you have any particular idea about what you want to do or do the ideas just bubble up from the depths?

HE: Well, I hope they keep bubbling. I guess whatever I say that I am trying to do could easily be disproved by the books themselves. I think probably the best advertisement for the books is the books themselves. But all three of the things you mentioned appeal to me. I hope that my books entertain. I hope I do some probing of the psyche and do some dissecting and talking about the society. I feel as though I am poking at it with a stick rather than probing with a more precise instrument. I like the idea of coming at the society from, not a new angle, but an eccentric angle with the character of Benny Cooperman. He has a kind of ironic detachment from the society; he is in it but not of it or he is of it but not in it. He has gone to school with his friends on the police force, or some of them, but he is not on the police force, he feels just a bit different. He is a bit of a spectator, a bit of an observer of life and so he sees things. In the first book, *The Suicide Murders*, he sees that some of the best families are up to their eyebrows in crime. It is interesting that there are people with names like Staziak and Savas who are doing all the work and people like Ward and Yates are collecting all the pay. In other books I would like to probe to what degree I can the human psyche but I don't think I could ever face it as a question like that. It'd have to come out of character. I like the idea of people moving and behaving in a way that is natural to them, either to be virtuous or villainous but to behave consistently and characteristically rather than be mangled about as rather large marionettes with me pulling the strings.

DCC: On second thought, I think I've treated Lovesey's, Macdonald's and Symons' intent too simplistically. Michael Smith has suggested that *The Suicide Murders* is too close to its Chandler/Hammett/Ross Macdonald models.

HE: I can't deny being terribly influenced by Hammett and Chandler. Perhaps Chandler mostly, although I think I admired Hammett first. What I was getting back to was the private-eye and the private-eye as seen by Hammett and Chandler, that is, the private-eye before the Baroque frills, before the sadistic overtones added by Mickey Spillane. He is in the tradition but coming out of the tradition fairly close to the source. I think that there is also a lot of the feeling of the Johnny Fletcher books written by Frank Gruber. He wrote stories about a couple of down-at-the-heel private investigators and he was writing at the same time that Chandler and Hammett were writing. There is a case where humor is added. Now, Marlowe says some very funny things, makes some funny observations and certainly his similes are wonderfully contrived and funny in themselves, but I don't think humor is the main thing that Chandler was after. However, humor was a little more up front in Gruber's novels and I think that I am trying to keep humor a little more up front.

DCC: Do you think that the assessment is fair to say that you are too close to those models?

HE: I think he is wrong. But I can see why he said it.

DCC: As you know, in the last ten or fifteen years there has been a considerable scholarly response to detective fiction. What do you feel about various attempts to discuss detective fiction in terms of mythic archetypes and patterns, the flight and pursuit, the escape and the struggle, guilt and expiation, the quest, initiation, sacrifice, knowledge acquired through violence, the exorcism of sin, the return to order and innocence? Northrop Frye for one has written about the detective novel in these terms. Do you think these critical methodologies are useful in application to the detective novel?

HE: I don't know that that kind of analysis does more than make the writer self-conscious. I'd be tongue-tied, I think, if Noam Chomsky started taking my sentences apart on a blackboard. Anything that helps the writer is fine for the writer but the critic has other functions besides helping the writer. He is helping other people, he is helping the reader to see what the writer has done and pointing out what is happening to the society based on what the writer has been doing. I think a mythic interpretation is legitimate. For instance, we know that Chandler did write stories about knights in shining armor for the *Westminster Gazette*. He wrote about saving people. His character literally was a knight in shining armor walking down not these mean streets but walking through flower scented glades and listening to the murmurs of delightful music. Philip Marlowe and all of the characters that were in the small short stories who weren't called Marlowe are really the same detective, the same knight in shining armor, a bit pock-marked, a bit splashed from the gutters. Nevertheless, his instincts are the same as that knight's.

DCC: I suppose I am playing the devil's advocate because I really do agree with you. I think that criticism is very helpful to a lot of people, not necessarily to the writer in terms of creating his work but in terms of enlarging the reader's perception. Pete Hamill, the journalist and novelist, has said that Raymond Chandler and Dashiell Hammett were better American writers than William Faulkner. I feel that is stretching it a bit. Do you think there is any point in this kind of comparison?

HE: It is interesting that Gide said that Hammett was the most impressive American writer because he never corrupted his art with morality. That is an important view of literature but to say that Chandler and Hammett are better writers than Faulkner, I would hate to say that. It is no accident that *The Big Sleep* was written for the screen by Faulkner with Leigh Brackett and Jules Furthman. But just as Carlos Fuentes thinks that Faulkner is a writer of the third world, a South American writer, I think that Chandler and Hammett can be considered serious writers. Anything that can break down the compartmentalization of writing is probably a good idea. I do think that Faulkner was a better writer than Hammett or Chandler but I think it is because of the size of his achievement, not because of the genre any of the people we are talking about were writing in.

DCC: I know that writers do not usually think of a particular reader or response when they are actually writing or creating their books. However, after the book has been completed, is there an appropriate response that you would like to your books?

HE: Let us see. No response can be nicer than a good review.

DCC: I don't mean "I like it" or "I don't like it." Would you like to see somebody do an in-depth semiotic analysis of *The Suicide Murders*, structuralist response, a mythic, archetypal interpretation of your books?

HE: Perhaps sometime on a very cold February evening before a fire, that would make good reading. I think the kind of reader that I am looking for is someone who can enjoy the book on all the levels that he can take in. Certainly I'd like to think there is more in the book than just the mystery novel. I am not slumming, I am writing as good a mystery as I can and I am trying to do it as well as I can. What is it Faulkner says, "kill all your darlings." I guess I have left some darlings unslain. One reader of the book in Paris wrote to me and mentioned some of my " darlings" and I was very happy to hear that she had seen those particular things. For instance, she mentioned "The Green Tower" that seems to brood over the city of Grantham and that happens to be the location of the solution of the whole story. That was good to see and also she saw some other things that I would like to think I thought of but I really can't honestly remember putting them in for those reasons.

DCC: You said that you call your work "my typing." Truman Capote once said of another writer's work that he was not a "writer" but a "typist." Capote meant that in the worst possible sense. I assume you don't.

HE: The first book happened so quickly and came out rather more easily than I ever imagined possible. I had written only eleven pages of a long poem before, so that to find that within a few months I had written a book.... I don't want to really disturb those circumstances and suddenly think of myself as a writer, someone who gives interviews and someone who appears on television programmes. I don't want to become a talking head, I don't want to become someone who is known as a writer. I want to just go back and do my typing. If that's the way to get it done then that is what I would like to do. I once tried to write a play about Ragueneau, the pastry cook in *Cyrano de Bergerac*. He was a very good pastry cook but a bad poet. He wanted to be a poet and he abandoned something he was good at to move to something he was terrible at. And I saw it as poignant, a small tragedy, of someone not recognizing who he is. So I want to save myself, I guess, from not making a mistake. Let me go on with my typing. Let me lisp in numbers because the numbers come.

DCC: You have written poetry, stories and you have mentioned a play. You will probably write novels outside of the detective genre in the future. What are the demands of the detective novel that other forms of literature do not have?

HE: There has to be a genuinely mysterious situation which will coalesce into suspense as your detective begins to turn over the stones, finding strange things wriggling out underneath. There have to be characters you care about. You have to care about the detective so that you identify enough to feel threatened when he is threatened. One of the attractive things about the genre is that your detective takes you to places you are not likely to go on your own. He can take you up blind alleys or into the back of pool rooms or into board rooms of large companies. He has to keep changing the scene for you and introducing you to characters who are diverting, and who represent problems for the detective; each one is a nut that has to be cracked in some way. In addition, I guess there is a feeling that the detective has made some of the bad in the world go away without redeeming it altogether.

DCC: Dick Francis would agree. He thinks of his detectives as almost the last bastions of civilization.

HE: I don't think that Benny Cooperman is a vigilante. He is not a Dirty Harry. He is not right wing in that sense. He's a "tidier," he is compelled to tidy peoples' lives. I don't think he has got grander notions about tidying up society in general or I don't think he would ever think of himself as a self-appointed Catcher in the Rye, someone to make things right. He doesn't believe that without Benny the world would fall apart. I don't think he would ever imagine that.

DCC: In keeping with the idea of the form of the detective novel, Thomas De Quincy in *Murder Considered as One of the Fine Arts*, wrote that "something more goes to the composition of a fine murder than two blockheads to kill and be killed.... Design... grouping, light and shade, poetry, sentiment, are now deemed indispensable to attempts of this nature." Would you agree with De Quincy and do you think that you've done this?

HE: Yes, but *Murder as...a Fine Art* reminds me of the murder in Agatha Christie or Ellery Queen. This is the murder where the crime has been contemplated many years and finally executed exquisitely with a silver tipped arrow which is replaced at the first opportunity by a silver stiletto. That kind of cerebral crime has a kind of fascination. However, I like Chandler's idea when he said of Hammett, "He gave murder back to the people who commit it, for reasons, not just to supply a corpse...," reasons of greed and revenge and malice, all of the reasons why people commit crime. I am not particularly interested in crime as such; I don't spend hours in criminological sections of the library. I am not interested in the transgressor or the delinquent offender. I am interested in the reasons for murder when life has people in a forked stick. How are they going to react on the basis of their individual temperaments?

DCC: What would you have liked to have done in *The Suicide Murders* that you feel that you failed to do?

HE: I would have liked to write great prose. I would like to have sold 15 million books. Obviously I am not complacent about it. When I look over it I see more than the odd "typo." I see lots of sentences that could be a lot better. I see opportunities lost as far as plotting and as far as writing goes. I'd like it to be a book that I would be very proud of. I am proud of it because I've done it but now I would like to make the next and the next and the next even better.

Interview with Ruth Rendell

Diana Cooper-Clark

DCC: You are obviously a great reader of books. Your novels always include references to Shakespeare, E.M. Forster, Arnold Bennett, Oscar Wilde, Dickens, Rupert Brooke. Why do you prefer to quote these writers as opposed to writers of mystery?

RR: It never occurred to me to quote writers of mystery in this way. I quote because I like reading and also because my readers have come to expect this kind of thing, especially from Chief Inspector Wexford who is a great reader. I am a very catholic reader and I suppose I read generally about five books a week. Also I have a good memory and so this stuff is stored and comes out. I find it pleasant for me and popular with my readers. Of course great writers do contribute to the detective—or, let us say, the suspense—*genre*. In spite of what Julian Symons says in his excellent book *Bloody Murder, Crime and Punishment* is a thriller. It's one of the world's greatest novels and if we don't think of it as a thriller, and would indeed be shocked to hear it called so, this isn't because its form and progress is not that of a thriller but because the writing and the examination of motive, guilt and remorse transcend to an amazing degree the usual suspense novel limitations. Graham Greene wrote a number of thrillers he called entertainments. Trollope came very near to writing a mystery novel in *Phineas Redux*. C.P. Snow and Kingsley Amis may be classed as distinguished straight, if not great, novelists and both have written detective stories. Any crime novelist with the talent can write a crime novel that will be regarded as a "novel" if he or she takes the trouble and ignores silly or hidebound opinion. Patricia Highsmith did in *Edith's Diary*.

DCC: Is it that you think that these writers of the mainstream are more profound or more eclectic in their vision than mystery writers?

RR: Certainly I do think Shakespeare, Dickens and Forster have a wider scope than most mystery writers.

DCC: Why? Is it a question of limitation in the genre?

125

RR: I think it is a question partly of limitation in the genre. The writers we have specified are some of the greatest writers that the world has ever known, and I don't think there is any mystery writer that I can think of that you would include in that category. Especially when it comes to *Shakespeare* who is possibly the greatest writer the world has ever known. I quote what comes into my mind, what simply has been stored and what comes up by association. I think there is a gap between mystery writers and others just as there is a gap between science fiction writers, the writers of romantic novels, and to some extent historical novels, and others. The requisite structure and form of *genre* novels curtail a novelist's freedom. They also make fewer demands so that it's not difficult within these forms to get away with sloppy writing and poor characterization so long as enough excitement, sex and mystery is injected. This therefore may make even the most aspiring and talented writer "not bother" or just give up trying. I think one sees quite a lot of this. Why attempt to create original situations, real or moving relationships, why try to give a picture of some aspect of the human predicament when critics will admit to being bored by this and readers become restless?

DCC: Since you think Shakespeare is possibly the greatest writer the world has ever known, which of his plays are most important in your writing?

RR: *Antony and Cleopatra* is my favorite play. There are more quotes from that play than any other in my books. That love affair has influenced the relationships of my characters more than any other, such as in the novels *Shake Hands For Ever* and *Make Death Love Me*. As a matter of fact, "Make death love me" is a quote from *Antony and Cleopatra*. This is a love affair between people no longer young; it is a destructive relationship. In *Make Death Love Me* that love affair comes to nothing because it is doomed from the start.

DCC: But it is not doomed necessarily by fate. The people seem to reflect more fully Cassius' words to Brutus: "The fault, dear Brutus, is not in our stars,/ But in ourselves."

RR: You're absolutely right. I also think a lot about *King Lear*. The title of my novel, *The Lake of Darkness*, was taken from that play. I really do think about *Lear* when I write about middle-aged children with their older parents. It is not fortuitous. It is a common theme and I use it a lot such as in *A Sleeping Life*. These children will reject their parents, will want to dispose of them.

DCC: Are there any direct parallels between characters in Shakespeare's plays and your novels?

RR: I tried to create a Cordelia character, Una, in *Make Death Love Me,* a truly virtuous yet interesting character. Also the character of Enobarbus in *Antony and Cleopatra*, noble yet capable of treachery, parallels my character in *A Sleeping Life.*

DCC: I suppose *Macbeth,* a play of murder, fear, betrayal and remorse, would seem a more obvious influence on a writer of mysteries.

RR: I like *Macbeth,* but it is not as important to me as the other two plays.

DCC: Your book titles are wonderful, taken from Shakespeare to Edgar Allan Poe. They are keys to the meaning of the novel. Is this how you begin a book, the title first, or do you start with an image of a character or a psychological perspective?

RR: Not all the titles are mine. They mostly are. *A Judgment in Stone* was thought up by a friend of mine. I would say that I have never started with a title, I have never started with a character, I always start with an idea and this usually comes from something somebody has told me. I don't mean saying, "I have got a wonderful idea for a novel," because that is usually hopeless, but telling me a story without any idea of its being material for a novel. If I read a story in a newspaper or somehow or other pick up something else, the two will be put together and from this conjunction the novel will come. For instance, with *A Demon In My View* I was at the time living in a flat in which I found a shop window model or torso made of a sort of plastic in a garden chair. I was sharing this flat with a cousin of mine at the time and he is called Richards. There was somebody who had another flat in the same house called Richards and their correspondence got mixed up so these two ideas came together and gave me the idea for *A Demon In My View.* Most of my novels were founded on this kind of conjunction, I think.

DCC: To get back to the detective novel as a genre, is it fair to say that earlier detective novels did not reflect the world outside, but instead offered a world where the status quo remained unchanged? In the drawing rooms and country estates of Lord Peter Wimsey and Hercule Poirot, all was right with the world. But, if good still triumphs over evil in the contemporary detective novel, their sense of evil is more ambiguous. In the words of Robert Browning, whom you quote in one of your novels, we are "on the dangerous edge of things."

RR: I suppose that earlier detective novels did reflect to a certain extent life as it was; I think that people did live like that, at any rate the upper class did. The concern with good and evil in the detective novel has something to do with the proliferation of the knowledge of psychology and psychiatry. Before that, although Freud and Jung were very, very well known in scientific circles, they were not known in popular circles so that before the Second World War black seemed blacker and white, whiter. I think that psychology has a very profound effect on detective novels. But this is a question for a dissertation! I can't begin to answer it. I can only touch on it here. Just an example—a novelist writing detective, or indeed most, fiction in the early part of this century has to show a girl child brought up in a household where child abuse regularly happened. The girl was beaten by her father and mother, as were her siblings. She grows up loathing violence, particularly violence against children, and herself becomes a gentle and kindly mother. The novelist writing today knows from psychological and sociological studies that this is most unlikely to be the picture. Battered children grow up into battering parents. A chain of violence is set up and the abused girl abuses her own children. One might say here that such a character might be a very likely protagonist in a crime novel while the old-fashioned, ignorant-of-psychology development of the character would make her more suitable for inclusion in romantic fiction.

DCC: Are you particularly interested in the question of good and evil and morality? Is this why you chose the detective genre to explore your ideas or your perceptions about humanity?

RR: I have to say here that I didn't choose it, it almost chose me. I wrote many novels before my first novel was accepted. I had never submitted one of them to a publisher and the first novel I ever did submit to a publisher was a sort of drawing room comedy, which is a very hard difficult genre for a young writer to try and deal with. This was kept for a long time and then returned to me and I was told that they would accept it if I would completely rewrite it. I wasn't prepared to do this and they asked if I had done anything else. I had written a detective story just for my own entertainment or fun and that was my first published novel, which is called *From Doon With Death*. It was quite successful for a first novel and I was caught up really because of this success within the genre. Having now established for myself a means of livelihood, I was constrained to work within the detective genre and doing so I found that I preferred to deal with the psychological, emotional aspects of human nature rather than the puzzle, forensics, whatever most seem to come within the ambiance of the detective novel.

DCC: In your recent novel *The Lake of Darkness*, you twice quote Arnold Bennett: "Humanity treads ever on a thin crust over terrific abysses." What is the "crust" and what is the "abyss" because that tone pervades many of your novels?

RR: Yes! It's something that I feel very much myself going through life; I feel that disaster is imminent. What is the abyss? It is very hard to say what the abyss is because, of course, one doesn't really ever confront the abyss. The abyss is some kind of disgrace, humiliation, suffering, pain, disaster, poverty, famine, starvation and death. The crust is that thin rim which one has established over it, on which one treads hoping never to break it, hoping that there will never be any kind of fracture of this because one will tread carefully and go easily. It happens a lot in my novels. I feel it, I have known people who feel it, I know people who live in this kind of way. We dread the postman's knock, the ring of the telephone because the foot may tread on it and you go through. It is a neurotic state, I wish I didn't have it. I have it. Many of my characters have this sense of disaster: if he had not answered the phone, gone out at this point, got up at this moment, things would have been different. I see that life is ruled by these particular things. Other people see it differently. Much of my life and my writing is ruled by these factors.

DCC: Is the crust the social rituals and the masks we create to inadequately cope with this deeper sense of reality, which is the abyss?

RR: I don't think the abyss is necessarily the deepest sense of reality. I see it in very much more fundamental, almost occult terms. It is almost a superstitious thing, as if the crust is created by ourselves, but if we tread very, very carefully and observe certain rituals we won't go through. This is probably fantasy but I think that is how I see that abyss. I see the abyss as always there and yet at the same time, I see that the abyss is probably nonsense. But it is very real to me and I have to tread. It is almost like the person who treads on the squares rather than on the lines, touches the wood to avoid going through, not anything so real as your social crust and reality abyss.

DCC: In *A Judgment in Stone* the narrator says that "there are age-old desires in man which man needs no instruction to practise," like murder. Do you think that murder dwells in the hearts of all people to be aroused like an atavistic knowledge when circumstances demand it?

RR: No, I don't think I do really, just in some people. I don't think murder dwells in me at all. I think that I have this in common with many people who write about crime, that to me, it is a most abominable thing and I can't imagine ever committing it nor that anybody close to me would ever commit it. It seems to me the most frightful thing and always will seem that way.

DCC: So presumably you would be against those critics who interpret detective fiction as a kind of mythical acting out of rituals in our past. The idea that there is the sacrifice, there is the victim. Do you think those critical observations are far-fetched?

RR: Yes, I do.

DCC: If the desire to murder, to follow these critical analyses, is an age-old one (and I am sure you have seen the analyses of the detective genre in terms of Cain and Abel and Sophocles and so on) what about the idea of the victim ritual? Colin Wilson, in one of his books, has written that the people who get murdered are of a definite type. Would you say that this is true of your victims?

RR: Yes.

DCC: How would we recognize them?

RR: I don't know, it is not something I have ever been asked before, nor is it something to which I have given much thought. I don't recognize murder victims but I recognize people of that kind. I am not one myself and perhaps that makes it harder. There seems to be some people who invite pain and I think it's quite distinct from masochism, quite a different thing. There are some people who seem to be forever on the defensive, forever expecting to suffer, forever expecting pain, forever expecting victimisation.

DCC: In novels of crime, the victim is not usually a fully developed three-dimensional human being; the killer is always more interesting. In your novels, like *A Demon in My View* and *A Judgment in Stone* you also find the killers much more interesting than the victims. You don't develop the character of the victims as much as you do the murderers.

RR: I suppose my victims are victims by accident normally. They are victims by chance. In some literature, the victim chooses to become a victim but in mine the victim doesn't choose, it is the killer who does the choosing, if choosing is the word. In *A Judgment in Stone*, the whole thing happens by chance. However, Eunice is not a killer by chance, she was going to kill somebody and she had already killed her father. So I think that what I am saying is that with me it is the killer that is interesting and not the victim.

DCC: You often refer to criminology. Do you read books on criminology?

RR: Not much. However, I do read Freud, Jung and Adler because psychology interests me so much. But I don't read much criminology because I think criminology is very unsound.

DCC: You mentioned Freud and Jung and they both felt that guilt brought about the ultimate punishment on murderers. Are you particularly interested in the effect of guilt?

RR: Yes, I am sorry that I am because I think that guilt is a horrible thing. I am amazed it goes on being so effective. Even if guilt doesn't seem to have been brought into people's lives, they make it for themselves. It seems as if they make it out of nothing. It almost seems to be an infectious thing and they take it out of the air and there it is to affect their lives. It is almost as if there is a need for guilt inherent in human beings.

DCC: In your novels the mundane often precedes passion and pain. Are you interested in that juxtaposition of the ordinary with the painful and the passionate?

RR: You do come across people to whom the ordinary and the mundane seem to be all, especially if you come out of an English middle-class. But the ordinary isn't everything. The passionate is also there. I try to bring the conflict out in my books, I think. So many people are unable to express their feelings. This is surely a twentieth century phenomenon. Victorian men, if contemporary writing is to be believed, used to weep freely in company. I think we're returning to a time when men won't think it unmanly and shame-making to cry when much moved. When I talk about people to whom the ordinary and the mundane seem to be all, I'm thinking a good deal about those who suppress all their feelings except small enthusiasms and small disappointments, the kind of people who are always saying, "Never mind," or "It's no good making a fuss." I have seen women of this kind flung suddenly into widowhood after forty or fifty years of marriage, seen them unable to cry, unwilling to talk, numb in their ignorance of how is the right way to act. In two cases I've known such women to have complete mental breakdowns a few months later. I'm also talking about their having, these people, shocks or occasionally astounding things happen to them. Then they burst into hysteria, exaggerated amazement or joy. In my work I am interested to show sad, shy, inhibited people moved to passion and expression of their feelings. Contrast is so important, isn't it? One of the things that keeps us interested, wanting more, turning the page. One of the ingredients of suspense often.

DCC: P.D. James feels that women writers are more attuned to that contrast, the contrast between the crime and its setting, the library, the rectory, or the respectable village. Would you agree that women are much more attuned to the contrast between the crime and its setting than men are?

RR: No, I don't think I would say that. I don't wish to make these differences between men and women. I don't think they actually exist.

DCC: Therefore, you wouldn't agree with literary critics who feel that there is a female narrative voice.

RR: No, I don't think there is such a thing as feminine or female intuition either.

DCC: Then Coleridge and Virginia Woolf were right when they said that all great minds are androgynous?

RR: Yes, all minds, whether they are great or not.

DDC: On the subject of women, it has been suggested that women are more ruthless than men, that the female of the species is more deadly than the male. The women in your novels, such as *A Judgment in Stone, The Face of Trespass, Shake Hands For Ever*, are certainly deadly.

RR: People are still shocked by the fact that a woman may have these feelings, these fantasies that men have, because if you look at my novels really the men are just as intensely evil or bad or whatever as the women, but these people are women and they are picked out. I don't think that women are gentler, kinder, more violent, more savage, or more subtle than men. I really don't think that there is any difference. There may be a difference brought on by conditioning but I don't really think that there is any basic difference.

DCC: Actually I would have guessed that you would feel that way. There was a British judge called Gerald Sparrow who wrote that the female mind is not logical, therefore, women murder by inward compulsions. He derived this theory, which I find a faulty syllogism, from years on the bench in various parts of the world. However, as you quite rightly say, in your novels men like Arthur in *A Demon in My View*, is a classic case of a man driven by inner compulsion.

RR: I think that women are driven by inner compulsions and I think men are too equally. If you were to look at John Christie and the murders which came out of his curious psyche, they were quite irrational. You could say the same for such killers as Hague and Hume and also for the women. I don't think many people who have murdered do so from rational motives. It will be quite hard to find famous or infamous or notorious murderers who have done so from rational motives. I wonder what Mister Justice Sparrow meant when he talked about that. Would he be able to produce murderers who have murdered from what would be a rational motive, to get a large sum of money or to rid one's self of somebody who is an actual menace? It would be terribly rare if you analyzed any murder case to find these people. These are not the motives from which people commit murder.

DCC: In *A Demon in My View* this definition of a psychopath is given: "The psychopath ... is in positive conflict with society. Atavistic desires and a craving for excitement drive him. Self-centered, impulsive, he disregards society's taboos." But elsewhere in literature this definition can be seen as positive, a throwing off of society's shackles, a bid for freedom, vision, a search for God in man. In *The Lake of Darkness* Finn sees killing as a fire baptism into the kind of life he wanted to lead and the kind of person he wanted to be. Is this a perversion of the creative instinct or is it Finn's negative exploration into awareness?

RR: I think I see his exploration as a creative instinct but it is not an instinct I would applaud. I think people do feel like that. I feel that this attitude is negative and that it's positively wrong and harmful for writers or anyone else to look upon it as in anyway part of the creative instinct. It seems to me to be just there, just negative, just wrong and almost not the kind of thing one should do.

DCC: Again, in both *The Lake of Darkness* and *A Demon in My View*, Finn and Arthur both try to master impulses; one does it by mysticism and the supernatural and the other by acting out the murder. What is the ideal balance between socialization and the so-called "natural man"?

RR: Both these people are ill, they are ill in the psyche, they are both psychotics, in fact, extreme psychotics. I don't know, are you asking what could be done for these people?

DCC: No. I am really thinking of the response that argues for a throwing off of society's restrictions. This is the negative definition of society, the Rousseaunian notion that man is in chains but he is born free. As I have said before, murder in some writers' novels is seen as a blow for a return to the natural man, when we were free from society's laws and rituals, like Arthur or Finn who act out their impulses. For Arthur, it is a way of preventing himself from committing the actual murder when he acts out the murder with the dummy. Finn also tries to master his impulses, which Freud believed is the price we pay for society, for civilization. We repress or suppress the instinct in order to master our impulses. Another school of thought would say in accordance with William Blake, "Sooner murder a child in its cradle than nurse unacted desires."

RR: That's terrible, isn't it? It is far better to feel these unsatisfied desires than murder a child in his cradle. Blake must have been having an absolute off-day when he said such a dreadful thing. I think that, for me, both Finn and Arthur are highly undesirable elements; they are there because they exist. Arthur knows that what he is doing is wrong. Finn doesn't, he is amoral, he has no idea. I think that I am saying Arthur knows that there is an absolute right and Arthur knows he is wrong. I feel that Finn is a lost soul. I don't think much could be done for Finn really, and I am talking in psychiatric terms. I think he is lost and gone.

DCC: Am I right then in assuming that you are opposed to these philosophical, psychological and aesthetic conversions of murder and psychopathology into philosophical methodology?

RR: Yes I am. I really think that a whole Nietzchean philosophy is awful and ultimately leads to Nazism. That kind of thinking disgusts me and bores me. Finn disgusts and bores me.

DCC: Is this why you make sure that Finn gets caught?

RR: But he doesn't.

DCC: The implication at the end is that he will.

RR: I left it open because I hoped to use him again.

DCC: I see. I thought that it was quite definite that he would get caught.

RR: He doesn't quite get caught, if you think about it, rather as James Bond doesn't get caught in *From Russia With Love*. It's probably an unwise thing to do because when these people come back they are never the same again, Sherlock Holmes wasn't. When I first wrote the end of *The Lake of Darkness* I thought that that would be the end of Finn and then I thought, well, maybe I will use Finn again and so I left it open. It is open, just.

DCC: Was Arthur killed because you felt that there was no other solution for him really?

RR: I thought there was no other solution for Arthur. I think it was better for him. Life for him was an absolute torment. There are a lot of people who are like him, they perhaps don't go to his extremes but I do think there are a lot of people in a sad psychotic state. I know a lot of people in a bad neurotic state. It seems that a number of people believe that most people that one encounters in this world are leading happy, rational, lucid and logical lives but I don't find that. I find that an enormous number of people I know are in a very bad state, a bad psychotic state. It appalls me.

DCC: Sometimes your novels remind me of Thomas Hardy's. I don't know if he is an influence but Thomas Hardy employed murder thematically as a means of embodying his tragic vision, in novels such as *Tess of the D'Urbervilles* and *Jude the Obscure*. I feel this is close to your work.

RR: My father was a great admirer of Hardy. When I was a child he used to get me to listen to him reading Hardy aloud. I used to have to sit on my father's knees and have great masses of Hardy read aloud to me, which bored me horribly, so I never read any more Hardy for many years. I went back to reading Hardy when I was about thirty. Yes, I do see things much the same way as Hardy saw them. You know I feel a bit humble about this because of course Hardy was a very great writer in spite of being so disorganized and such a mess. Hardy is very close to me in a visceral sort of way. I'm not sure what this means. That's probably why I didn't answer it! Life *is* tragic, though this need not be taken in a maudlin or sentimental way. Murder happens in my novels because I write within the crime novel *genre* and because I like writing melodrama. Graham Greene says in his *Ways of Escape* that this was the answer he gave to people who asked him why he wrote such thrillers as *The Ministry of Fear* and *Our Man in Havana*. He enjoys the vicarious living with and handling of melodrama. So do I. I would always have the tragic vision whatever kind of novels I wrote because it is my temperament to regard life as terrible, fearful, marvellous and awe-inspiring. Murder is the way I express this concept in my books. If I were an historical novelist I daresay I should do it through battles, if a writer of science fiction—but, no, I can't for a minute imagine myself a writer of science fiction!

DCC: Human relations are crucial in your novels. First of all, sexual love is clearly a prime concern of yours; lovers are either destructive or they are redemptive, there seems to be no middle ground. For example, Wexford and his wife are an example of a redemptive relationship, they have a wonderful marriage even though he does tend to see it as a kind of sanctuary which can have its problems as well. Burden and Gemma Lawrence in *No More Dying Then* also have a nourishing relationship. The destructive relationships, however, seem to outnumber the redemptive ones—Nell, Tate and Vedast in *Some Lie and Some Die*; Fabia and Margaret in *From Doon With Death*; Francesca and Martin in *The Lake of Darkness*; Gray and Drusilla in *The Face of Trespass* and many more. Sexual love is invariably full of deceit and very often leads to murder. In *A Judgment in Stone*, Melinda precipitates a disaster course which leads to the death of her family because "she was in love." In *The Face of Trespass,* we are told, "O Love, what crimes are committed in thy name." Would you say that this is a fair evaluation that I am giving?

RR: Yes, I would.

DCC: Are you primarily interested in sexual love relationships and the consequences of them?

RR: Yes, I suppose I am. I would have thought that most people would say that intense sexual relationships led to pain and unhappiness rather than to happiness and fruition. When relationships are very intense and these are very intense, they are fiery, they are full of passion. Therefore, if you were going to talk about Wexford's relationship with his wife, it is one that has worked out over the years, it has calmed down, it has become probably not very sexual and it is the way a sexual relationship ought to come to its final flowering. I do think anyway that very intense and violent sexual attraction leads to disaster rather than to happiness and calm.

DCC: Another aspect of human relationships is of course the family. People are often troubled within the family, estranged or blighted as children, like Arthur in *A Demon in My View*. The family motif is explored extensively in *Murder Being Once Done*; in *The Best Man to Die,* Wexford's relationship with his daughter,

Sheila, is used to counterpoint the essential selfishness of another family.

RR: Family relationships are important to me. While I have no siblings, I still have a very large family. I think relationships are terribly important and one should know who one is. In order to make Wexford a real person it seems to me essential that he should have a wife and children and grandchildren and forebearers and I can't imagine writing a novel with a protagonist who isn't deeply rooted in his ancestry.

DCC: The relationship of servants to their employers is also explored in *A Judgment of Stone* where the class structure and the changing contemporary mores lead to murder and death. Do you think that this interrelationship between people, whether it is a professional or private one, is the crux very often for murder?

RR: Relationships in general interest me and I am always watching them and watching how people react to each other. The family relationship is very important as an impetus to murder but what makes people commit the murder is something that seems on the face trivial. It seems to happen superficially about some very small trivial thing, about what time you have your dinner or whether you come in late or what time you are getting up in the morning or that sort of thing. I think these things are in families and I write from what I have experienced or seem to think I have seen or think I have sensed.

DCC: Murder is the central motif in your novels. Rebecca West once said that it is easier to write about the dynamically bad than it is to write about the dynamically good.

RR: Yes, I think it is easier to write about the bad whether it's the dynamically bad or just the bad. I suppose that this is something to do with the fact that the good is always the same and the bad is very different. The bad is more diverse. I think Somerset Maugham wrote a story trying to work this one out. It is an Italian story and I think it is just called "Giovanni." It is about a man who is an Italian peasant who leads an ordinary life with his wife and children. He is born and he marries and he has children and he dies, and as Maugham himself says, "I have managed to hold your attention to the end and I have written about someone who is entirely good." But he really doesn't hold your attention, the story is very dull. I think that because goodness, saintliness is dull, it is always the same. It simply observes the rules, it proceeds in a pure fashion. It is not interesting to us because we demand excitement and variety which evil has in almost an infinite progression.

DCC: Do you think that even though we hold goodness to be an ideal and therefore unattainable, that underneath all the philosophizing and socializing we, in fact, think that evil is more exciting than good?

RR: I think it is perhaps more exciting because goodness is channelled into one perfection and evil is more diffuse. Do you think people who are actually good and pure exist? I have known several of them but I would hesitate before I put them on paper. It is something that Balzac could have done but not me. Yes, I do think that we feel closer to evil than good but we should go to psychiatry to find more suitable terms. We are now beginning to know that we are not as good in a nineteenth-century and a pre-nineteenth-century sense. In other words, we have these desires and needs and wishes that don't fit into that kind of terminology or world view.

DCC: Your working out of good and evil is much more complex in your non-Wexford novels. Approximately half of your books, however, employ Chief Inspector Wexford. What attracts you to the use of Inspector Wexford and let's say the detective genre, when you're obviously pulled toward the more complex exploration of human nature and murder outside the format?

RR: I should say money.

DCC: Wouldn't your novels sell as well?

RR: I really don't quite know, but I have a great fan mail for the Wexford novels. They say, "Please can we have another Wexford." I feel that I had better go on doing Wexfords for these fans who long for him. I would rather write the other kind of novel and I do now write more of the other kind than Wexford. I brought out a collection of Wexford short stories last year to keep up the Wexford and my new book in May will be a Wexford. I will go on producing them. I quite like the man. I am very fond of him really because he is me and he is my father.

DCC: Well, the erudition certainly is you.

RR: I think he is me. He is an Aquarian, you see, and I am an Aquarian. We have our heads in the clouds and our feet on the ground and so I don't mind going on doing him. I do prefer doing the others. I will eventually kill him in a posthumous Ruth Rendell.

DCC: Why did you make your literary alter ego a man? Why not a female detective or police inspector? I guess they don't have female police inspectors.

RR: I think they do. You have to remember first of all that Wexford was born at the age of 52 in 1963 or 64. Things were not as they are now. If he had been born today, he would probably have been a woman and he certainly would have been about eighteen to give me plenty of scope. He was also a man because like most women I am very much still caught up in the web that one writes about men because men are the people and we are the others. I was very much caught up in that in 1963, much less now, of course, and so, he was a man because a policeman, a judge, a lawyer, whatever it was, was a man in 1963 and for many people it would be so today.

DCC: Have you ever thought of writing a novel now wherein you make Inspctor Wexford a younger man? Jean Stubbs told me that she made a mistake in her first Lintott novel because she made him too old. She will eventually write a novel and recreate him at a younger age.

RR: Yes, I have thought of it, but, you see, the thing with me is that I find it rather hard to write about any age except that in which I live. I have written a very long historical novel about the Oxford movement in which I was very much interested. I did an enormous amount of research into Newman. Well, I am sure that at the time I was almost a world authority but it was very dull and I found that although I could do all this, I was never happy with it. I feel that I have to write about the here and now. If I were to take Wexford back into the 1950s I could do it but to do all this without the feeling that I know exactly what's going on does not appeal to me; I would rather keep him artificially younger than he should be.

DCC: Jean Stubbs also has the advantage that Lintott is in a different historical period.

RR: That's right, she is not dealing with her own period anyway.

DCC: You are often compared with Agatha Christie, which I don't understand, because you couldn't be more different. You can correct me if I am wrong but do you not find Agatha Christie superficial?

RR: Although she had some wonderful plots, marvellous ideas, I don't think she ever bothered to go into her characters in depth. I don't think she ever studied the time that she was living in and her novels are peopled with a group of stock characters. I don't believe that in the 1930s one was simply hedged in by the judge, the solicitor, the model, the secretary, the colonel, the maiden aunt, and it cannot be that in any age there were more stereotypes, I would think, than in any other. That is why I would say that she was superficial and I don't think I am. I wish I could think of her plots and her wonderful surprises and in that way she was vastly superior to me, but I don't think she was my equal in characterization and emotional content. I think her emotional content, the relation between her characters is non-existent.

DCC: I would agree. On the other hand, you admire Patricia Highsmith and Julian Symons.

RR: I admire Patricia Highsmith for her peculiar slow buildup of tension. I can't do it. I don't quite know how it is done and it ought to be very dull but it isn't. It is very exciting. I admire the texture, the detailed background. I always admired the kind of writing that deals with the food people eat and the furnishings of their houses and the music they listen to. I am always quoting Somerset Maugham and I don't know why because I don't really much admire him although I did when I was very young. He says that what we want to know about people is what they had for breakfast and we do know with Patricia Highsmith. I want to know that; I don't think you can ever have too much detail in texture and I like that with her. I like this mounting tension and I like the understatement.

DCC: How about Julian Symons? He is quite different.

RR: I like very much the English suburban environment and the people. I like the marriage situations. Again I like the family relationships and the horrible tensions and the houses. I am very fond of houses in London and the streets and the suburbs and he is very good on that.

DCC: Which other writers do you admire?

RR: My favorite novel of all novels ever written is *The Way of All Flesh* by Samuel Butler. If I had one novel that I could take to the desert island, I would take *The Way of All Flesh* because it is an understated, down to earth novel, with complex human relationships and a family. I am very interested in the relationship between parents and their children.

DCC: But you always include murder; you don't write novels where murder doesn't exist. Why didn't you write your version of *The Way of All Flesh*?

RR: When you start writing about murder and within the detective genre, it is very hard to get out of the genre.

DCC: Are you affected by your reviews?

RR: Yes, I am very much affected by them. Bad ones upset me very much and good ones give me a lift but they don't give me such a lift as the bad ones upset me. I suppose I think it is rather awful that one is more easily made unhappy than happy. I hope I learn, I don't know.

DCC: Have you found that there have been reviewers or scholars who are particularly perceptive and sensitive about your work?

RR: Ah, I don't know. You see one tends to think that those who say that one is terribly good are perceptive, and those who say that one is bad, are not. (Both laugh.)

DCC: One critic singled out your use of atmosphere as an illustration of your talent and another critic referred to this negatively as "an overdose of atmosphere." Now that is very strange and very confusing, of course, for people who think that critics are creating a kind of absolute aesthetic criteria. Do you have an ironic distance from this critical conflict?

RR: Yes, I suppose so, because you see when you get to that point, it is ridiculous. Yes, I would think that was nonsense just as it is nonsense for Patrick Cosgrave in the *New Statesman* to say that he didn't like *The Lake of Darkness* and bring back Wexford. I am very much affected by critics but I hope I am not absurd about it. Yes, I do create a lot of atmosphere. I am very fond of houses, districts and people. What would they have me do instead?

DCC: Is the conflicting critical response toward your work a good thing because it shows that your work can't be categorized into neat analytical parcels? Would you say that this conflict is a good thing because that way the boundaries of what you are doing are far larger than if everyone agrees that, "Yes, Ruth Rendell is turning out yet another Dostoevskian exploration of human nature in this particular way," and so on?

RR: What I would really like would be for everybody to say in very large 48 point type on the front page of the *Guardian* every day that I was like Doestoveski. (laughs) Yes, I would like that but they aren't going to do that.

DCC: Your novel, *Put on By Cunning* (*Death Note* in the United States), which is a quotation from *Hamlet*, was published in May of 1981. All of your books seem to come out in May.

RR: All of my books come out in May because one of the nice critics said a new novel from me is like a breath of spring, you see. You can imagine that when my publishers got a grasp on anything so catch-on as that, they grabbed hold of it, never forgot and never will forever. So even when I am long dead they will go on bringing out reissues of Ruth Rendell in May. As a matter of fact, my next collection of short stories, *The Fever Tree and Other Stories*, will be published in Autumn 1982, in time for Christmas gifts.

Interview with Janwillem van de Wetering

Diana Cooper-Clark

DCC: In your book *The Empty Mirror*, about your time in a Zen Buddhist temple in Japan, you said that you were a guerilla fighter in eternal combat with the establishment. Some people, like Joseph Wambaugh, feel that the police are the last bastion of civilization, they protect the establishment. It seems to be a contradiction that you are writing detective novels.

JVW: It was a bizarre incident in my life that I had to become a policeman; it was either that or I had to join the army. I left Holland when I was nineteen and I got leave from the army, and I came back when I was thirty-three. The age in Holland for the draft is thirty-five which I didn't realize, so I was drafted for the army, and I refused. They said, "Well, you can't refuse, we'll put you in jail." I said, "But I don't want to go in the army, I'm thirty-three, I've got a job." And they said, "Do something else, serve the Queen, join the police for four years, two years in study, two years patrolling in Amsterdam." I thought this was such an idiotic thing for me to do that I did it. I didn't think it would give me material to write books, I just thought that me in a police uniform would be the absolute opposite to whatever I thought I would do. It was funny. Then when I got into it, I found I liked it. But I was never a regular constable, although I had the regular uniform, the arms and the authority. I never made an arrest. I was always very pleasant to people who were arrested by other policemen. I led a strange life as a cop.

DCC: Did you stop being a guerilla fighter?

JVW: No, no! I've always been against really any establishment, although I see that there has to be one, that there has to be some sort of law and order. I described that in *The Maine Massacre*. The commisaris said that even at Woodstock, for instance, where all these free hippy and flower people were doing their thing, they had the Hell's Angels as police. And the same thing happened in Holland. It seems to be a universal thing that you have to maintain

145

law and order. So I can see there is a purpose for it.

DCC: Why did you start writing detective novels as opposed to any other kind of novel?

JVW: There was no real purpose. The business I was managing at that time was getting into France and the only way to do business in France is if you can speak French, and I could only speak school French which wasn't good enough. My brother suggested that I should read Georges Simenon in French because he is easy to read. I read practically every Maigret there is, and I was appalled by Simenon's refusal to work out Maigret beyond certain borderlines. And then I thought, I can do better than that, I can go much further. I read an interview that Simenon gave to two American psychiatrists and in that interview it's very clear that he has a definite line that he will not cross because if he does he might go insane. And in Maigret you can see that. Maigret ultimately doesn't care, although he does a good job. I like that, that's a very Buddhist point of view too, to do as well as you can without really caring about the results. There is a book by Simenon called *Le Clochard* in which the criminal can only be apprehended through a statement by a witness and the witness is the guy who was nearly murdered by the criminal. And the witness is a clochard, he's a down and out tramp in Paris who used to be a great society doctor, a very wealthy man in Marseilles, and he gave up everything to become this drunken bum in Paris. And he won't give the testimonial. And Maigret says, "But the guy threw you in the water, he nearly drowned you; you nearly died." And he said, "So what?" And Maigret said, "But I must have your testimony in order to arrest the guy." And the man said, "I don't care whether you arrest him or not." Maigret agrees with that in his mind and you can feel that in the book, Simenon won't work it out. So I thought that I can go a little further than that and create a detective who would do a good job and really not care and still be a great man, or be a great man because of that. But that was just a thought. Then I had some trouble in the business; it was doing so well that I got bored with it. One evening I was listening to some really boring conversation about the business, my partners and the accountant, and my mind switched off from it. And suddenly I had four complete plots for four different books, very clear. They are the first four books of the series. I thought, "This is it; I'll do that to keep sane," and I went home and wrote the first in two weeks, I think, in English, and sent it to America, and got a contract for it. Then I wrote the others immediately afterwards. And they took very little revising. Later I had to do a lot of revising on my further books because I didn't want to go into repetitions and I wanted to show different aspects of my characters. But the first four just came out.

DCC: I know that a character does not necessarily reflect the author's point of view.

JVW: Oh, mine do.

DCC: I wondered whether or not you agreed with Madelin, in *The Maine Massacre*, that death is perhaps the basis of all thoughts. I thought that maybe for this reason the detective novel encompassed a lot of your major concerns.

JVW: Yes, sure. But I never meant to write detective novels or get established in that genre or get literary fame out of it.

DCC: Do you feel that you write in the detective genre, or do you feel that you just write novels that happen to be about detectives?

JVW: I wouldn't even go as far as that. I'm just writing. Then you get all these critics and reviewers and professors who try to define what I'm writing but it doesn't concern me. I really don't care what people will say that I do.

DCC: Why do you write your novels in English? Is it because you can't express subtle thoughts in Dutch as your character Cardozo says of Spinoza?

JVW: I can be subtler in Dutch and I am too, I think. I re write all of these books in Dutch, I don't translate them. There is only one book that I translated, and that was *The Blond Baboon*. That was such a tight book that I couldn't change it. But all the others are changed a lot when I re-write them. They become much longer and even the plot changes and characters change, extra characters come in or are left out. I write them in English, I think, because I like English so much, and I think in it a lot, and I read it a lot; and when I started typing it came out in English, so I went on with it.

DCC: Your characters articulate different attitudes to life, and in the least restrictive sense, philosophies. In addition to entertaining the reader, what else are you trying to do in your novels?

JVW: I don't think I'm trying to do anything.

DCC: So it's a mistake to assume beforehand that writers have a vast, aesthetic methodology, a philosophy of writing, a concern with the function of the novel?

JVW: Well, maybe some writers have that attitude but I could never find it in myself.

DCC: I came across a saying by Seng-T's An, the Third Zen Buddhist Patriarch, and I wondered if this saying is reflected at all in your writing. He said: "To set up what you like against what you dislike. This is the disorder of the mind."

JVW: Oh yes, of course. Because then you start classifying and it's nonsense. "What is pleasant and what is unpleasant?" the commisaris says someplace, to my surprise. I thought that was a very good thing for him to say, that there are no calamities, there are only events. And that is very true. If you are at an airport and you have to wait eight hours for your next plane, that is not a calamity. It's not a positive thing, either, it's just an event, and you can use it any way you like. You can get very concerned, you can complain at the desk, you can hang around, you can get drunk, or you can sit and have some really good thoughts, or you can really look at an airplane and see how it's been designed, or you can look at the colors of the sky and you can have a great time or you can have a miserable time.

DCC: Zen Buddhism has been an important part of your life and in *The Blond Baboon*, Grijpstra asks, "Why, why, why? There'll never be an end to it, and even when you find the answers they invariably lead to more questions." The detective genre traditionally has been one that gave answers to questions of cause and effect. Crimes were solved rationally, detectives deduced, they found the killer through rational modes. Your detectives don't really do this. Nevertheless, does the detective genre, for want of a better word, illuminate this experience in life better than other forms of literature?

JVW: I don't know about the detective genre. I know that in real police work there is a certain amount of rationalization and logic, and there is a tremendous lot of intuition. If a man was in the room where the guy got killed, or could have been in the room, and he had a motive and at the time he could have been there, he is a major suspect. If you look at the guy, you very often know that he couldn't possibly have done it. You don't know why you have come to that conclusion, it's just your intuition, he's not the sort of guy. And then, you don't work with logic. The commisaris does a lot of that and that's real detection.

DCC: There are a number of characters who are trying to awaken to life and who express a Buddhist attitude towards life, like Vleuten, the blond baboon. He is trying to go against the flow, get out of the half-conscious dream, unlike Bergen, the businessman, who lived on the surface, doing what he thought was proper, following the stream without ever bothering to consider where it was taking him. Would these people, with the exception of van Meteren, be unlikely to commit murder?

JVW: No, they might. The Papuan, van Meteren, in *Outsider in Amsterdam* did commit the murder. And Vleuten, I am sure, would be able to commit murder if he saw a purpose for it. I think you should forget the Buddhist part of it. As soon as you say, "Is this a Buddhist attitude?" then you're getting back into a genre again, into a very limited point of view. The blond baboon probably never read anything about Buddhism and the Papuan never did either. Buddhism is just one of a thousand methods to get at reality but all the other methods are valid too. And all the combinations of the various methods are valid. I don't think you can say this is a Buddhist book, unless the guy writes the word Buddhism on every page. But the word Buddhism never appears in my books.

DCC: I was thinking not so much about content as about structure. There are people who have tried to incorporate their experience of Buddhism in their writing, the use of empty spaces in poetry or painting, the use of silence. Peter Matthiessen said that he wanted to create more air around his words. I had thought that perhaps there was something of this in your novels. Objects and actions speak for themselves so that the reader will not have to perceive things through the screens in the minds of the characters.

JVW: No, I'm just trying to tell a story.

DCC: The detective novel has been defined by A.E. Murch, because there are a number of people who are trying to create definition, as one in which the primary interest lies in the methodological discovery, by rational means, of the exact circumstance of a mysterious event. But the commisaris, for instance, says in *Death of a Hawker* that anyone who says he *knows* is a fool or a saint. Also, your detectives always find the killer, although not necessarily by those methods as defined by Murch. In what ways do your detectives' methods differ from other mystery writers'?

JVW: The only books I really admire in mystery writing were by Raymond Chandler and his plots are impossible. If I try to define one of his plots, it's the biggest lot of nonsense you can imagine. That part of it doesn't interest me either. But he writes so well. If a character in Chandler crosses a street in Los Angeles when it's raining, the reader gets wet. When a car starts, you can feel the movement of the car. And the character Philip Marlowe is such a marvellous character. This guy lives in a horrible little apartment, has this stupid little office, and he gets into all these heavy adventures for minimal pay; that's a good find. But the detection part of it is bullshit, which I like. I've read some thrillers too where the detection is not bullshit. It is a nice little puzzle with all the right data provided and all you have to do is fit it together and then you find out who the killer is. But I never liked puzzling and that part of the book wouldn't interest me. The way my characters work is what I saw in the police. You draw as many lines as you can, any little lead you get, you follow, and form a line and these lines will cross. Now, where they cross, that's the interesting little point. It is that "A" knows the killer, and "B" knows the killer, but "A" and "B" know each other too, so you have a triangle there. Then there is another character who knows "B" but not "A," and he didn't like the corpse, and he wasn't there, but he is interested in the death. So you follow that a little. You sniff around the area where the murder was committed. You study the corpse, you go to the place where the corpse lived when he was still alive, and you just sit in the room and try to find out what sort of man he was. And then some of the leads will combine into interesting facts and you work on those, and you manipulate continuously everybody who is connected with the case and, of course, the manipulation is always feared; it shows in these books. They just ask somebody to appear at the police station at two o'clock in the afternoon, they don't arrest him, they don't even phone him, they just write him a little note, through the regular mails which will take two days to get to the guy, and he's supposed to get there, at the station at, let's say, two o'clock. Everybody has fear; he's worried about something or other. So he's already softened. His resistance is further softened when he gets into the room where he is going to be questioned, and then there's coffee, and asking him about sugar and milk, they discuss the weather, they give him a cigar, and the guy says, "Am I under arrest?" And they say, "No, why should you be under arrest, why did you say that? Do you think we should arrest you?" Think of *The Corpse on the Dike.* There is an accountant who never committed the murder but he was there at the time when the murder was committed. And they keep on asking him to come to the station until the detectives themselves start worrying about him because they know that they're destroying him and maybe he had nothing to do with it. They remember another case when they did that and the guy actually went crazy and divorced his wife, and almost committed suicide, and he had nothing to do with it. So they are very careful about what they do and what they don't do. The commisaris is always very concerned about that, not to abuse the power that the police have. And all those things are very valid in Dutch police methods. I was really quite impressed by the way the detectives operate in Amsterdam which is the only area where I ever worked.

DCC: Your police detectives also differ in the way they reason. They dig about in the endless chain of cause and effect. But the commisaris can push the line of cause and effect and force it into another direction. It is suggested that this method improves the men who work under him.

JVW: There's no real detective work, I think. The commisaris, of course, is a very weird guy because ultimately he really doesn't care. He's the only enlightened figure I ever tried to write about. You can't catch him, like certain parts of my own mind and of anybody's mind can't be caught, because he always seems to escape any definition. The only steady thing about him is his friendship with his turtle, the pain in his legs, and the fact that he is a little old man. He inspires all three of them, Cardozo, Grijpstra and de Gier. Grijpstra is the part of my mind that is the solid Dutch part, the law and order part which, of course, I have because it's part of my super ego. I was born there in that country. He is completely non-violent, he is not too clever, he is conservatively dressed, and a lot of his opinions are boring and steady and average but there is something in him that is continuously attracted by the commisaris' strange mental behavior. Grijpstra wanted to be a policeman when he became a policeman. De Gier became a policeman by accident because he didn't know what to do, and somebody said, "Maybe you should be a policeman," and he went to an examination and was accepted. De Gier is almost always ready to freak out and to leave and he only stays because of the commisaris. I show that in my book, *The Mind Murders*, and even more in the book after that, *The Streetbird*.

DCC: Their relationship seems to get closer and closer in each novel.

JVW: Well, they were always pretty close.Cardozo is a very complicated character too. He belongs to an old Jewish family of merchants, not big merchants but small household dealers or street sellers. So he's got all that practical wisdom and he's tremendously eager; you give him a little lead and he runs his legs off to try and get to the bottom of it. But he also has a certain stupidity which he shouldn't have because he's a Jew. However, he's still young and he's always being corrected by the others. He's also very attracted by the commisaris' teaching, although the commisaris doesn't teach, he just does his job.

DCC: In most fiction about crime, murder and detection, reason always triumphs and irrational forces are seen as chaotic and destructive.

JVW: The irrational force could be destructive. There's a theory in brain surgery now and in psychiatry that the brain consists of two parts. One part is the rational part that pays the bills, makes the money, keeps the appointments and everything; it's a functioning apparatus. And the other half is chaotic but that's where all your inspiration comes from, all your better ideas. But it could very easily be destructive if the other half of the brain wouldn't control it somehow and this connection between the two parts is a physical brain channel. Now, if a man gets drunk, he gets marvellous ideas. Those ideas are really excellent, you have to get drunk sometimes to get them but very often they are impractical. That's why you have drunken accidents. You feel that now you want to drive 80 miles per hour, it's the right time of the night, you've got this powerful car. You're not going to drive at 55 miles per hour, you drive at 80, so you have an accident. That connection between the two brains, through alcohol, gets distorted and there is no more discipline. That's when it becomes destructive. But you don't have to be drunk to get the chaotic part of your mind to function. You can do it in meditation. Every man has his own recipe. I know that in the morning if after breakfast I smoke my first cigarette and have coffee, I get brilliant ideas. Some of them I write down or I remember them somehow but the other part of my brain tells me that I have to sit at the typewriter for a number of hours and work steadily to get this out. So, what I am trying to say is that the inspirational part of the brain is not destructive, just that it could be if you don't control it. It is neither positive nor negative, it's just a marvellous apparatus to initiate a lot of happenings in your life.

DCC: Do you agree with the commisaris that "humanity has an inborn need for order. It cannot function in anarchy"?

JVW: Yes. Again, that is the right part of the brain. If there's no order, you can't function. How can you rent a car and get out of this place and go home if you're not rational? There is a basic need for order.

DCC: In *Death of a Hawker*, Louis Zilver is a very interesting character.

JVW: Yes, an unusual character, I like him.

DCC: He thinks that public order is sheer boredom, a heavy weight which throttles citizens.

JVW: Yes, but look at him, he doesn't function. He had to be saved by the other character, Rogge, set up on his legs, made to function. Zilver had brilliant ideas so he made a man, a human figure, out of beads that hung in the doorway and was moved by the draft. All that was his own projection of his own mind, that's all it was. And he finally took that thing down and threw it in the garbage can because it wasn't doing anything for him. It is Rogge who made him work at the street market and made him go on trips and got him organized, made him function.

DCC: In *The Maine Massacre* the commisaris also affirms that organized life in what we call civilized society can be very boring, so the adventurous, the unusual, the creative, the originals, will try to make things happen, and, expectably may break the law in the process.

JVW: I don't have any real moral ideas about murder. I think if I had an option whether I die or the other guy dies, I'd rather die myself. Not because of a moral reason but out of laziness, I think. I don't think life is that important, or my life, that I should go and put a bullet in another man, or hang him, or push him down a cliff or anything like that. If he wants to murder me, I'll try and get away from him. I'd certainly do everything I could think of to escape, just for the hell of it, but I don't think I'd murder him.

DCC: Grijpstra says to de Gier, "We didn't join the police to become heroes, we are supposed to maintain order."

JVW: Grijpstra has that idea but de Gier has a different idea. He joined the police to be a hero, to have these adventures.

DCC: Exactly. Grijpstra describes him that way in *The Japanese Corpse*. He sees him as "our adventurer, our knight on his eternal quest. Fighting evil and supporting Good, under the banner of the Goddess of Beauty." How ironic is this description?

JVW: This is an internal discussion in my own mind. I know that I liked joining the police because I knew I would be driving a patrol car with a siren going at some ridiculous speed, *legally*, through a marvellous city like Amsterdam. That always appealed to me and I did it many times. Every time I was told to pursue a stolen car or get to an accident in minimal time, I loved putting on that siren. I really felt very heroic in that silly little car, dashing through the city. And I loved the feeling in America when I was riding with the sheriff.

DCC: That's described in *The Maine Massacre*, isn't it?

JVW: Yes. That was very dangerous what we were doing, going a 100 miles an hour over an icy road, and for what, to get to an overturned car somewhere. There was nothing we could do about it anyway but the sheriff said, "Well, this is why I joined the force." And I completely agreed with him although I was shit scared. I had a marvellous time.

DCC: In *The Japanese Corpse*, de Gier says that, "The victim is Japanese, maybe we've got ourselves into something subtle for a change.... A case with a delicate flavour." Grijpstra replied that if the case is "subtle, we could never solve it."

JVW: Grijpstra couldn't. Yes, because that super ego, that traditional, solid sense of morality that Grijpstra embodies could never solve a subtle crime. But he can solve it because he's got de Gier with him.

DCC: We see this subtlety in *The Blond Baboon*. The commisaris says that the suspects are trapped already but not by the police. The police will reverse the strategy. They will release the suspects.

JVW: That's the idea.

DCC: Another thing that I find interesting is that the commisaris says there is a strong connection between the killer and the victim. What is that bond?

JVW: You can say that the victim wants to get murdered otherwise he wouldn't get murdered. I thought of that during the war when I saw these transports of Jewish people marching to the trains by their own volition. All they had was a letter, a printed letter in the mail that they were expected to be at the railway station on such and such a day, at such and such a time. And there they were, thousands of them, tramping to the station, no guards, nothing. They were just told to go there. And although they were telling each other that they weren't going to be killed, that these were just work camps, every single one of them knew that he was going to get killed there. And in some strange way, they wanted to get killed. I think the victim in a criminal case really sets himself up to get killed and offers himself up to that. In psychiatry, where people are treated who have been in the concentration camps and escaped or somehow have come through alive and have these traumatic experiences in their later lives, they found that the guards of the concentration camps and even the children of the guards who lived with that guilt feeling, responded to exactly the same treatment as the inmates of the camps. This horrible thing is experienced from two different sides but it is the same thing. If you find out who the corpse was and what he thought, and what he did, and what he liked, and what he disliked, and how he tried to get through his life, you will find the killer too. Except in a case where you have a killer who takes a high powered rifle and he sits on the turnpike and he shoots up a lot of cars. If you study those victims in the cars, it won't lead you to the killer because that's a very strange set of circumstances. But when it's a motivated killing, if you can analyse the corpse you've got the killer too.

DCC: And just as there is a connection between the victim and the killer, the criminal often mirrors the policeman. In *Outsider in Amsterdam*, the murderer is a former policeman; in *The Japanese Corpse,* the leader of the "Yakusa," the Japanese mafia, is a Zen master figure similar to the commisaris; in *The Maine Massacre*, the BMF gang reminds the commisaris of the police, "a darker more romantic version but essentially the same."

JVW: I know of an author who might interest you. My favorite French writer is a man called Raymond Queneau. He is very well known in France, very surrealistic, very intellectual. There is a scene in one of his books where there is a little hut somewhere and there's a strange hermit who lives in the hut and a man comes in, his enemy. The enemy bothers the hermit to the point where the hermit brings out a derringer, one of these little pistols, and points it at his enemy. The enemy says, "Are you threatening to kill me?" And he says, "Yes, get out or I'll shoot this pistol at you." And the enemy says, "Gimme that pistol, I'm sure it's not loaded." So the hermit gives this pistol to the enemy, the enemy opens it up, sees it's loaded, closes it, and says, "My God, it is loaded," and gives it back to the hermit. Now that is really a very subtle situation which I plan to use in my next book. This is really marvellous. Somebody will point a gun at the commisaris, the commisaris will say, "That thing isn't loaded," and the guy will actually give it to him. He opens it up, sees a cartridge in the breech, closes it again and gives it back to him. It would be a marvellous thing not to explain it any further, just leave it.

DCC: In the same way, there isn't an explanation for van Meteren's escape at the end of *Outsider in Amsterdam*, other than the fact that the murder seems to be justified in a sense. Van Meteren killed a heroin pusher in order to stop him—a law unto himself. His escape also seems sanctioned by your sympathetic portrayal of him. The chief inspector calls it "an act of God."

JVW: Yes, but the last word of that book is God. That's like saying "Zen" or "Tao" or any of these fantastic words that are a contradiction. You can't call God, God; you can't say that that's his name because then you limit him. You can't say that God is good; Jung has pointed that out, to me, anyway. It must have been pointed out many times in human history. The first time I saw that was in Jung's book *Dreams, Reflections and Memories*. God isn't good, of course he isn't; he couldn't be because then he is something. You can't say, "Zen is...." What is Zen? Zen is the Japanese version of Ch'an, Ch'an is the Chinese version of Dyana, Dyana means meditation. That's a meditation sect. If you say, "That man has a lot of Zen," you're talking bull. What sort of statement is that? And if the chief inspector says, "This is an act of God," he is merely making a weak statement. He's trying to push his own guilt away; he was very silly in this case. He never realized how clever his opponent was. He got manipulated by the Papuan and the Papuan escaped so he called it an act of God. So the commisaris says, "Ah, yes, God." And that's the end of the book. Of course it's an act of God, everything is an act of God. But the chief inspector slipped up there.

DCC: I think at this point I'll conclude because if I ask you any more questions, I'll really be soliciting a kind of response which is contrary to what you are doing. There was a wonderful statement that the commisaris made: "Humanity consists of mindless forms groping about."

JVW: They are very · interesting mindless forms. It's worth describing what goes on, and it's worth getting into like the commisaris does continuously. In the first part of *The Mind Murders*, nothing happens. It's Friday and they are just about ready to go home for the weekend. De Gier stopped smoking (I had stopped smoking at that time) and he knows that if he goes home, he'll smoke because he'll have nothing to do, so he's looking for work. Grijpstra doesn't want to go home to his wife because his wife is even fatter and more horrible than she ever was before. So they run into a little accident with a drunk who is in the canal swimming around which is very normal in Amsterdam. There is always a drunk in the canal; they fall in and the police try to get them out. And the police are there, the uniformed cops are there trying to get this guy out and the guy doesn't want to get out. He's fighting them with his crutch, he's an invalid. This is a bizarre happening but if you walk through Amsterdam, you'll see bizarre happenings every five minutes. So they get into this and they fabricate on very flimsy evidence that could be explained any old way, a murder case. They reckon that it is a murder case, although there is no corpse. And for a whole hundred pages they work on this case that never was there. It was just really a figment of their minds and by fiddling around with this, they finally bring it to a conclusion that there is nothing there, although lots of stuff has happened all the time. The beginning of the second part of the book is that they run into a real murder case that comes out of that first non-existent murder case but then they have a corpse. And it's called *The Mind Murders* because of the fumbling about. The commisaris is very amused by this whole case because it proves a lot of his theories and he gets into it too in the end, he actually solves it. There you have a crime, a murder that is completely committed by mental manipulation. They cause a death, the criminal side of it causes the death of the victim by playing on his mind and legally you can't pursue that, you can't convict a man of doing that. I could do it to you or you could do it to me, anybody can do it to anybody. If I know you well, and I know what irritates you and what gives you security, if I give you enough factors that irritate you and enough factors that destroy your security, you will develop a psychosomatic disease which might kill you. And in this case, it's ulcers that cause the bleeding of the stomach, the guy dies of it. The commisaris then manipulates the killer and gets him into a similar situation and the killer dies but he dies more by his own karma than by the activity of the commisaris.

Interview with Patricia Highsmith

Diana Cooper-Clark

DCC: I recently read, and you can clarify or correct me, that you are not enamored of the human race. Is that accurate?

PH: Not really. I often talk with a sociologist friend and her opinion is that most people are quite ordinary, that universal education hasn't brought the happiness and beauty that people had hoped. I think human beings are very interesting, however. It is like talking about "a better life." Not everybody wants it, not everybody likes aesthetic things. Why should they? It is a matter of taste. It is one thing to make millions of people literate, to enact labor laws that provide leisure. The individual then decides how he spends that leisure time.

DCC: This particular reporter was from *The Observer* and the slant of the article was that you were misanthropic.

PH: That isn't true. But like many writers, I like solitude. I have had two rather bad interviews with *Observer* people who shall be nameless. In fact, I don't even remember their names. I remember distinctly that I had a nice lunch but it was a silly interview. Lots of my friends saw it and said it really wasn't like me. I didn't even keep it in my scrapbook.

DCC: You have said: "I like to entertain and to stimulate in an emotional way." Is emotion diametrically opposed to intellect or are they part of the same thing for you?

PH: It could be part of the same thing but I know that I write to tell an entertaining story, and that I am not trying to make a point. I am not trying to be an intellectual.

DCC: So you have no particular philosophy of criminology or murder as some people do who write?

PH: No. I think unfortunately that most criminals, in fact the vast majority of the people who are in jail, have not got a very high IQ. Therefore, they don't interest me very much.

DCC: You wouldn't agree then with George Bernard Shaw's idea that the artist is very close to the criminal? Colin Wilson also picks that up.

PH: I can think of only one slight closeness and that is that an imaginative writer is very free-wheeling; he has to forget about his own personal morals, especially if he is writing about criminals. He has to feel anything is possible. But I don't for this reason understand why an artist should have any criminal tendencies. The artist may simply have an ability to understand.

DCC: In *A Casebook of Murder*, Colin Wilson wrote that he regarded murder as a response to certain problems of human freedom: not as a social problem, nor a psychological problem, nor even a moral problem, but as an existential problem. Is that what you meant before when you said that you are writing to entertain rather than for a didactic purpose?

PH: Yes, I still stand by what I said. I would much rather be an entertainer than a moralizer but to call murder not a social problem I think is ridiculous; it certainly is a social problem. The word existentialist has become fuzzy. It's existentialist if you cut a finger with a kitchen knife—because it has happened. Existentialism is self-indulgent and they try to gloss over this by calling it a philosophy.

DCC: In *Ritual in The Dark* and some of his other novels, Wilson explored the idea of the criminal, the murderer who is trying to move away from the boredom of life, searching for the meaning of life, going beyond the taboos of society. I think it is in this sense that he means freedom. He finally comes to the conclusion that murder really is a perversion of freedom but he is still sympathetic to it as an attempt for freedom.

PH: Yes, Dostoevski was toying with this idea too. It is extremely interesting if one writes a story about that but I wouldn't want to imagine a world in which everybody tried this.

DCC: Would you associate Bruno in *Strangers on a Train* with some of these notions? He often speaks on this subject.

PH: Yes, but he is also a psychopath. He is really mentally sick and either doesn't realize or doesn't care about the consequences of these ideas if he carries out all these projects; he is without a conscience and without any understanding of what he is talking about. He is simply not right in the head.

DCC: Often the criminal is the hero in your novels. Is this because, for a while at least, this particular person is not bound by society?

PH: Yes, in fact I once wrote in a book of mine about suspense writing that a criminal, at least for a short period of time, is free, free to do anything he wishes. Unfortunately it sounded as if I admired that, which I don't. If somebody kills somebody, they are breaking the law, or else they are in a fit of temper. While I can't recommend it, it is an awful truth to say that for a moment they are free, yes. And I wrote that in a moment of impatience, I remember distinctly. I get impatient with a certain hidebound morality. Some of the things one hears in church and certain so-called laws that nobody practices. Nobody can practice them and it is even sick to try. I get impatient with that and so I made a rather hasty statement that at least for a short period of time the criminal is free.

DCC: And many people picked that up.

PH: Yes, Julian Symons has quoted it, and he said the equivalent of what I said, which was that neither the law nor nature cares about real justice. I mean frequently in court the guilty person goes free, either through mistakes or a crooked court which is quite possible. In nature it is the survival of the fittest. You cannot call that justice, you just call it a scheme of nature, a jungle.

DCC: Many contemporary novels, those of Colin Wilson, James Dickey's *Deliverance*, Walker Percy's *Lancelot*, Saul Bellow's *Mr. Sammler's Planet*, Graham Greene's autobiography, *A Sort of Life*, to name a few, explore the idea that human beings murder and seek violence in a search for meaning, as a relief from ennui, as a challenge to society in order to find the potential in themselves. Although Bruno is a psychopath, these ideas are touched upon in *Strangers on a Train*. Is it ever justifiable to convert murder into a philosophical and aesthetic experience?

PH: I simply don't agree with it. Murder, to me, is a mysterious thing. I feel I do not understand it really. I try to imagine it, of course, but I think it is the worst crime. That is why I write so much about it; I am interested in guilt. I think there is nothing worse than murder and that there is something mysterious about it, but that isn't to say that it is desirable for any reason. To me, in fact, it is the opposite of freedom, if one has any conscience at all.

DCC: I think that is important. Critics just don't discern that aversion to murder in your work. They seem to want to create categories of responses. Do they ever say anything that you consider accurate?

PH: In regard to murder I can't think of anything. Just now, I am going over the past two years of reviews. I have neglected them for two or three books, and I'm interested in the negative things. The new book out, *The Boy Who Followed Ripley*, is an interesting case. By the way, Ripley very much resembles Bruno psychologically because Ripley has done about eight murders by now, of which the first was the most important to him. I mean, he thinks back on the first murder and he feels shame. In the later murders he is killing people who—except for one honest man who is about to spill some beans, Murchison—are evil themselves. But he is also singularly lacking in normal conscience. So naturally the critics are going to pick up the similarity or they will make the remark about Ripley that he has no conscience. This is true. But, on the other hand, this is not true in a book like *The Blunderer*, in which the man gets to the brink of killing his wife, when she takes the bus trip, and can't bring himself to do it, only to have the wife throw herself over the cliff. Mostly my heroes are rather like Walter in *The Blunderer*, I think, by which I mean that whether they kill somebody or whether they don't, murder is not a casual thing to them, it is of great importance, it is a very serious crime.

DCC: I find that interesting because it is so much at odds with what other people seem to glean from your books. I think that if someone read all of your work he or she would see what you are saying. Perhaps part of the problem with reviewing is that many of the reviewers have not read a large quantity of your work. If you read only one of your books, I think it is easy to select certain striking features that are quite antithetical to what you are doing on the whole.

PH: Yes, but I can hardly blame them now because I have about twenty books.

DCC: It is a large undertaking but a fascinating one. I have read many of the reviews of your latest book, *The Boy Who Followed Ripley*, and they do seem to stress the negativity. To go back to what you were saying about guilt, you have previously said: "I suppose the reason I write about crime is simply that it is very good for illustrating moral points of life. I am really interested in the behaviour of people surrounding someone who has done something wrong, and also whether the person who has done it feels guilty about it, or just, 'so what'." Very often the people in your novels around the killer think that he is mad or close to madness, and very often he is: David in *This Sweet Sickness*, Syd in *Suspension of Mercy* (in the United States, *The Story-Teller*) Robert in *The Cry of the Owl*, Vic in *Deep Water*. What interests you about this particular reaction?

PH: I suppose in the case of Vic it makes the story much more alive. One can identify with a so-called normal person who is looking at Vic and suspecting, because anybody can identify with a person who has a suspicion, you see, in fact more easily than they can identify with Vic. It is just like a 'background' in writing, a necessary element or a very useful element.

DCC: Freud and Jung both felt that murder can exact its own punishment in that the murderer feels tremendous guilt and punishes himself. In *Strangers on a Train*, Guy says that "every man is his own law court and punishes himself enough." Guy certainly is tortured by guilt but several of your characters do *not* feel guilt: Philip Carter in *The Glass Cell*, Victor Van Allen in *Deep Water*, Tom Ripley. Do you find the effect of non-guilt just as interesting as guilt in a murderer?

PH: Yes, I do. Ripley as I said before is a little bit sick in the head in this respect of having very little conscience. Vic is becoming deranged in the book, he is a bit schizophrenic at the end. I try to explore as much as I can the part of themselves that these murderers are keeping secret from the public and even their wives. I try to tell how they deal with what they have done.

DCC: And Philip?

PH: Philip was changed in prison when he saw the riot and his best friend Max was killed. He became hardened, you might say, and detests the man he kills at the end.

DCC: In what way does amorality interest you in a character like Tom Ripley?

PH: I suppose I find it an interesting contrast to stereotyped morality which is very frequently hypocritical and phony. I also think that to mock lip-service morality and to have a character amoral, such as Ripley, is entertaining. I think people are entertained by reading such stories. The murderers that one reads about in the newspaper half the time are mentally deficient in some way or simply callous. There are young boys, for instance, who pretend to be delivering, or who may help an old lady carry her groceries home, and then hit her on the head when she invites them in for tea, and rob her. These are forever stupid people but they exist. Many murderers are like that and they don't interest me enough to write a book about them. Somebody like Ripley, however, who is reasonably intelligent and still has this amoral quality, interests me. I couldn't make an interesting story out of some morons.

DCC: It seems to be a *sine qua non* of crime fiction that order is restored and good triumphs over evil but sometimes your murderers do get away with murder; again, Philip Carter and Tom Ripley.

PH: This is the way life is and I read somewhere years ago that only 11% of murders are solved. That is unfortunate but lots of victims are not so important as the President of the United States. The police make a certain effort, and it may be a good effort, but frequently the case is dropped. And so I think, why shouldn't I write about a few characters who also go free?

DCC: You have often been accused of carrying your identification with your psychotic characters to the point where you actually seem to be preferring their interesting evil to the mediocre virtue of their victims. Would you agree with that assessment?

PH: Yes. I think it is more interesting to talk about something off the beaten track than it is to talk about a so-called normal person. That's one answer to your question. Another might be, that in some of my books the victims are evil or boring individuals so the murderer is more important than they. This is a writer's remark, not a legal judge's.

DCC: Is this why you might perhaps find amorality more interesting than immorality, because it is more unusual?

PH: Yes. I suppose it is such a subtle question because it is such a subtle difference. Amorality such as Ripley's is rarer than immorality. People in the Mafia or pimps, people in any kind of wretched occupation, know that they and their work are strictly in the gutter, that their activities are disgusting, and they don't care as long as it puts a little money in their pockets. This is immoral but the Ripley type is amoral.

DCC: In *The Tremor of Forgery* the hero is both detective and suspect, accused and accuser. He is faced with the question of whether or not he must recognize the violence within himself. Conventional values and ethics seem lost in Tunisia and he is faced in his own life by the novel's statement: "Whether a person makes his own personality and standards from within himself, or whether he and the standards are the creations of the society around him." Which do you think come first?

PH: I am quite sure that the standards of morality come from the society around; a child within the jungle is not going to invent his own sense of right and wrong. In *Forgery* he leaves America and comes to a place where murder is taken a little more lightly.

DCC: Your exploration of the criminal mind is ever-fascinating. There have been so many conflicting insights about the criminal mind: murderers are innately evil; Lombroso believed that criminality was a trait inherited from degenerate ancestors; sociologists maintain that criminals are victims of urbanization, family disintegration, poor schooling, unemployment, mental illness; and a recent study by Yachelson and Samenow stated that there *is* a criminal personality. Where do you believe the ability to murder comes from?

PH: I happen to believe more in heredity than I do in environment. There is certainly such a thing as a no-good family. Families always have a history, and I have heard of families where the grandfather was an old crook, never quite in jail. Within one household one can find sometimes an atmosphere of flaunting the law to a greater or lesser degree.

DCC: Do you believe in the "bad seed" theory?

PH: Yes, I think there is something in that; it doesn't mean the individual would always turn out badly but as I said, I do believe in heredity more than environment. The phrase "poor schools" makes me laugh. I went to several. What counts is individual motivation. Ambition and drive count.

DCC: Do you think it is a mistake to try to reduce the original impulse to murder to one thing or another.

PH: An impulse to murder is surely based on anger. Premeditated murder is different. I think of the two young Australian girls. One was eleven and one was thirteen, and they murdered the mother of one of them on a garden path I believe, for no reason. They just got together and said, "Let's do it." That comes under mental derangement and as I am not a psychologist, I can't make any intelligent statement about that except that any court would probably say that the girl who was the leader of the two was mentally deranged. Where does that get you? It's just a term. But there was something wrong with her brain even though she was only about thirteen. There is something wrong with anybody who is so inhuman as to kill the mother of a friend.

DCC: In P.D. James' novel *Death of An Expert Witness* the murderer states that a murderer sets himself aside from the whole of humanity forever. It's a kind of death. Do you believe that murder is a kind of death for the murderer?

PH: It certainly would be for me but I don't know if many murderers take it that seriously. I had two dreams in my life in which I had committed a murder and only in one could I identify a certain person whom I disliked years ago. But in each dream I was very disturbed by the fact that I was ostracized from society, or at least I felt that I was. In the dream, if I went to a store to buy a newspaper, I felt that people were looking at me and saying, "There goes a murderer." It was a truly dreadful feeling but I think the world is also full of people walking around the streets in Chicago and Marseilles who have killed somebody and they sleep quite well.

DCC: In *Strangers on a Train* Bruno tells Guy that "any person can murder." Do you think that is true?

PH: No, I don't. Maybe I thought it was when I wrote it but at any rate it comes out of Bruno's mouth. I don't believe that at all. I don't believe that everybody can be coerced into murder. In war, yes, I guess it is different. But I don't think everyone can murder, not even for money. It is all relative because if you were to go to some primitive place, the Far East or Africa, and offered a fantastic sum to some humble person to kill somebody he doesn't know, then you or your paid agent could do it. You could find maybe the same thing in America if you looked hard but I think I have to ask myself what kind of people I am talking about; the poor, the middle-class, or people like you and myself. I don't think you could be coerced, you couldn't be persuaded, I dare say you would not be able to kill somebody even for a considerable amount of money or whatever else.

DCC: What if we eliminate the question of punishment, jail, so that one would not weigh the consequences against the act? Many people think that it is the spectre of jail and punishment that prevents people from committing acts of violence.

PH: Again one has to ask what intellectual level of person is one talking about. Of course the more primitive the person is, if you eliminate the punishment, then the more likely the person can kill somebody for money. But I mostly write about middle-class people and they would have too much awareness of what they had done, just as I had in the dream. It is the awareness of it that is the torture rather than being put into jail. Koestler spent some time campaigning against hanging in England, and with success, because he proved that capital punishment is not a deterrent but insignificant. Yet its advocates are again trying to call it a deterrent.

It's revenge they want and that's as barbaric as the Old Testament.
DCC: I agree. Graham Greene, in his introduction to *Eleven*, wrote that you create a claustrophobic world which we enter each time with a sense of personal danger. Do you see danger everywhere in life as it seems to be in your writing?
PH: No. I am inclined to be naive in my personal dealings and I am not inclined to lock the door and have padlocks everywhere. I don't know what Graham Greene means but in my short story "The Terrapin," about the little boy with the tortoise, the story is seen through his eyes. I don't know why it is claustrophobic anymore than any story, considering that a short story has to be intense and is usually seen through the eyes of one person. You are within the little boy's atmosphere. I don't know why that is claustrophobic.
DCC: Just to continue with that, danger can also lurk under the rules and regulations of society. Vic, in *Deep Water*, feels that "People who do not behave in an orthodox manner are by definition frightening." This juxtaposition of the ordinary and the respectable with violence creates a chilling atmosphere in your books because we are dealing with people who are middle-class, who are respectable. Do you purposely create that kind of atmosphere because you know it is all the more frightening?
PH: No, it is because it is the atmosphere that I know, because it is my own class more or less, a very ordinary American. My family was neither rich nor poor and I couldn't write about peasants. In New York once, when I was a teenager, I tried to write a short story about an Italian family because I went to school with many Italians. I found I couldn't do it because I had never lived in their households with ten or eleven people sitting at the dining room table. I never finished the story. In other words, I have to write, any writer has to write, about the class of people that he knows. Therefore the contrast between class respectability and murderous thoughts is bound to turn up in most of my books.
DCC: You often return to the theme of a pathological conflict between two men, in *Strangers on a Train, Deep Water, The Blunderer, The Glass Cell, The Cry of the Owl*, and others.
PH: The ideas come to me in that way. The idea for *Strangers on a Train* came as an idea for an exchange of murders. For the exchange, one needs two men, two people.
DCC: You don't really explore that conflict with women though.
PH: No, the only female protagonist I suppose in my novels is

Edith in *Edith's Diary*. But I have a lot of short stories that have women protagonists.

DCC: Are you more interested in the conflict between men as opposed to conflict between women?

PH: No, perhaps I find men more violent by nature than women or more able to use physical strength, but that is obvious. In the American schools, at least in my generation, around fourteen years of age, they separated the boys from the girls in the Junior High School. It wasn't to keep the birth rate down at all, it was because the boys were difficult to handle, they were disobedient and the teacher would have to slap them in the face in those days and pull their ears. It was much more fun when I was going to school with boys before the age of fourteen because they have a sense of humor, much better than that of the girls, I must say, and it was amusing. And suddenly from fourteen to seventeen there was a bunch of girls before university learning things by rote. Pretty boring. Young women these days are less passive, thank goodness, but they've still a long way to go.

DCC: In a time when people are interested in the portrayal of women in literature, I found your book *Little Tales of Misogyny* really quite unique.

PH: That was like a book of jokes.

DCC: Yes, but I find that in a number of your novels the women seem despicable in trivial ways. They are often cheats, Melinda in *Deep Water*, Hazel in *The Glass Cell*, Alicia in *Suspension of Mercy*, Miriam in *Strangers on a Train*. And the women are totally unsympathetic in *Little Tales of Misogyny*.

PH: I must say that it certainly looks like that but actually I have quite an esteem for women's strength. I think the women portrayed in my writing have rather bad characters but I don't think that personally. I think that women can be quite strong. I can remember my grandmother who was the head of the household in a very pleasant way when I was a kid, and my mother's character was stronger than my stepfather's. Unfortunately in *Strangers on a Train*, Miriam, the wife, happened to be a silly high school girl. The early marriage of Guy and Miriam was based, as you might say, on falling in love around high school age. This was a mistake for Guy and so the girl Miriam is the type who would flirt and make another stupid liaison of some kind. And then Melinda, who was Vic's wife, was always flirting and having two or three lovers. I simply needed that for the story because it gives Vic a motivation for murder. Unfortunately, the whole picture looks as if I suspect that women have narrow characters which is not really true. It is not my personal feeling at all.

DCC: Julian Symons has pointed out that you are drawn to the attraction exerted on the weak by the idea of violence, such as in *The Two Faces of January* and *Those Who Walk Away.*

PH: Well, I don't plan these things. When I start to write anything, I think of the story first. I think of the events. Is it interesting or is it amusing or is it unexpected or is it almost unbelievable? That comes first, rather than thinking one character is weak and one character is strong.

DCC: Critics often discuss your obsessions and fixations and the one they usually mention is paranoia. Clearly from what you have said, you don't believe that you particularly have obsessions and fixations in your own life.

PH: Well, maybe there is a bit of paranoia in David in *This Sweet Sickness,* but I don't find it in *The Tremor of Forgery.* Vic, in *Deep Water,* is just the opposite of paranoid; he is quite sure of himself. He kills one man, then the second man, and he thinks he is completely in the clear. As for myself, I don't think I'm paranoid, but as I said before, rather trusting and optimistic about personal and business relationships.

DCC: Maurice Richardson has said that you write about men like a spider writing about flies, and another reviewer has maintained that reading one of your novels is like having tea with a dangerous witch. Both are compliments I might add; they weren't meant to be negative. We talked before about reviewers. Do you read, now or in the beginning, material about yourself?

PH: Oh, definitely! I read reviews as I was beginning to write. Now I finally read the critiques, sometimes after they've been lying around the house for months. It is the last thing I look at in the Sunday paper when I know I have a review out. I am not exactly eager to read my reviews but I have always been interested in the negative comments.

DCC: Do you notice a change in the responses to your work, from your first novel, *Strangers on a Train,* to your latest, *The Boy Who Followed Ripley*? Do you see an evolution in the response? Is it the same, is it very different?

PH: No, I don't find it very different. I don't notice any change in them.

DCC: Do you feel that your literary reputation has suffered, as some people think, because crime is at the centre of your books? Or do you really worry about your literary reputation?

PH: I don't care about it at all. The publishers always want to categorize you and they think it helps them to sell books. *Edith's Diary* was rejected by Knopf in New York and because the publishers can't categorize every book I write, this is why in New York I must have been with five publishers by now. I would rather stay with one but they get so fixed on a certain category that if I write something out of line, then it is a rejection and my agents have to take it to another publisher which up to now I have always been able to find. In England, Heinemann is less rigid. I won't say they will take anything, but my work has a fair amount of variation, if I consider *Edith's Diary, Little Tales of Misogyny* and the animal stories, but Heinemann is content to publish them all, mainly because they can sell them. So this business of categorizing bores me. I couldn't tailor my inspiration to that.

DCC: You mentioned *Edith's Diary*, which was a departure from the murder element that is in most of your books. It was a wonderful novel. Are you interested in writing more novels in the future that don't deal with murder?

PH: Oh, yes, definitely. In fact, I might go to the States to live for a few months in order to freshen my memory and my information, in which case I might write another American-set book with quite a different theme. I am interested in morale just now, not morals, but how one keeps up one's morale. It doesn't sound like a very exciting theme, and isn't until I attach it to a story.

DCC: I think it is crucial to anybody who is alive today.

PH: Sometimes one has the mental habit, well, really tricks, to continue to be cheerful and to continue to imagine that one's making progress when one really isn't. I speak not of myself but of many, many people.

DCC: Why have you never written a detective novel as such?

PH: I think it is a silly way of teasing people, "who-done-it." It doesn't interest me in the least and I don't know anything about the police procedure or the detective methods of working; that is an occupation in itself. It is like a puzzle and puzzles do not interest me.

DCC: I am interested in the movies that were done from your novels. What did you think of them?

PH: The Hitchcock film, *Strangers on a Train*, is very dated now but I think it is a good film. *Purple Noon* is an entertaining film even though Ripley gets caught in the end. *The American Friend* I thought came off quite well. That's Wim Wenders doing *Ripley's Game* with Dennis Hopper. I saw that twice. I like to see any film that I'm interested in twice. *The American Friend* is a good film. I like it all except the ending. I thought they did the train scene very well.

DCC: I know that some writers, once they have sold the rights to their book, don't care what the filmmakers do with the movie after that. Do you like to be involved?

PH: I do care. My agents want to put into the contract that I have the right to see the script, and if I don't like it I can remove my name. I care quite a lot because I like to have a reputation for not only writing amusing books but books that are capable of becoming good films. Of course that depends on the quality of the director and script writer.

DCC: Was it an augury that you have the same birthday as Edgar Allan Poe, January 19th?

PH: I don't believe in astrology. It is also the birthday of Robert E. Lee, so I used to have a holiday down south in school. They recently stopped having holidays on his birthday though, too Confederate. (laughs)

Interview with Julian Symons

Diana Cooper-Clark

DCC: You have said that the only way to envisage public violence is through private crime, given the violent age that we live in. Presumably you meant in fiction. Could you expand that?

JS: Novelists, in general, if they are dealing with something as vast and horrific as the Viet Nam War find that it's really not possible for them to treat it directly and realistically. Instead their approach is like that of Robert Stone in *Dog Soldiers*. Although in a sense this fine novel is about the Viet Nam War, certainly about the effects of the Viet Nam War, and although it asks questions implicitly like, "Is running drugs any worse than killing entirely harmless Vietnamese?" it doesn't confront the war head-on. Nobody has directly confronted the Viet Nam War or the German concentration camps, dealing with them straightforwardly and realistically as Tolstoy did in *War and Peace*. It may well be that the best way of dealing with what is generally agreed to be a very violent time indeed is to envision public violence through private violence. We had a very horrific series of murders in England a few years ago, which were called the Moors Murders, in which a young man and a young woman got hold of children and tortured them. I have actually written a book which has got a relationship to that (it is not a direct account of the Moors Murders or anything like it) and people were rather upset by my doing it. They felt, "Why should anybody want to write about something so horrific!" Well, for two reasons. First of all, I would feel that if you label crime writing an entertainment field simply, in a way you are down-grading it. One ought to be able to do more than that. I don't say one should have to, certainly not, crime writing is first of all an entertainment but it should be possible to do more with it than merely to entertain. That is one reason why I felt impelled to write about the Moors Murders, or to deal with them at an indirect angle. The other reason is that I do feel that for most novelists, if they want to envisage the violence of the time, it is easier to do it through private violence than in any other way. Through private violence one can pose, implicitly at least, questions like, "What is the guilt of Brady and Hindley, who were the two people in the Moors Murders, compared to the guilt of Lieutenant Calley?" I am not saying that there is any simple answer to that question but only that the question is important.

DCC: You seem to be interested in what you have called, "the respectable face of violence," shown in your novel, *The Players and The Game,* where the killer is a highly respectable professional man living in a highly respectable dormitory town. Is evil essentially banal and ordinary as opposed to exceptional and unique?

JS: I don't think evil is essentially banal; no, I know it's not, although it was a fashionable thing to say and believe. My feeling would be much more that evil is unique, that it makes much more sense to think of somebody like Hitler, not as a little banal man who somehow happens to have been put into the position of being able to order very evil things to be done, but as a unique expression of a period.

DCC: But you're more interested in violence that comes out of what seems to be a respectable situation than, for instance, the violence of the Mafia or criminals.

JS: Yes, the private face of violence fascinates me. My belief is that one good recipe for writing a crime story or for the plot of a crime story would be to think of people that you like very much, your friends, lovers, wife, husband, and then imagine under what circumstances you could conceivably want to murder them. No sooner has the thought come into one's head than, in almost every case, it is really quite easy to think of circumstances in which you would want to kill people whom you hold in great affection. Between the thought and the action there are, of course, for most of us, all kinds of barriers but these dangerous thoughts are very absorbing. About five years ago, a young BBC television producer made a film about my books, which he called *Games.* The theme of the film was that in all of my books or in almost all of them, people are playing games, and this was something I hadn't realized myself. I think that although he pushed it a bit far, it is a perfectly true thesis that in almost all of the books that I intend at all seriously, and I know that I have perpetrated some disastrous mishits, everybody is wearing a mask. We are all potentially different people in our own minds from the figures we present to the world, and sometimes the different person we are in our own minds goes over into action. This is fascinating to me.

DCC: Crime is also seen as a kind of game with dire consequences. How do you define "game" in terms of crime, considering that most people think of games as frivolous, non-serious, perhaps a diversion, a safety valve?

JS: Games are safety valves quite often in my books. One of my characters, Lowson in *The Players and the Game*, is a masochist. He goes to see a prostitute posing as a doctor, and he is subjected to various indignities. She says, "Good Lord, you wet your pants again," that kind of thing. Well, this is a game of a harmless kind, perhaps not to some people an agreeable kind, but it is a safety valve. That would be one sort of game. Of course there are many others. In *The Players and The Game*, even the villains start out by playing games, with one of them pretending that she is Bonnie of Bonnie and Clyde and the other one is imagining that he is Dracula. That is a game and so far a harmless one. A fantasy life, or Walter Mitty life, is led by almost everybody.

DCC: Yes, that's true. You have also remarked: "I am particularly interested in suburban man. I mean, the sort of person who lives in Blackheath. That character of mine, Solomon Grundy for example, is pure Blackheath. It was a world that seemed to me to incorporate the three great themes of the English novel—class, childhood and sex." Why are the English drawn to these themes more than any other culture?

JS: I would say that these themes are used much more in the mainstream novel than they are in detective stories or crime stories or whatever you would like to call them. Crime writers, with some exceptions like Ruth Rendell, are not very greatly concerned with the themes of class and childhood and sex. I wouldn't call sex a particularly English theme; class and childhood certainly are. Class, because England has been always and still is, although much less so, a class ridden, class organized society. It's out of class, out of distinctions in class, which are often almost imperceptible to Americans and Canadians even though they speak the same language, that many English novelists have made classic English comedy. One of the distinctions in Jane Austen's books is the distinction of class. There are all kinds of class distinctions, of the most subtle kind, in Trollope, and to come up to date, in Anthony Powell's *Dance to the Music of Time*. This is something that can flourish only if your society is a class-conscious society which

English society still is.

DCC: In an essay on your mystery fiction, you wrote: "What I have consciously been trying to do in most of my crime stories is to use an act of violence to point up my feelings about the pressures of urban living." This is explored in *The 31st of February, The End of Solomon Grundy, The Progress of a Crime.* Is there a direct relationship between violence and the pressures of urban living? Or is murder an age-old desire?

JS: Obviously, murder has always existed in every society. In almost all societies it's not merely the ultimate act, since it deprives somebody else of life, but it's also ultimate in the sense that in many societies the murderer has to be cast out. This is Auden's idea that the course of a crime story is the commission of this ultimate crime and then the casting out of the wrong-doer. There is the discovery, first of all, of the one bad apple in the barrel and his being cast out from society. As to the pressures of urban living, yes, I think we have lots of different, more sophisticated crimes now, which wouldn't have been so likely to take place a hundred years ago.

DCC: There is much debate about whether or not murder is an innate instinct as opposed to the behaviorist notion that it is society that creates the impulse to kill.

JS: I would be on the side, not perhaps totally, about eighty percent, on the side of the environmentalists in that. Certainly I wouldn't be on the side of pure heredity as the basis for murder.

DCC: Would you disagree with the Russian writer of detective stories, Arkadi Adamov, who has said that the Russian detective novel has much more moral, social and public weight than those of the West?

JS: I don't know his work. Obviously, I would expect any crime stories written by an orthodox Russian living in the Soviet Union to be basically political, so, from his point of view, yes, they would express that, from mine, they wouldn't.

DCC: In *The Detective Story in Britain*, you wrote that the detective story would have considerable significance for future sociologists trying to interpret the nature of twentieth-century man. Do you find the detective novel the best way you can express as an artist your concerns about society and Western civilization?

JS: (laughs) I dare say it isn't the best way. I think I should talk a little personally here. My first crime story was written as a kind of joke. I had always liked reading crime stories; read Sherlock Holmes at ten and so on. I had a close friend, who was the Secretary of the Surrealist Exhibition when it came over to England in 1936, the first time most of us had ever seen any surrealist paintings; we were so provincial then. He suggested that it would be fun to write a crime story together. We would put all our friends in the book, we would have a kind of mock-art movement, and we would kill off the friend we liked least. We would make the murderer another of our friends, and so on. We tossed the idea around; he used to send little notes across the square in which we both lived, and I would send notes back to him. He, in fact, never wrote any of the book, although he suggested a lot of ideas. I wrote it, but it really was a joke rather like Dylan Thomas' "Death of the King's Canary." I didn't do anything with it, I just put it away in a drawer, it never occurred to me that it could be published. Years went by, the war came, I was called up, and I got married to the wife I am married to now. After the war, to my astonishment and disgust, I found it rather hard to get a job. We were quite poor and my wife happened to come across what was a yellowing manuscript by now. She read it and said, "Well, it is quite funny in bits, you might make some money from it." It is a very, very dotty book. By chance I sent it to the only publisher in London, Victor Gollancz, who appreciated the book's zany comedy. After writing three books that were rather like the kind of academic detective story Edmund Crispin and Michael Innes wrote very much better, I moved into something that did much more nearly approach a novel. I realized then that this was the sort of thing I wanted to write. I regard books like *The 31st of February* and *The Progress of a Crime* as novels. I know they are not mainstream novels, although they seem to me as good as a lot of mainstream novels. One is simply aiming at a larger audience, a rather different audience, by putting the points one wants to make about society, politics, or whatever, in the form of a crime story. So you can do what Eliot said one can do in a play; you can have a story operating on two levels. One level is, if you like, for the groundlings. That is to say, the book can be read simply on the level of, "This is a crime story with no other implications." Or you can read it as a crime story but also get the plus of some ironical or tragic or serious comments about the society we live in. That, at least, is my intention. I am more or less precluded, or I felt I was, from writing a mainstream novel by the fact that I started to write detective stories but I have tried to put at least some of the elements of mainstream novels into my crime stories.

DCC: I would agree that you have done that. Does the idea of murder as expressed by some writers as a perversion of the creative instinct, freedom, transformation and vision appeal to you?

JS: I think on a philosophical plane that is nonsense. Clearly murder can have or does have a sort of connection with the creative instinct. Yes, I suppose I'd agree it is a perversion of the creative instinct. But to talk about murder providing psychological freedom for the individual seems to me nonsense. Murder is the expression of something quite contrary to that, of something deeply wrong with the individual. The only kind of murder, I suppose, which I would think entered into that category you're suggesting would be a murder which was quite consciously committed in opposition to the existing state of society, or something like that.

DCC: You said before that you feel that murderous impulses are caused mainly by environment. Does that mean that you don't think that there is a distinctive murderer's personality? A recent study by Yachelson and Samenow in the States indicates that there is a distinctive murderer's personality.

JS: I'm not qualified to offer an opinion which ran counter to an expert's view. But, for what it is worth, my belief is that the psychopathic personality, which would still spring in my eyes more from environment than from heredity, certainly exists. However, that this could be defined simply as a murderous personality, I should find very hard to accept.

DCC: Ross Macdonald disagreed with your statement that the detective novelist should always investigate "the springs of violence." Macdonald felt that this was to fall into what he called "the scientist fallacy," because the value of the detective novel lies in obeying the laws of narrative, which are not derived from either the chemist's laboratory or the psychologist's Rorschach test. But I don't think you are denying narrative importance in the novel.

JS: Of course not. I would just observe that if anybody goes into the springs of violence in relation to personality more than another detective writer, it is Ross Macdonald.

DCC: Meaningless violence seems to be of particular interest to you. We see an example of this in *The Progress of a Crime*, based on a real incident, when a crowd of boys pulled another one from a bus and killed him.

JS: The violent nature of our society interests me more than it would interest most people. To amplify the point slightly, such violence is often organized by authority. In relation to America, the wilful destruction in Viet Nam is a very good instance of it. Obviously, there are other instances, some of the English behavior in Northern Ireland, for example. But the violence that particularly interests me is meaningless in the sense that it springs from individual frustration, like violence in English football matches, or the actual murder that was the basis of *The Progress of a Crime.* I am interested in the nature of violence and these seem to me two aspects of it in our time, individual violence and the kind that gets authority's stamp of approval.

DCC: Do you pay any attention to criticisms about the violence in your books?

JS: No, I don't pay any attention to that.

DCC: Do you read reviews of your work?

JS: Yes.

DCC: Do you find them illuminating?

JS: Not often. The most illuminating thing from my point of view has been the film that this young TV producer did on games in my work. He put me through a searching interrogation for some hours. I began to realize things about my own books that I really had not understood before. I regard myself as a better critic of my own work than almost anybody else around. It doesn't really affect me much if people say books that I think are good are not good; I still go on thinking they are good. Nor, certainly, would it affect me if they said, "Well, this is very unpleasant, I don't like it." I wouldn't quarrel with that. If they find my books unpleasant, I can't argue with them, but I feel strongly that there is absolutely no subject that a crime writer shouldn't be able to approach, any more than any straight novelist. There are certain pieces of crime writing which I find very disagreeable indeed. I detest them and I think they are socially bad, but all this means is that I wouldn't want to read them myself. I have in mind writers who appear to me to luxuriate in violence for its own sake. One of the essential features of their work is that the good guys are even more violent than the bad ones. The bad guys commit violence, the good guys are more violent in return, and this is depicted to the reader as being all right because the people who do it are good. I found the film *Dirty Harry* very dislikable and distrustable. The violence was gratuitous and we were expected to approve or condone the violence because it was the good guys who were doing it.

DCC: Yes, Anthony Burgess explores that idea in *A Clockwork Orange*. He is saying that to commit violence with the intention of doing good is just as bad as the kind of violence done by the main character who is a delinquent. The authorities condition the violence out of him.

JS: The principle of my objection is that an author is implicitly asking us to condone an act committed by one person, which we wouldn't condone if it were committed by another. The important thing in my eyes is the "act"; you either condone it or not.

DCC: The detective novel is getting more and more critical attention. What do you think, for example, of analyses that see this genre archetypically, mythically, that see Apollo as the detective and Dionysus as the murderer? In other words, the whole stream of critical methodologies that are applied to the detective genre?

JS: Some of it seems to be very interesting, some merely pretentious. I don't see much interest involved in talking about Apollo as a detective or talking about detective stories in the Bible. It seems to me that those critical responses are so far removed from detective fiction or from the crime story, which I think has developed out of the detective story, that they are irrelevant. Marxist criticism of the detective story is another matter. Or psychoanalytic criticism, of which there has been extraordinarily little. I think that might be extremely interesting and valuable. But I am not perhaps quite up-to-date with some of these matters.

DCC: I would think that you would find analyses of detective fiction, like those which speak of the "crime of existence," too far-fetched.

JS: Yes, I think it is going too far. If I were going back, I would go back to something like Frazer's *The Golden Bough*, because the essential theme of the pure detective story is the casting out of evil.

DCC: Would you agree with Howard Haycraft that the detective novel flourishes in a stable, democratic country that recognizes and accepts established principles of law and order?

JS: Yes, I would go along with that almost totally. I think Dorothy Sayers has put it even better in saying that until there was an organized police force there really couldn't be a body of detective stories. Poe, who wrote at a time when there wasn't an organized police force, is a marvellous exception to that but he is an exception. A Marxist view of the crime story would be that it is the perfect bourgeois art form because its object is the protection of the rich or the well-to-do, and its object is further to show that those who tried to take money or to take away the lives of the well-to-do are, in fact, wicked people. Leaving that aside, the detective story really can't exist in anything other than a stable and fairly open society. I wouldn't feel that anything like the detective story or the serious crime story could exist in the Soviet Union or indeed under any other dictatorship.

DCC: You have said that the detective or crime novel can't be taken as seriously as Tolstoy even at its highest level. Do you still hold to this and why?

JS: I do indeed. We have to lump the detective story and the crime story together, although they are to a certain extent separate things. But like the spy story, they are all parts of sensational fiction and sensation is the object of it all. A book like Wilkie Collins' *The Moonstone* is marvellous on its own level. As Eliot says, it is absolutely as good as it can be in the line of sensational melodrama. But this is not what great novels are made of; one can't really compare Collins, however much one admires him, with the greatest Victorian novelists. If Dickens had been merely a writer of sensational fiction, he would not be a great novelist. Most of us who are working in the various different aspects of the crime story are all writers of sensational fiction and this limits us. The basis of great novels is the exploration of the springs of motive and character. The best crime writers know this but they are limited and hampered by the fact that they are bound to introduce sensation, rather as an addict needs his fix. The best crime writer operating today is Patricia Highsmith but you couldn't possibly call her a great novelist. Her intentions are as serious as those of most novelists around but the material she deals with and the way she deals with it is a limiting factor. The crime story is very interesting and it can throw a lot of light on the nature of modern society but that doesn't mean to say that crime stories as such are great novels. I think I would apply this even moving higher up in the scale really. I would apply it to Graham Greene, to the Greene crime stories; I would tend to apply it to books like Conrad's *The Secret Agent* and *Under Western Eyes*, though they are awfully good.

DCC: Why then do you write detective novels instead of novels outside of this genre?

JS: Probably because something in me flinches from (or is unable to write sufficiently well) writing in the mainstream. That would be an uncongenial answer to me but I dare say it is the true one. Another answer, to be just a little more cheerful about the nature of the detective story and the crime story, is that in a time when the novel has very much disintegrated in that it has lost its sense of narrative, the detective story and the crime story does provide this absolutely. This is the first essential of the crime story. So, if I were being more flattering to myself, I would say that I do want to have a story. The thread of narrative is important to me as a writer and I wouldn't easily relinquish it. Up to a certain point, you can say things in crime stories which are not so easy to say in the form of a straight novel. But if one is putting it on a higher plane than that and asking, "Can a crime story be up to Tolstoy or can it be up to Dostoyevski or Dickens," well, it could be, but, in fact, it isn't. If it is going to be, then it's got to do something more. Dickens and Dostoyevski were not really concerned with crime, although their books often deal with crime. They move through the crime into something more important and this crime writers don't do.

DCC: Do you think that part of the reason that detective literature has been designated an inferior position in literature is that the literary revolution called modernism was ideologically and aesthetically against the Aristotelian tradition? What I mean by this is that the critical and literary world tended to reject stories with a beginning, a middle and an end, to reject prose in favor of poetry. By this criteria, the detective novel would seem hopelessly narrow and outdated.

JS: Again, I am not sure that I am totally qualified to answer this. But yes, the detective story is rather opposed to modernism of a free flowing kind, of the kind you are talking about. One ought to bear in mind as contrary to that, that a writer like Robbe-Grillet can be claimed rightly to be using the form of the detective story to a certain extent, at least for his own ends. But one rather better reason why the detective story is regarded as such an inferior article is that in ninety-five cases out of a hundred it *is* an inferior article. Like science fiction, most detective stories are really very much worse written than it would be possible to believe. If you have made deep incursions into the field, you will know this is true. The ninety-five percent absolutely are commercial articles, not worth very much because they don't bring much money to their authors. But they are commercial articles really of the lowest kind and this is one reason for the scorn that the detective story is exposed to. It is one favorite complaint of crime writers that they are put into a ghetto, in a critical sense, that they are shut off and reviewed by Newgate Callendar in *The New York Times* or in the English papers are reviewed under a special section called Criminal Records. They complain about this but what they don't realize is that if it weren't done in that way, if their books were simply sent out as straight novels along with the other straight novels, they wouldn't get reviewed at all or only very, very few of them.

DCC: Would you care to give some examples of the best contemporary writers of crime fiction, aside from yourself?

JS: These are the people that you are interviewing. Patricia Highsmith is very good indeed, although she's gone off lately. Ruth Rendell is awfully good. P.D. James is very good in a traditional style that I am astonished to see flourishing so well and so brilliantly in her work. In America, I admire greatly Ross Macdonald.

DCC: What are the essential differences between contemporary American and British authors of the detective novel?

JS: Well, how closely would you want me to define the detective novel or the crime story in general?

DCC: In any way you want.

JS: I don't think there are great differences. English books seem to be more popular in America than on the whole American books are in England. On the other hand, I have just been writing something about Chandler and Chandler was not only given much more critical appreciation in England, well, he had none in America, but also his books right from the beginning sold much better in England. This is really very surprising because the English market is not anything like as big as the American market. Obviously, there are differences of language, there are differences of approach; American books make much more use of what is at times a very considerable knowledge, so it seems to the English, of criminal life. There is nothing in England that approached Chandler or Hammett or has approached them since in their writing about the criminal scene. On the other hand, we do have our own virtues.

DCC: What made you look back to the Victorian period in *The Blackheath Poisonings* and in your recent book, *Sweet Adelaide*, given that you usually explore contemporary society?

JS: Well, two reasons. One was that I had never written a period crime story and I wanted to see if I could do it. This is perhaps a purely personal thing but I would have the feeling that it is a healthy thing for crime writers always to be pushing away at the limits of the form in some way or other. As P.D. James, for example, after starting very conventionally, moved into a really quite gruesome description of murder in *A Shroud For A Nightingale*, and then, my word, what audacity, she actually set a story in a home for incurables in *The Black Tower*, very good indeed. That is something that couldn't conceivably have been done in their time by writers like Christie or Sayers. So I am all for pushing outwards. Another reason is that as one grows older, one inevitably loses touch with the way in which people, or some people, talk. As I have said before, I know the good things about my books. I know the way in which the kind of people I am writing about, talk. I wouldn't know the way in which (this is one of the reflections of English class society) upper class people really talk to each other. I know the way they might talk to me, but they might talk to each other differently. Among the kind of professional classes that I write about and among the young people I wrote about, I felt myself perfectly at home. I am no longer so much at home and this is simply a matter of age. In depicting the conversation of young people, I know how my son and my daughter-in-law talk to me but I don't really know and I can't fully envisage how they talk to each other. When I see films which the young enjoy very much—by the young I mean anyone under thirty—I often dislike them so much, and I find them so trivial and boring that I can't understand how intelligent people, and a lot of these people are intelligent, can enjoy them, what they can get out of them. I am not saying that all intelligent young people like trivial boring things. But this does rather preclude me from writing about the young now so I have been trying not only to break a bit of new ground with Victorian crime stories, but also to find a way around the difficulty of growing older which is, I think, a difficulty for all writers. The Victorian crime story *Sweet Adelaide* is based on an actual Victorian case. It is about a famous Victorian murder case involving a woman named Adelaide Bartlett. I shall do one more and then that will be it. I don't want to produce mere Victoriana. What will come after that, I don't know.

DCC: *Murder Ink* lists *The 31st of February* as one of the five best detective novels ever. Is that the book of which you are proudest?

JS: There are three or four which I think are pretty good novels and also I hope pretty good crime stories. Certainly one of those would be *The 31st of February*. Another would be *The Man Who Killed Himself,* another *The End of Solomon Grundy*, another still *The Progress of a Crime*. I mustn't extend the list too far because there have been some real disasters. *A Three Pipe Problem* was fun to do and I enjoyed doing it. I had always wanted to write a sort of pastiche Sherlock Holmes story but I didn't actually want to introduce Holmes, so this was a way of getting around that. Oh, just one more thing I would like to say although you haven't asked me, and that is that I have never wanted to be simply a writer of crime stories. I do write a lot of other books.

DCC: I most certainly am familiar with your other writings—your first-rate biographies of Thomas Carlyle and A.J.A. Symons, for example. You indeed have many faces. You have turned your hand to so many things—history, literary criticism, novels, and, as I said, biography.

JS: The reason I am going to Canada next March to a place called Douglas College is to give the opening lecture in a conference on the art of biography. I don't actually write all that many crime stories but in a way part of the answer to why I don't write a straight novel would be that I find an outlet for what I don't get in crime stories by writing biographies, some military history, some criticism and so on.

Interview with Amanda Cross

Diana Cooper-Clark

DCC: Why do you write your novels under the name of Amanda Cross instead of Carolyn Heilbrun?

AC: Well, I began them in 1963 and I hadn't yet got tenure at Columbia University,and I felt that if they knew I was writing detective stories, it would impede my chances of getting tenure; so I simply kept it a secret. And it was a well kept secret until about 1972.

DCC: That's what I thought. Reed Amhearst tells Kate: "The truth's a slippery thing. Perhaps that's why only literary people understand it." Many detectives are literary: Kate Fansler, Lord Peter Wimsey, Adam Dalgleish, Sherlock Holmes, even Lew Archer, Ross Macdonald's character, reads Zeno. Is that what makes Kate a good detective? Is it necessary to let ideas leap about illogically to solve a crime?

AC: It is for her, I guess. Of course, I began writing these novels obviously following the vision of Dorothy L. Sayers. I have moved further and further away from the Sayers model but the early Cross novels were quite imitative. I sometimes think I began writing them because I didn't have any of Sayers' novels left to read. And the mind of a literary person who loves quoting, loves conversation, a comedy of manners, in short, is what appealed to me. I admit that I do like novels where people quote. P.D. James's latest book, *Innocent Blood*, is not a detective story, it's a novel. (It's wonderful by the way, how successful she's been. She's now sixty and it's just so exciting to me to see this kind of success late in life.) In it she has a woman come out of prison after ten years and she's quoting literature. As to having your mind jump around, I think all detective writers' minds jump around; most of them carefully cover up that fact when they plot the story.

DCC: Is Kate a university professor because you agree with Kate that detectives in real life are annoyed by complex ideas and find the need for ambivalence distasteful? Is murder beyond the hardness of facts?

187

AC: The answer to the first question is yes. She's also a university professor because I am and because you have to use a setting that you know well. Obviously, you can get up facts but you can't get up the feel of a profession. As to murder, you raise the old question, debated by Auden and Chandler, as to whether murder in books should take place among people who murder regularly, like the Mafia or, as Auden puts it, "in a Vicarage," among people who don't expect a body and therefore find their whole world endangered by a murder. Obviously I'm on Auden's side.

DCC: In *The James Joyce Murder* Grace Knole said that the murder was a crime of a metaphoric mind, a literary, a Joycean mind. What is the nature of a metaphoric, literary crime?

AC: Good heavens, I haven't a clue what I was talking about. I haven't read that book in years. I really can't imagine what I meant. How embarrassing!

DCC: Michael Innes said that he can't remember any of his books either.

AC: I don't reread my novels though I had to go back to *The James Joyce Murder* because I reused a character in it and had to look up his name. But I can imagine what I thought Grace Knole was saying. Either you murder someone simply because he's in your way, taking over your customers, or whatever, or else the murder is an act with a great deal of other significance, it stands for something else, it is something else. I imagine that's what she was saying. In these novels you don't murder a person simply because he's in your way. The victim also comes to represent or to stand for something. I suppose that's what I meant. It's just a guess. (Both laugh.)

DCC: Why do you structure your novels around particular writers such as W.H. Auden, Sophocles, Joyce, Freud?

AC: I don't all the time. My latest novel, *Death In A Tenured Position*, isn't structured around a particular writer and *The Question of Max* didn't use a single writer in that way. Still, the notion of building on the framework of a classic does intrigue me. Modern British literature is the period I teach and, of course, Joyce did use the structure of *The Odyssey*. The chaos of modern life is such that, as Eliot said, it is easier if you start with a scaffolding or a structure for what you are doing. Besides, it allows your work to reverberate more. Although I like form in works of fiction, I'm obviously not a great novelist—if I were I wouldn't be writing these detective novels—so I need all the help I can get.

DCC: That's interesting. Why would you think that if you were a great novelist you would be writing something else? What would you be writing?

AC: Well, novels.

DCC: You don't consider the detective novel in the same...

AC: —class. I think it's a lot better than many of the books that are published as novels. Don't misunderstand me. Detective novels are intelligent, they're well crafted, and I certainly think that they're as good or better than nine-tenths of the stuff sold in airports. But I teach great writing. I know very well what it is and I know that I'm not a great writer. It's just that simple. I don't know how many novelists writing now will eventually be called "great" but I do know that some of them have a quality of imagination, a complexity of mind, that I just don't have. Doris Lessing, for example, or Margaret Drabble. I would love to have it, I might even give everything in my life for it, but I haven't been so blessed.

DCC: If you were writing novels outside the detective genre, what themes would you pursue?

AC: They would be clearly the themes of the modern world, the perception of the breakdown of conventional moral categories, with the disorientation that brings, but at the same time, the liberating effect of new ideas and new possibilities of lives for both men and women. I think it takes enormous talent to embody this in fiction and I think there are a lot of people doing it very well. I'm not enthusiastic about the contemporary American novel, however. My field is modern British. Shirley Hazard is a wonderful novelist but she wasn't born in America. Toni Morrison is an exception. I have great admiration for her work but in an important sense she's an outsider. I think that Eudora Welty is a brilliant writer, Flannery O'Connor is too. I admire their skill and their craft and their art. But it doesn't catch me, it doesn't catch my breath about the possibilities of life. They say what I know better than anyone else could, and they say what I can't know about the South or about being a Catholic in the South. But something in the vision of British writers, or Henry James, who of course was an American, reaches me at a different level. The male American novelists do not, other than James, interest me.

DCC: Murder and academe have a long association in literature from Dostoevski to Michael Innes, Dorothy L. Sayers, Josephine

Tey and others. It has been suggested that this tradition in literature always shows academia finally to be sound, rational and orderly. Do you agree?

AC: Yes. That is again back to Auden's "Murder in the Vicarage." You start with a society of highly intelligent people. If all its members were capable of murder, the society, in fact, could not exist. Yet there is a terrible moment when you don't know that they aren't all capable of it even as you know that only one of them *could* be capable of it. So the sense of order is threatened by chaos; but order is then restored. Basically, that is the pattern of the detective novel that interests me. Plus the chatter along the way.

DCC: What about the question of order and morality and evil? What you just said reminds me of Hannah Arendt's notion of the banality of evil, that, in fact, we would be more secure if we really believed that Hitler and Mussolini were aberrations, that they really weren't like our next door neighbor.

AC: Yes, I think what Hannah Arendt meant is not that Hitler and Mussolini were ordinary people but that those people who murdered on their behalf were just, as they said, doing their job. I worry terribly about people's inability to see the meaning and implications of their own acts. That is another reason for using very intelligent people in detective stories. They are usually not shortsighted, not given to saying things like, "Let's get back to the old values," because they know that the old values were never what they're cracked up to be. Having intelligent people in the story allows one to play with ideas in a way that I enjoy doing. Besides, it takes an extremely talented writer to portray a non-intelligent character well. I'm not up to doing it. Everybody talks the same in my novels. I know that and it's a flaw. But then everybody talks the same in Henry James' novels and Meredith's novels, so I take some comfort.

DCC: Your detective, Kate Fansler, has remarked that detectives are like knights on a quest. What is that quest?

AC: They believe that there is truth and it can be found which, of course, is a fantasy. But it's a fantasy that one holds to. I teach modern literature in which, again and again, there are no truths. In the detective novel, you do at least return something to order. This is a Greek pattern. All that happens at the end of the Greek tragedy is that order is again restored. But one isn't any further along. In fact, one is usually several paces backward. I think that many people believe in religions because they want to be convinced that there is somewhere a mind that knows the truth. The hardest thing to live with is the anxiety of knowing that this simply is not true. Obviously, that's why we have this tremendous return to fundamental religion now. There's a need to be secure, to have a structure, not to be anxious.

DCC: Marjorie Nicholson, in an article written a long time ago called "The Professor and the Detective," asserted that "scholars are, in the end, only the detectives of thought." Would you agree that that is the essential nature of scholarship?

AC: I don't know if it is the essential nature but the excitement of the chase is certainly very much a part of being a scholar. Altick wrote a book called *The Scholar as Detective*. Following out a clue or making a case or proving something, yes, I think that's very much a part of scholarship. And, of course, the readers of detective stories as well as the authors have tended to be intellectual people.

DCC: I have observed that. How much of yourself is in Kate—the unplanned only child or only child in effect, feminist, professor of English at a big New York University?

AC: Obviously a good bit. But still, not too much. That is to say, I made her rich because your detective has to be rich. You can't have a detective who's too poor to leap on a plane at a moment's notice. And I made her a woman, and this was before the woman's movement, because I knew how women talk and behave and because I thought it would be fun. I made her beautiful which I now rather regret. I made her too much of a fantasy figure. It's rather awkward because everyone expects me to look like her. Even apart from that small awkwardness, I now wish I hadn't done that. Actually, the only thing about Kate that was taken from an actual person is her looks which are the looks of a woman friend of mine who is tall, willowy, the possessor of a lovely face with the hair back and no make-up.

DCC: In *Reinventing Womanhood*, you have written about the failure of imagination, the problem of creating a self, that most women novelists have had in creating a female character. Have you surpassed this problem in your creation of Kate Fansler?

AC: She's very widely criticized because Reed either solves the crime or rescues her in the end. Now obviously someone has to rescue someone, I mean, that's what makes detective stories, but I took this criticism seriously so that in *Death In A Tenured Position*, Reed is gone. He's not there. He's off in Asia or Africa or somewhere, and she's alone and she is not rescued.

DCC: Do you think that women novelists create very good male characters?

AC: George Eliot certainly did. But, you see, even men who have done great women characters have had problems with young, nubile women. They are hardest to draw well because it's immediately a stereotype. It is interesting that Colette who did marvelous men characters wasn't acclaimed by the establishment because she is one of the few women who has seen men as sex objects. In *Chéri*, for example, the man is just seen as beautiful and, of course, that is simply to see the man as the woman has always been seen.

DCC: That's what Erica Jong did in *Fear of Flying* too.

AC: I think that American women writers are doing better men than the men are doing women. The women characters created by most American male writers are terrible. Just terrible. Or else they're not there at all. And I think the women have done a lot better.

DCC: Do you dislike the writing that came out of the so-called tough guy, hard-boiled school of writing?

AC: I don't like it at all. No. But that's just a matter of opinion. I don't like violence and certainly not for its own sake. And I don't care for what Jacques Barzun calls "sex as a spectator sport." I just don't like those tough guy worlds. Now Chandler, of course, really wanted a moral man and Marlowe became more and more moral. Chandler really wanted to write like the English.

DCC: Didn't he study in England?

AC: Yes, and he was very split on this whole question. I used to enjoy reading Chandler but I don't read him much now. Dashiell Hammett I like, but although he's considered greater, I like him less than Chandler.

DCC: What about Ross Macdonald, do you see him in the tradition of that school?

AC: I have a problem with Ross Macdonald because I cannot get up any interest in his people. He has attracted Geoffrey Hartman who wrote about Oedipus in the work of Ross Macdonald but I just don't find his people interesting.

DCC: I find them fascinating.

AC: Well, it's my drawback. I'm not trying to make a critical statement. It's just that I like reading about people who are at least as intelligent as I am. I suppose that makes me into what is called "a snob."

DCC: But Lew Archer is as intelligent.

AC: He is but the other people aren't. I'm sure Macdonald himself is a wonderfully intelligent man. This is obviously a failing on my part. I'm just so English-oriented in writing. I teach English literature and I like English literature and there it is. It's just a drawback. On the other hand, which may anticipate a question of yours, I don't much like Julian Symons. So I don't like all English writers, either. Symons again goes in for too much sadism, too much nastiness. He's too Marxist in his criticism. I think his criticism of Sayers is grossly unfair. Colin Wilson at least is humorous about it, though I don't agree with his judgments either.

DCC: About Sayers?

AC: About Sayers and about snobbery in general. It's the sort of judgment that F.R. Leavis used to make on the Bloomsbury Group and I think it arises from a total misunderstanding. And Leavis and Symons are far greater snobs than Sayers ever was.

DCC: Martin Green's position in *Children of the Sun* is very much the same.

AC: That's right, he hates Sayers and he hates Woolf; he's written another essay on it in Trans Atlantic Patterns. He hates Sayers with a passion. And a lot of people that I've talked to who came from the working class in England who are now professors and nine times as intelligent as I am, can never forgive her, for some reason or other. Leavis and Queenie Leavis detested Sayers as well as Woolf.

DCC: Kate is an avid reader of detective stories. Are you?

AC: No. I read very few now because, as I say, the kinds I like aren't being written. I read P.D. James, I read Dick Francis and I read my favorite Englishman, and he has long been my favorite, Michael Gilbert who I think is just wonderful. His sister wrote me a lovely letter once, recognizing one of his plots in one of my stories and she said, "I'm sure you were writing about him." There's something in his tone of voice I like. I think *Smallbone Deceased* was brilliant. One of the things that has just occurred to me about Gilbert, and I literally never thought of it until about a week ago, is that his murderer oftens turns out to be a woman. P.D. James is terribly interested in adopted people or people without parents, it's a scene that obviously intrigues her because she returns to it again and again and again. That is interesting. Michael Innes is just too spacy for me and also a tremendously male-centered novelist. I read a novel of his about a year ago and the joke was that all of these boys had gotten together and raped some girl and wasn't that cute, and I just don't think it's cute. And he makes fun of the wives of dons and that kind of thing. I guess I'm getting to be doctrinaire, aren't I? (laughs)

DCC: In *The James Joyce Murder* Grace Knole states: "The whole point about mysteries is that it is so nice to read about other people doing things without having to do that sort of thing oneself." What is the fascination of that kind of vicarious experience?

AC: Ah, well, that's what storytelling has been about together with suspense and narration. What I like about Michael Gilbert is that he will tell a story that has a special kind of knowledge of the law, and, for me, that's fun. Or in *Smallbone Deceased*, he gives the hero some sort of odd disease where you never sleep. I find all this fascinating. I love expertise in detective stories, even if it's gotup, provided it's well gotup. The best example, of course, is Sayers and bellringing in *The Nine Tailors*. It's wonderful to read about lives that one can't possibly live. A lot of people write just one detective story perhaps about death in the ballet, or in the opera, or in whatever world they happen to inhabit, and I usually find it fascinating.

DCC: "Supercivilized" is the one word that I have seen more than once in reference to your work. Yet each novel has involved a death and very often a murder with the exceptions of *The Theban Mysteries*, *Poetic Justice* and *Death In A Tenured Position* where the deaths were accidental or suicidal. I think the order of literacy and civilization makes the chaos and the dissolution even more marked. Kate often longs for a statelier, less untidy era. Jorge Luis Borges has said that he is drawn to the detective novel because it preserves a world of order in a collapsing world. When literature was becoming more obscure, the detective novel insisted on a beginning, a middle and an end. Would you agree?

AC: Oh, yes. I think Borges is one of the great writers, I wish they would give him the Nobel Prize. I totally agree. But to come back to the point you made before. There were two things I wanted to do with Kate. One of them was to give everything to a character and then see what she does with it. We all think we want enough money, enough looks, enough position, lovers, brains, so I said, "Give someone all this and see what happens." But the other thing that interested me is the combination in Kate of liking the manners of another era while also being rather revolutionary socially. This intriguing characteristic is something I share, and it's totally contradictory. I like manners and courtesy of a certain sort very much but I understand the price is too high and a lot of it is silly. And, at the same time, I can't bear the frozenness of that world. I belong to the Cosmopolitan Club and I like it because it's gracious and stately. But there are many women in clubs like that who in their courteous "way" are abysmally rude to someone they don't think is worth talking to. Courtesy comes from the heart. In my latest novel, a woman Kate is dining with bursts into tears and they leave the restaurant and the woman takes the napkin with her to weep into and Kate worries that she will forget to return it, which is the sort of worry, you know, while everything is going on, that nobody has anymore.

DCC: The plots of your novels seem to be secondary to other main concerns: gentility which often overlays evil, order versus chaos, the self-determining woman. What is the "hook" that begins the process to create one of your novels?

AC: I don't know. I'm asked that often and I honestly don't know the answer.

DCC: Do you start with a scene, an image, a metaphor?

AC: No, I start with a place or a situation.

DCC: How did *The Question of Max* originate?

AC: I thought that I wanted to write a novel which would include the early lives of several minor English novelists whose lives are more or less in there, in a slightly garbled form. The setting described in *Max* is at May Sarton's. She lives in a house that has a path to the sea but you cannot see the sea except from the second floor of the house and that setting intrigued me. I was up there once and I went for a walk with her dog who's a Shetland collie and I climbed down onto the rocks at the edge of the ocean and the dog followed me. I suddenly looked back and I couldn't see land and there was the dog sinking in a sort of pool. With all that hair I was afraid he would get wet and really sink before I could pull him up. And I had a moment of almost blind panic. *That* is what initiated *The Question of Max*. The body found there is a very small moment in the story but that's where it started.

DCC: Were the women writers in that novel based on real writers?

AC: Yes, I shifted the lives for my purpose. The childhood of the woman who lives in Maine is taken largely from the childhood of Rose Macaulay. The two women who were friends were inspired by

Vera Brittain and Winifred Holtby. But only very loosely. It is true of Winifred Holtby that she wrote novels and left the proceeds to Somerville College, as I think I indicated in the book. Holtby's last novel, *South Riding*, was a huge success, it's been a movie and it's been on British television. So now there is enough money at Somerville for scholarships. That is all true but the other things I moved around.

DCC: What about *The Theban Mysteries*?

AC: Well, *The Theban Mysteries*, which is by far the weakest of the novels, and I'm somewhat...

DCC: That is one of my favorites...

AC: Good. But it's got too much solid *Antigone*. I've written my novels at three year intervals but that one I wrote a year after *Poetic Justice* because I needed the money. One of my children wanted to go to Europe and if I finished it I could get the rest of the advance so that she could go. And it was forced. I was writing *Towards A Recognition of Androgyny* at the time. That's why there is so much Antigone in the novel. And clearly I was very worked up about the Vietnam war. A lot of people do like it but I worry if someone picks it up first because I think it's just a little bit too *solid*. I like some of the things in it, though.

DCC: What writers have been an influence on your novels?

AC: The only direct influence is Sayers. Sayers, Josephine Tey, and to some extent Ngaio Marsh, whom I no longer like much but liked very much at one time. Josephine Tey I like enormously. But, otherwise, I live so much with literature and the literature I teach, I couldn't say. Forster, Woolf, have been an enormous influence, and I am clearly much too involved with them to put any aspect of them into a novel. I'm much less involved with Joyce which is why I could make use of him, and of course that's how Joyce wrote novels, using his material in a very intellectualized way.

DCC: What is there specifically about the work of Dorothy L. Sayers and the others that influenced you?

AC: Again, it's the intelligent, cultivated, courteous, Symons would say snobbish, way of life. The thing that all the people in novels I like share is conversation. They like to talk. And they like to talk with intelligent people and they like to explore ideas. And to have time for conversation, you need leisure, so you tend to have people from the upper classes. Obviously you need a certain kind of person; that's another reason for the academic setting.

DCC: That's true because your books are highly verbal and conversational.

AC: A good deal too much, I think.

DCC: I'm drawn to that myself.

AC: Apparently some people are because my novels are beginning to get a following.

DCC: I'm glad. Who are some of the other writers in the past that you have admired in the detective genre?

AC: Wilkie Collins to start with, who I think is superb. Then, a man named Edmund Grierson wrote one novel called *The Second Man* which has a woman barrister in it and I like that very much. Cyril Hare I like enormously. I guess that must be about it, isn't that awful? Of my contemporaries, I like P.D. James and also Patricia Moyes. Do you know her? She has a Scotland Yard detective with a sort of "house-wifely" wife who keeps getting involved. She wrote a novel called *Murder à la Mode*, I think, about murder in the fashion industry which she knows; it's fun. And she's married to a diplomat so her novels keep taking place in embassies, in Washington, in Switzerland. She again doesn't have very interesting women but I recommend her.

DCC: Do you find sexism in Dorothy L. Sayers' work? The women, for example, in Lord Peter Wimsey's "Cattery" do the tedious drudgery necessary for successful detection and get little or no credit in *Strong Poison*; his biography gives Harriet Vane two lines—her distinctions are as a wife, daughter, mother; Harriet calls Peter "my lord" in *Busman's Honeymoon*, and there are lots of lines like that throughout the book. Although Sayers is not ignorant of the problems of single, intelligent and independent women, she is ambivalent.

AC: I'm interested in Sayers' life, she is one of the women about whom I write in *Reinventing Womanhood*. She shares one problem with a lot of other women detective story writers: they create a male detective, then they create a female who stands by his side and then gradually the female recedes. I don't think you can call Sayers sexist at all, certainly not in *Strong Poison*, where, after all, you have to take into consideration how Lord Peter is working. *He's* giving jobs to people. Of course, it's true that Sayers marries Harriet Vane off and then abandons her and many people feel that *Busman's Honeymoon* is a betrayal of Harriet Vane. I'm not sure that's true since it seems to me that Harriet's to go on writing under her own name, making her own career. The stories that follow are certainly distressing, particularly the last one where Harriet and Lord Peter end up with three sons. That's awful, without a doubt. So it's a two part answer. I don't think Sayers is sexist but she in the end is drawn back to the male point of view. It's a pattern I've written about in women, the anxiety of maintaining a female protagonist who is not "feminine."

DCC: Do you find sexism in other writers of detective fiction?

AC: Oh, yes! You find it in all writers and more in American than English or European. The Americans, with the exception of Hawthorne, clearly do not produce women characters of any depth at all. I wrote about that years ago in an article called "The Masculine Wilderness in the American Novel." So, of course, there is sexism, but it's diminishing. That's why Dick Francis, you see, interests me. He began just as the Women's Movement came along and he put so-called "liberated women" into his books. I think that's fun. I did a piece about the connection between spinsters and virgins as independent women, but that metaphor, of course, is now thoroughly out-of-date. You find so-called "sexism" everywhere. I like to make the joke that the only really good marriage in English fiction is between Holmes and Watson. (Both laugh) It's marriage of a sort that no one ever pictured between men and women. Holmes is very much the husband. And Rex Stout, another writer I like, wrote a piece saying that Watson was a woman. Certainly he is sexist, but again I just admire the intelligence. British detective novels, by the way, are less sexist than other British fiction.

DCC: What about Margery Allingham?

AC: She is very sexist and she's a frightful bore, I think.

DCC: I don't really like her work either. What do you think is the link between the detective novel and writers outside the genre like Faulkner, Marguerite Duras, other noveau roman writers, Dickens? Or is this going to far?

AC: I find that dreary. Johns Hopkins has just published a book about the theme of the detective story that starts with Oedipus and ends by putting down Agatha Christie. It's the most pompous possible nonsense. But, obviously, the theme of suspense in *Oedipus* is a detective story; he sets out to find out who the murder of Laius is, and so it is a very central human plot. It's also the plot, obviously, of psychoanalysis.

DCC: It's also a plot in Robertson Davies's Deptford trilogy. The major question is, "Who killed Boy Staunton?" The answer also leads to a discovery of the self.

AC: That's right. There is this close connection but the detective story has rules. *Edwin Drood* is a fascinating work and I think it shows that Dickens was moving. He was getting tighter and I believe better about women. I wish he had lived to finish it. Henry James wrote a detective story called *The Other House.*

DCC: Does the detective novel require a different critical methodology from those applied to novels outside the genre?

AC: In a sense, I suppose so. Obviously, if you don't like detective stories, you don't like detective stories. But if you go as far as Barzun does, for example, in liking only the puzzle and not wishing to go into anyone's personal life, I think you're carrying a distinction too far. I would say that my test of a detective story is that if I know how it comes out and I still enjoy rereading it, then it must be good. And, therefore, the plot is not the major thing. That is why I never reread Agatha Christie. But I reread the ones I do like all the time. Josephine Tey is an example. I remember the solution perfectly and I still think she handles it extraordinarily.

DCC: I agree. A Russian critic, I. Revzin, did a semiotic analysis of Agatha Christie's detective novels and other Russian scholars I've noticed have applied formalism to the interpretation of the detective genre. Do you think these are valid approaches?

AC: Oh sure, it's easier. It's obviously easier to do a semiotic study of Agatha Christie than it is to do one of Shakespeare. Or Henry James. It reminds me of the time when stylistics was a very big thing and they used computers to discover that John Dickenson and Dickenson Carr were the same writer. But of course we all knew that anyway. Computers also discovered that Madison had written most of the Constitution, which we also knew. But it's fun to practice criticism and some people have done it on me with the most hilariously foolish results. I have often maintained that everyone who teaches literature should write and publish at least one novel because until you've done it, you really do not know what the connection is between life and fiction. Too much nonsense is written about the connection between real characters, for instance, and fiction, as though an author could just take a real person and drop him or her whole into a book.

DCC: I do think that there are tremendous gaps between the scholarly interpretation of the work and perhaps what the author thinks is happening in the work. But there's much that is valuable even if it's just to watch the mind in motion, even if it's wrong.

AC: There is a difference between writing about a great novelist of the past who speaks to the future world, often unconsciously, that's part of the genius, and writing about someone living now and making guesses about what they're doing or what they mean. You can certainly look at a writer's works and say that he or she is interested in this or that theme, but to announce that they did a particular thing because they were influenced by something specific is preposterous.

DCC: Your use of Joyce in *The James Joyce Murder* is intriguing. The characters bear the names of characters in Joyce's *Dubliners*; each chapter of your novel is titled after one of the stories from *Dubliners*. The names Padraic Mulligan (perhaps a composite of Padraic Colum and Buck Mulligan), M'Intosh, Mr. Artifoni, all appear in *Ulysses*. Paul Pickrel suggests that Sam Lingerwell is based on Lincoln MacVeagh who published some of Joyce's early work in *The Dial*.

AC: He isn't though. He's based (very loosely I may say) on a man I knew. The daughter business and the Nunnery are fictionalized. But Sam Lingerwell is modeled on Benjamin Huebsch who founded the Viking Press, and who was one of the early publishers of Lawrence in this country. I went to school with one of his sons. Huebsch was one of the great men of publishing, he and Knopf, in the days when publishing was not yet altogether "hype." He was courageous and fine and I was extremely fond of him. He lived to a ripe old age and was, I suppose, the source of that character. Anyone in publishing with a long memory will know that name. He published first under the name of B.W. Huebsch and then started Viking together with Ginzberg, the father of the present publisher.

DCC: What are some of the other connections between your novel and Joyce? Other than the names and the chapters and so on?

AC: Well, of course, the plot hinges on a Joyce manuscript. It's all very Joycean. I know that there were a lot of Joycean jokes in it.

DCC: Newgate Callendar has said that your novels are for specialized tastes because they are literary and highly verbal. Does this truly reflect the kind of person who reads your novels? Do you have any feedback on your readership?

AC: I do get more and more now. Let me add, by the way, that I don't read reviews and don't pay any attention to them. That's the sort of statement that no one believes but it's just quite simply true. When I speak now, people often want to talk about the Amanda Cross novels and have read them. They are selling, they sell upward to 80,000 copies in paperback which sounds like a lot to me, although it doesn't impress a real paperback publisher. And so I'm developing a following. I get a lot of letters and the books are being mentioned more and more frequently in various articles. I have always been terribly shy of publicity of any sort and which is, I suppose, a form of vanity. I just don't like it. I'll talk to a very large audience, but I don't like hype, I don't like anything about it. I do think that there are people in this country who are reading books, often borrowing them and so forth, that are just never talked about. I'm sure Robertson Davies is an example of what I mean, widely read, respected, but not the sort who would ever be given the bestselling author treatment by the *New York Times*.

DCC: I believe his books were bestsellers. Part of the problem too is somewhere between the publishing houses and the bookstores. The last time we were in New York, I was looking for your books. They were just not available.

AC: This just came up with *The James Joyce Murder*. It's the only one that hasn't gone into paperback, probably because of the title. Publishers apparently think it's too erudite and my husband says that I should rename it *Love Among the Haystacks*. (Both laugh.) Anyway, Dutton's now reprinting it in April, 1981. Someone came into my office with a copy for me to sign and he had just paid $45.00 for it. I said, "You aren't serious." He said, "Yes, that what they're bringing." It pays not to have a big first edition, not that the author gets any of this.

DCC: One thing that I'm always questioning when I'm reading your novels is this. Is it professionally ethical for Reed to confide so much police information to Kate when working on a case?

AC: I think so. It's a certain amount of "poetic license." But I've known assistant district attorneys and they were amazingly free to talk. I got a lot of the legal information that I've used from an assistant D.A. that I knew. He didn't know I wrote detective stories, of course. And I didn't quote him, but, for instance, while writing *Poetic Justice*, I asked him how you get into an apartment when you don't have a search warrant, and he told me all that's involved.

DCC: You obviously have a bit of Kate in you. Elizabeth Janeway has said that Kate and Reed remind her of Nick and Nora Charles of The Thin Man series. I hadn't really thought of that similarity, frankly, but I wondered if you see any similarities between them?

AC: I keep getting them mixed up with William Powell and Myrna Loy. She doesn't work or anything, and she is not central. But I think, obviously, there is some sort of connection there, types who say funny things and drink a lot.

DCC: I've waited a long time for *Death in A Tenured Position* and I liked it.

AC: I wanted to call it *Kate Goes to Harvard*, which is where the whole thing takes place but I guess the publisher didn't care for the Nancy Drew overtones. The plot involves the first tenured woman in Harvard's English Department. At the time I wrote it, they'd never had one. Oddly enough, they have since appointed a woman in the same field as my fictional character. Life imitating art, once again. The book's been a long time in the works; I've changed publishers so it was a bit delayed in coming out, but I've enjoyed my new editor at Dutton. I'm fond of it but I'm always fond of the most recent one.

204

Interview with Anne Perry

Diana Cooper-Clark

DCC: You first published *The Cater Street Hangman* in 1979. As a novelist who is relatively new to the world of detective fiction, what kinds of problems have you encountered? In getting acknowledged? Having your books available? With sales? Advertising?

AP: In America I have had few problems, although I don't know about advertising of course, not having been there. In Britain unfortunately I have had almost every problem—neither advertising nor reviews, except one in a local paper. I took my book to the paper myself because I happened to know the journalist. But other than that, nothing in Britain. I have been very fortunate with reviews in America which my publisher has sent me, and I have received letters from readers.

DCC: In the last three years you've published four detective novels and you have written two more. In addition, you've written two non-mystery novels. How do you account for this prolific output? Are you bursting with things to say?

AP: Yes, I am. I love to work morning, afternoon and evening. I love to describe things, I love history, I love to try and take a reader into the world that I see, to feel it, taste it, smell it, hear it, to feel as the people concerned feel. There's an old proverb that I believe comes from this part of the world: if you could only walk a mile in the other man's moccasins you'd know how he felt. I suppose this is what I'm trying to say. Historically, everybody has something in common with us today. There's an old French proverb, with which I don't entirely agree, which says that "to understand all is to forgive all." I wouldn't go so far as to say we should forgive all, but to understand all is perhaps at least to love if not to forgive, which is not necessarily the same thing. The essence of my writing is the exploration of the nature of self-mastery, courage and compassion.

DCC: Your books reflect this. They remind me of Thoreau's admonition to "Be a Columbus of the mind."

AP: I think that's wonderful. I'd love to be a Columbus of the mind and a Marco Polo and a Magellan.

DCC: In what sense?

AP: To be somewhere that I have not been before. I would also like to shed new light on the old possibilities. How is that for a compromise?

DCC: Why did you choose to write Victorian mysteries? What is it about the period that attracts you? Was it perhaps the dichotomy and schizophrenia of Victorian society—the woman as whore or Madonna, the very rich and the very poor, the moral rectitude and moral decadence, the violence and obscenity lying under the mannered surface, or as you say in your novel *Paragon Walk* the nasty little secrets that snap through the civilized veneer?

AP: Exactly. I couldn't have put it as well myself. It is all of that and I also love the civilized violence of some of their conversation, I love their insults, and I like the sense of wit that's wrapped so neatly but is so barbed. I like the sense of period dress as well; it's wonderfully elegant on the exterior. These dramatic contrasts are most interesting.

DCC: You can see that cultural dichotomy even in their dress. The well-dressed Victorian woman went out of her house with ten to thirty pounds of clothing on, yet she maintained the illusion of fragility and delicacy.

AP: It's the contrast between illusion and reality which is very satisfying for a mystery writer because after all the essence of mystery is that you should uncover a little at a time and that things should not be obvious. Therefore, I think that the Victorian period is ideal for a mystery writer because so many things are not what they seem.

DCC: Yes. In your novel *Resurrection Row* Aunt Vespasia says that "society is all to do with what seems, and nothing to do with what is." Is that what you're talking about through the character of Aunt Vespasia?

AP: Yes, to a certain extent. She goes a bit further than I would, but a great deal of society is what seems rather than what is. The Victorians had a marvellous ability not to see what they didn't wish to see. They carried it to an even greater art than we have today. Of course, they had to. If they were to look at what was really there, it would have been unbearable, wouldn't it? But I think we today still have a great ability not to see what we don't wish to see.

DCC: I agree with that. On the subject of historical mysteries, Peter Lovesey has written: "And how productive the nineteenth century was of motives for murder. The need to achieve security by inheritance, or life insurance, or marriage; the risk of losing it when scandal threatened; the equating of sex with sin; the stigma of insanity; the things that went unsaid. Our world of social welfare and easier divorce and psychiatric care has removed many of the bad old reasons for murder. How uninspiring, too, by contrast with times past, are the modern weapons—the gun with telescopic sights, the car bomb and hypodermic syringe. Give me Jack the Ripper's knife or Neill Cream's bag of poisons or Lizzie Borden's axe."

AP: He's said it all there. I think in a good mystery story the reader should identify with the criminal and feel that in those circumstances, "I might well have felt compelled to do the same thing if I was frightened enough and cornered. It's not outside understanding that a person should do this." I don't like motives of just pure greed or just pure malice unless there is a very strong reason. I like to feel that the reader would identify with the criminal, with all the people involved, and with the detective. I always feel that insanity or just pure basic greed are cop-outs. I don't exactly want the reader to feel "there but for the grace of God go I," but at least the reader should understand why it was that this person felt this way. I agree with Peter Lovesey. There were so many more motives in Victorian society. They were far more restricted. Other alternatives were not there.

DCC: Do you think that everybody's capable of murder, given the right circumstances?

AP: I should think most people are, yes, if they are frightened enough and they have to act quickly enough either in defence of themselves or in defence of somebody else they care for deeply and the means are at hand. I don't know about absolutely everybody but a great many people. But whether it would be classed as murder or self-defence or whatever, I'm not sure. May we say capable of killing rather than capable of murder?

DCC: That's perhaps a better distinction.

AP: Murder presupposes a certain guilt whereas killing can be justifiable homicide. I would think most women were capable of killing to defend a child, probably most men to defend their children or their wives or their homes, especially if they didn't have time to think, to find another way out. Time is a strong element.

DCC: Would you be capable of killing?

AP: I don't know. I would think probably, if I felt that it was the only answer. Almost certainly, yes, if I was defending somebody else.

DCC: I'm thinking here of your character Dominic, because one of the points that you make in two books is that he doesn't have the passion or imagination to kill. Do you think that somebody with, let's say extreme sensibility and intense emotion within themselves, would be more capable of killing?

AP: Yes, but Dominic might kill if he was cornered and it was a matter of self-defence, but he'd have to be driven very hard.

DCC: To change the subject, is your "sleuth," Charlotte, the new emerging woman that Thomas Hardy speaks about in his novels? She's a woman who dares to defy convention by marrying a policeman, Thomas Pitt, a man who is socially beneath her.

AP: Charlotte is just me. If she wants something badly enough she'd do it and think afterwards; she'll do it and pay the price, thinking later, "good heavens, what have I done, what has it cost me." But it's an emotional thing, it's not sitting down and thinking, "should I do this or shall I do that?"

DCC: So Charlotte isn't really a feminist?

AP: Not consciously but probably subconsciously. You see, I have never been consciously a feminist unless I see a particular case of injustice. I've always been brought up in a family where I have been treated as an equal with my brother so I've never had to fight for intellectual and social equality. Therefore the idea of having to fight for women's rights has only come to me relatively recently. The character of Charlotte is not written with the brain; she's written with the emotions and the guts. She is a lot of me.

DCC: In *The Cater Street Hangman* Charlotte is not a "sleuth." But in your subsequent novels she is. How do you acount for this change?

AP: It probably never occurred to her that it was possible for her to do it. She really didn't have much of an opportunity until the murder happened in her own immediate area and then, of course, when she married the policeman she discovered that meddling was rather fun.

DCC: Peter Lovesey and Jean Stubbs have suggested that the vicarious need for excitement in very dull lives was important in the Victorian upper class.

AP: Oh yes, I think so. Everything that I have read would indicate that that was very strongly so, and a lot of their excesses sprang from boredom. Imagine if there was nothing that you needed to do how quickly you would get bored. If you go on holiday, the first day of doing nothing is marvellous, the second day is less marvellous and by the third day it's driving you crazy. If you have a life where you are unnecessary really, it breeds not only boredom but a lack of self-worth.

DCC: That's important to Charlotte.

AP: Yes it is. It's important to everybody even if they don't realize it. Many of the people who indulged in some of the peculiar Victorian vices and the general wasting of time—gambling, crazy carriage races, wild flirtations and affairs and what have you—behaved this way because it sprang from boredom. Sometimes this behavior springs from a need to convince yourself that you're alive, that you have a purpose, and that you have an identity.

DCC: You're right that everyone needs self-worth but the definition of worth for the beautiful ladylike Victorian woman was that she was useless. It was a way of defining yourself as beautiful—the privilege of not having to work. Uselessness was aesthetic.

AP: Yes, that's true. But if society says that, does it necessarily make for happiness?

DCC: That's a good point because Charlotte certainly doesn't accept society's definition of her role in life.

AP: And her sister, Emily, increasingly is finding the static upper class life less satisfying; she enjoys a jolly good meddle as well.

DCC: Usually detectives are male and either celibate or with a wife firmly in the background. But Charlotte Pitt is not only highly visible and incorporated into the story, she also becomes involved in the detective work. This is unusual in the Victorian mystery story. Of course, she is married to a policeman, and she and her sister Emily can infiltrate the world of "Society"; they can hear things Thomas would not. When you were thinking of the character of Charlotte, is this one of the ways in which you thought you could ease her into her role as sleuth?

AP: I started by wanting to show both upstairs and downstairs in a Victorian household and thereby get both sides of the story. I used Charlotte and her husband, Thomas Pitt, to do this. I'm not sure honestly which idea came first, it sort of happened. This was one way to explore the dichotomy you were referring to earlier. One person wouldn't see both sides behaving naturally. If Charlotte had gone downstairs to the kitchen, the servants would have immediately altered their behavior and if Pitt had gone upstairs into the drawing-room the upper class likewise would have altered their behavior. So in order to see both worlds naturally, I had to have two people from different classes.

DCC: I'd like to get back to the subject of women. Women were extremely limited in the Victorian period. Charlotte's father would not allow her to read the newspaper because as the narrator writes in *Callander Square*, newspapers carry "little else but crime and scandal, and such political notions as were undesirable for the consideration of women, as well, of course, as intellectually beyond them." In addition, men did not like a tongue as frank and undisciplined as Charlotte's.

AP: It's still not so popular for a woman to have intellectual opinions and be quite as frank as Charlotte. I hadn't realized this focus until you asked the question but probably it's a good deal of my own feeling coming through because I've found myself a little less than popular on occasion for being articulate, having opinions and perhaps being less reticent than I might have been about expressing them.

DCC: To continue with that, throughout your novels we see that Charlotte has political convictions with regard to Reform Bills in Parliament such as the Poor Laws. Why hasn't her interest (given that she is a woman who is more than aware of the unequal position of women in her society) focused on Women's Property Rights, the Divorce Laws and women's suffrage? Dependence in the Victorian period was a part not only of woman's supposed nature, but also it was incorporated into English law. I wonder why Charlotte has so much compassion and sympathy for the poor when she herself is in a position that is inferior by law and by society.

AP: Give me time, I'll get around to it (laughs). I think it's a very good idea. It's possibly a jolly good motive for another crime. I feel I ought to deal with one thing at a time or it's going to become too confused. But you've given me a good idea, I'll get around to that. We've had quite a number of women suffrage programs on television and I just didn't want to get on the bandwagon. Also women's property rights are now fairly well settled and some of the other things that I've dealt with, in some cases, are still open wounds. You'll have noticed that I've covered child pornography quite a bit; well, you know that's currently on the rise. That is a valid thing to be concerned about because a significant number of children are still abused. Quite a lot of the things I've covered are current whereas women's suffrage is not. We do have the vote and for goodness sake we've got a lady Prime Minister (laughs). We haven't got anything like equal representation in Parliament but there's nothing the law can do about that.

DCC: You have a proportionately high number of female murderers in your books. In five novels, you have three female murderers. Why?

AP: Because women were so limited, as we've said before, in their dealing with things. The law didn't give them an opportunity to get out of their difficult situations and when you are as restricted as that you have to take matters into your own hands if you're going to solve the problem to your liking. The more restricted you are by outside circumstances the more inventive and perhaps the more violent you tend to be within those limits. Perhaps it is also because I am a woman that I can think of situations in which a woman might do those things, not that I'm suggesting that it's acceptable or excusable. Possibly the women's motives were stronger because Victorian men had so many other ways out of their particular problems.

DCC: Your ratio of female murderers is statistically high but then literature is not sociology.

AP: Also the idea happened to occur to me. When I start to write, the first thing that comes to me before anything else is motive. Now what is a strong motive for a crime? Then I build upon the motives that have occurred to me and it just seems to have been the ones that have been the most appropriate for women.

DCC: You said before that Charlotte is yourself, a kind of alter-ego.

AP: A part of me anyway.

DCC: I'd like you to clarify those parts and also what about Thomas Pitt? He seems to be a part of you, although perhaps in a lesser way.

AP: Charlotte is physically quite a lot like me or at least when I was her age. I think probably her speech patterns, her thoughts, her instinctive ideas, and much of her behavior is me. But she doesn't have my darker side. I'm more of a fighter than Charlotte. I don't think there is a character that's really as close to me in the detective stories as there is in my historical ones. In my historical novels there are people who are more like me. Also Charlotte has no particular religious conviction, therefore, that whole side of my life which is possibly the most predominant side, is not there. I would like to be as compassionate as Thomas Pitt is, and I would like to have Aunt Vespasia's sense of humor.

DCC: Is Charlotte in any way a fantasy for you? Other writers have admitted that their main characters were. The reader is told several times in several novels that Charlotte is Pitt's haven.

AP: Not really. I think if I were going to identify in that sense with either one of them it would be Pitt. Charlotte is far more domestic than I am. I would love to wear the clothes of that period, but that's about as far as the fantasy goes. If I wanted the life of any one of those people it would be Aunt Vespasia's. She has tremendous courage, she's outrageous, she's a fighter, she's compassionate, she's at the top of her tree socially, and there's a streak of ruthlessness in Aunt Vespasia—ruthlessness and courage in fighting for what she wants but yet with great compassion. I don't admire ruthlessness in itself but I admire courage and single-mindedness. If you have power, you have the responsibility to use it well. Power is opportunity; it's opportunity to do well or do badly. If you make a mess of it the penalty is very dreadful but if you do it well what you can achieve is enormous. One of the things that I admire in Aunt Vespasia is that she feels responsible; she has the best qualities of her class, of knowing that every privilege carries a very great responsibility.

DCC: She's involved in the Poor Laws.

AP: Yes, she has power, therefore, she knows that she must be responsible for change, for improving things, for seeing that those who do not have the power are cared for. I don't think she would ever walk by on the other side. I hope Charlotte is going to become like her but I can't do it in a hurry because Charlotte is still only young. You see, Charlotte is quite a bit younger than I am.

DCC: P.D. James has said about women who write detective fiction: "I think women like writing about human beings and their reaction to each other, and detective novels...as well are about human beings and their reaction to extreme stress. I think that we often write about a fairly domestic situation; the contrast between this and the horror of the actual murder is very effective." Do you agree with that?

AP: Very much, she's put it beautifully. I am really less interested in "who did it" than I am in the stress of the investigation afterwards, and all the other little sins you turn up, as well as the major crime. It's the little sins and what people will do to hide them that I find the most interesting and the most enthralling. It is like peeling the layers off an onion.

DCC: We can see this interest in all your novels. In your next novel, *Funeral at Rutland Place,* the narrator says that "the mystery of murder was ephemeral, even paltry: it was the emotions, the fire of pain, and the long wastelands afterwards that were real." In *Callander Square,* we're told that "murder and investigation reveal to us so many things about each other which we would rather not have known." In *Resurrection Row,* Pitt wonders whether Dominic is "afraid of the scandal and all the dark, corroding suspicions, the old sores opened up that investigation always brings." In *The Cater Street Hangman,* nobody can trust anyone else. Charlotte understands that it's "like ripples on a pool, and perhaps the rings would never stop." As recently as 1980, the police urged British women to think carefully about all the men that they knew, including their husbands and fathers, in case one of them was the dreaded Yorkshire Ripper.

AP: This is exactly what I'm trying to write about—the distress and the suspicion and the fear and the re-examination of everything that you've previously taken for granted. I can remember frequently the radio, television and newspapers advising us to not exclude anybody. I wrote *Cater Street* before this happened but it's just this sort of situation and really I'm only using the crime as a catalyst to peel off the layers of everything else in people's lives and lay bare the truth. Truth has a fascination for me even if it's an unpleasant truth. There is something beautiful even in the most naked, bare or otherwise ugly truth simply because it *is* truth and in the end you have to return to it. Maybe you can't take it all at once but there isn't anything else to build upon.

DCC: Do you read detective fiction?

AP: I've been reading quite a bit since I came here to Toronto and haven't had a television. I've been buying different authors and reading maybe three or four of their works and studying them and I've learned a lot. Before that I've thoroughly enjoyed people like Josephine Tey but really I have done very little reading. I was only writing to my own needs, instincts and obsessions but not to a formula. I do plan my book out before I start because I couldn't possibly just start writing and hope it would end up in the right place. I have to know the end before I write the beginning. Even in the historicals I'm writing toward a conclusion the entire time.

DCC: You've written two (as yet unpublished) non-mystery novels. Do you fear that fans will tie you to Charlotte and Thomas Pitt Victorian mysteries? Ruth Rendell's fans clamor for more Wexford novels every time she tries to write a non-Wexford and she'd like to do other things. Or are you still at the stage where you're very happy that people are clamoring for Charlotte and Thomas?

AP: I'm delighted that people like Charlotte and Pitt. I'm aware that there is a difficulty with the historical novels I write because they are not "romantic." I know that there is a difficulty in classifying them but I'm not prepared to alter them. I'll just have to let my agent and such publishers as might be interested worry about what they're going to do. They might have to be published under a man's name because I understand that historical novels written by a woman are automatically slotted into "romance" but when they are written by a man they are slotted into perhaps the more political power struggle. My novels focus on the political power struggle. If readers see a woman's name on the jacket, the ones who want the political focus will not look at it and the ones that want romance will look at it and see that it's not what they wanted and put it down. As a result nobody will buy my book (both laugh).

DCC: Do mystery and non-mystery stories satisfy different parts of your literary being and if so in what way?

AP: I suppose they do. I hadn't really thought about that but, yes, they do satisfy different parts of my personality. I enjoy constructing a mystery and then peeling it off bit by bit. The Victorian era is very different from the other historical periods that I have chosen. I think lots of people like a mystery. It is the same as filling in a crossword puzzle or discovering anything little by little. There is in most people something that likes to unwrap layer by layer and spin out the pleasure of discovering a mystery. My historicals deal with fictional people observing very tumultuous and conflicting real events. I just love the drama and the knowledge that this really happened. Human beings like myself experienced these things and were torn apart by these fears, terrors, beliefs and ideals, and writing about it is the next best thing to going back and actually seeing it. In fact, it's even better because you have all the excitement and the internal knowledge without the actual pain or physical danger. I have written a novel about the Spanish Inquisition called *Thou With Clean Hands*. I think the Spanish Inquisition period for the ethical conflict was one of the most fascinating. Many of the conflicts, particularly over "free agency," are still very apposite today. We don't these days feel passionately about religion but we do about politics and we'll bomb other people to death for their own good (laughs).

DCC: That's like the Crusades.

AP: Yes, "better dead than red" or whatever it might happen to be which is the same basic feeling as "better dead than a heretic"—"we must cut out this infection before it spreads any further; you may not realize this, dear, but for your own good, better we should kill part of you than that all of you should fall to whatever it is that we don't like whether it's communism or Lutheranism or Catharism or whatever it might be." One can understand that there was a certain genuine feeling with the Inquisitors, "I'm saving your soul and if it has to be at your body's expense, well, that's dreadful but better your body perish than your soul." I must respect that. I can exalt, preach, teach, love and plead with you but if at the end of that you choose to believe differently that is your right. It's a very difficult conclusion to come to and even now we all try to persuade people who are closest to us of our own way of belief and we feel we are doing them a favor and that we have a responsibilty to do so. It's very difficult to allow people you care for to go the way that you believe is a mistake. I have also written a novel about the French Revolution, *Lower Than The Angels*. The more I look at the tragic revolutions that we keep having in the world (how many we've had in the last forty years!) they do almost always seem to follow a very similar pattern. The French Revolution was perhaps in some ways the most dramatic because it had so many larger-than-life figures in it and it's sufficiently distant from us that we can see it more clearly now. Yet it's sufficiently close to us that there's a great deal of record about it down to what people actually said and what they wore and many diaries still extant. I think it is a valid thing to explore because we know a great deal about it and the pattern seems to persist tragically.

DCC: The Victorians hadn't accepted the combination of good and evil in one person. They could not accept ambivalence. Martha Prebble in *The Cater Street Hangman* is a good example of this. There's always a sense of irreconcilable pain and suffering in your novels. This creates tension between the Victorian rigidity and the Victorian disorder.

AP: I would like to think that I don't tie these important experiences up because life isn't like that. Any crime is going to scar. Crime is a tragedy and it is going to scar a lot of people. It isn't going to be tidied away and the police can't put it in a bag and carry it off and that's the end of it. It's bound to leave wounds behind in almost everybody it touches. I would like to make my novels true to life at least in that respect.

DCC: In *Paragon Walk*, Pitt says that he dislikes hanging although it was "a part of society's mechanics to purge itself of a disease." W.H. Auden has talked about this and so has Julian Symons.

AP: Characters at one time or another say a lot of things that I don't necessarily agree with. In the most recent novel I've written (which is as yet unpublished), *Bluegate Fields*, I made a fairly strong statement about hanging and that's what I really feel. Until such time as we can be absolutely sure that we are justified, I question hanging as a solution to crime. And even so I like to give people the opportunity to repent because people do change. I believe very, very passionately in the opportunity to repent. I can't afford not to have the opportunity and don't want to refuse it to anybody else. As far as hanging people is concerned, many mistakes have been made through British law. If you put somebody in prison and you discover afterwards that they were not guilty, that is bad enough; you could never give them back those years and the damage you've done them. But if you hang them, there is nothing at all you can do. If God were the judge, all right; He doesn't make mistakes but we do. Therefore, we can't afford to do something irreparable.

DCC: Would you feel that way if your mother or father had been the victim of a murder?

AP: I don't know but I hope so. The fact that a person is my mother or father doesn't make them any more valuable than if they were somebody else's mother or father or nobody's mother or father. A wound to me is not more serious than a wound to anybody else.

DCC: Don't you think then that revenge is in any way mythically purging or psychologically purging as some people do?

AP: No, it compounds the wound. It may have been Bacon who said, "He who revenges himself upon his enemy is equal, he who forgives him is superior," and I believe that very strongly.

"Vengeance is mine sayeth the Lord, I will repay." If you harbor hatred, you may damage somebody else but you certainly damage yourself. So, no, I don't agree that vengeance is purging. I think you've committed a second wrong against yourself.

DCC: You've written novels that belong to the tradition of murder as *the* inexcusable act and justice as the inevitable end. But in some of your novels the murderer escapes society's kind of justice. Nancy Wingate, who wrote a very good article on characters in detective fiction who have escaped society's retribution, believes that the satisfaction of the traditional mystery story comes *not* from the reader's certainty of the immanence of justice but from his/her certainty of the immanence of truth. It doesn't matter who does the killing, but only that the reader knows who did the crime. In your next novel, *Funeral at Rutland Place,* the reader discovers the murderer, but Charlotte lets the killer go free. Do you agree that detective stories gratify a passion for truth, not a passion for justice?

AP: Yes, I agree. But while I believe that morality is absolute, it is also complex. I think we are becoming much less rigid in our requirements of detective fiction. We used to be very black and white. Killers were always beyond the pale regardless of how harshly they had been provoked and the law always had to catch up with them or they had to be killed or commit suicide or whatever. We're now getting away from the black and white and nearer to the shades of gray. The public will accept that the killer doesn't necessarily have to either shoot him or herself or get carried away in handcuffs to find a satisfactory end. We're getting much subtler as time goes by. And we're beginning to learn that there are an awful lot of other sins that are not necessarily crimes because it isn't practical in law to have them as such. Nevertheless, there are other things which are almost as unpardonable as killing.

DCC: Such as incest or child pornography?

AP: Child pornography, yes, depending upon whether your mind is deranged. Incest, I feel, is a crime of distress and so is pederasty. Usually the people who offend are even more pathetic than the victims.

DCC: You are a Mormon with strong beliefs. Harry Kemelman uses the rubric of detective novels to convey the world of Judaism and his beliefs. Father William Kienzle does the same for Roman Catholicism in his detective stories. How do you incorporate your Mormon faith into your novels if you do?

AP: It's there in my philosophy, in my beliefs, but it's never stated. It's coming through subconsciously. It must be in my characters' standards, their values, their beliefs, their sense of responsibility, and the sense that every human being is a son or daughter of God, that there is no separateness from any person regardless of age, sex, color or whatever. Yes, I am my brother's keeper; there is somebody to whom I am answerable. I'm answerable to God not only for what I do but for what I say and what I think. God is my father. To me, a father is somebody who has absolute standards but who will love me even though he doesn't always approve of me and who in the last extreme will do everything he can to save me.

DCC: I remember that you talked to me about the pragmatism of the Mormon faith. And Charlotte and Thomas are very pragmatic. Could you explain what you mean by that because I thought it was beautiful?

AP: There is a great deal of deep doctrine which does touch on things of God, things of Holiness, but, yes, it's a very practical religion. It teaches you everything that you need to know to make your life more satisfactory, to help you realize your fullest potential. Mormonism teaches, "man is, that he might have joy," which, to me, is a wonderful thought. Everything that is, exists so that it might fulfill the measure of its creation, whatever it is. If it's a bird, it exists so that it might be the best possible bird; if it's a human being, it exists so that it might fulfill every good potential within it. I suppose Mormonism is such an ingrained part of my life, and it should be, that it comes through everything without having to be said.

DCC: And it comes through in Charlotte and Pitt.

AP: I'm delighted. That's the nicest compliment you could possibly pay me.

DCC: Charlotte may be more you, but Thomas, as we said before, has your compassion. Did you choose the Victorian period because the gap between the 'haves' and the 'have nots' is so starkly and painfully emphasized?

AP: Yes, because they are so closely side by side. I do love the dramatic, I must admit. The Victorian period is marvellously picturesque too, isn't it, it's beautifully visual. And the two extremes really rub shoulders in the street. I mean, the Devils Acres is in the shadow of Westminster. It's because they are so closely positioned side by side that the effect is so dramatic.

DCC: One of the things that strikes me about your novels is that

Pitt only explores the upper class, the aristocracy. Why never the lower and middle class?

AP: For a start, the aristocracy is more articulate, therefore, it gives me more scope for generally expressing my feelings and for getting a little bit of humor in. I like the scenery of the beautiful clothes and again, if you are entirely with the less well-off people, you don't get the dichotomy between the two totally different classes. Maybe it's a little bit of wishfulfillment but I identify much more easily with the upper class; I can imagine myself in that situation. We have many really excellent writers in Britain who write of the working class background and its people. I don't feel competent to handle it because I know that I don't understand it although my own grandparents and great-grandparents and great-great-grandparents, certainly on one side, were very ordinary people. I didn't know them, I've not been brought up in that background and I really think I'd probably make a hash of it. I can glimpse it, I hope, but I feel far more comfortable with the other people. It is more fun to get these catty drawing room parties. The upper class people are much more devious whereas the poorer people would be less subtle perhaps; they wouldn't need to mask things, they wouldn't have the leisure with which to develop these abilities and therefore I think it would be less fun to write about.

DCC: Also it allows Pit the opportunity to exercise his psychological perception of people in an age where there was no forensic medicine or other modern tools of investigation.

AP: Added to which again, the sort of motive I deal with is more likely to crop up in the upper classes where they have something to protect. If you are very poor, your motives for murder are not likely to be those of protecting your situation or reputation.

DCC: In *Funeral at Rutland Place,* Charlotte wonders if people who get murdered have some "flaw in them that invites murder.... Like Shakespearean tragic heroes—one fatal deformity of soul that mars all the rest that might have been good." In a way that disturbs me because it means that the victim is responsible for his or her murder.

AP: I'm not thinking of murder for gain or chance victims; I'm thinking of domestic situations where the person who is the victim and the person who is the offender have known each other for a long time and it's the result of a relationship. I believe most murders are domestic. There is very often a flaw or something that has provoked the situation because murder is an awfully extreme way out of anything. In any relationship that is unsatisfactory it's very, very seldom contributed to by only one party. Nearly always both parties contribute to it and that was what Charlotte meant.

DCC: Victorians called them 'bed' murders. What kind of research do you do for your books—newspapers, books on fashion and furniture, history books, books like Kellow Chesney's *The Victorian Underworld?*

AP: Yes, particularly *The Victorian Underworld.* It's a marvellous book. I've got a whole shelf of books at home right from Kellow Chesney up to the High Society. There is a lovely book called, I think but I'm not sure, *The Party That Lasted a Hundred Days* about the London High Society Season. Also I've got two enormous copies of the illustrated *London News* for a couple of years in the 1880s and I go through those as well for the advertisements. I do use the books more. I've always been afraid of over-researching since I've been criticized for it earlier on and stories should be about people. Your research should only prevent you from making mistakes. There's a tremendous temptation when you find research fascinating yourself to cram in every fact you know and kill the story and thereby kill the relationship between people.

DCC: Your novels are complete stories in themselves but they are also linked. There's an evolution. When you wrote *The Cater Street Hangman,* did you have a plan for a series or did it just evolve organically?

AP: It just happened. When I wrote *Cater Street,* I only intended to write one novel. I got rather taken with the idea and I thought this is a lot of fun.

DCC: What did you think you'd write after *Cater Street?*

AP: I was thinking of going back to historicals again. But when *Cater Street* was accepted that was absolutely marvellous. That was the first book I'd ever had accepted. I think it was my agent who said to me, 'Have you thought of doing another one?' Besides I enjoy them.

DCC: How did you think of Charlotte and Pitt?

AP: Occasionally, if you're fortunate, you get a character that does more than you expect just as sometimes you get characters you think are going to be great and they die on you. You realize you've written five chapters and you haven't mentioned them again. Pitt, however, sort of charged in and took over. I hadn't particularly intended him to come to life so much but I think I was a little enamoured of him myself by the time I had finished.

DCC: Many detective novelists such as P.D. James and Friedrich Durrenmatt, believe that the detective and the criminal are mirror images of each other. I don't see that in your books at all.

AP   It isn't there. It's something I've never seen myself. I hadn't even thought of it until I'd heard other people say so.

DCC: Writers like George Bernard Shaw and Colin Wilson have written about the relationship between the artist and the criminal. What do you make of these analogies?

AP: You see, I'm just writing a story; I'm not trying to be as symbolic as that. I'm not being consciously intellectual. Of course, my protagonists have a capacity for evil but one's capacity for evil is pretty much governed by your situation and how tempted you are. Charlotte has a capacity to sometimes be thoughtless as we all are and her evil is usually unintentional, but then a lot of people's evil is unintentional. It's mixed with fear, confusion and stupidity. Charlotte has hurt people along the way, said and done silly things, which after all is the level of evil that most of us reach. Very often if the evil that you do is greater than that it's because the circumstances have compounded to make your actions result in something much more evil.

DCC: In *The Cater Street Hangman*, Charlotte said that when Verity was killed, she had been abrupt with her, sharp with her, and now she was dead and she couldn't make it up to her. We talked a little before about how you create a plot. I believe you said that motive comes first.

AP: The motive and the crime comes first because I believe very strongly, as you probably observed, in making the crime spring from a very strong feeling. I was thinking the other day about the basic motives for crime that I find satisfactory—fear is one of the strongest, not necessarily physical fear but fear of losing something that is desperately important to you such as reputation, prestige, or status. Also hatred, if you've been offended against so desperately that you simply cannot bear it. Anger must be a red hot thing or else outrage that somebody is surviving and is going to continue to do something so monstrous and there is no way within the law that you can prevent them. Greed is a motive but there are times when it's a satisfactory one. I don't like the motive that hinges on inheriting money, I would rather it be the capacity to make more money and somebody stands between you and it. I think I've used that once or twice. I don't like cold-blooded motives; I like people to be driven into corners because then you can identify with them. I view crime as a tragedy, not as an intellectual exercise.

DCC: What do you mean?

AP: I suppose here you come back to the Mormon philosophy. Mormon philosophy teaches that the whole of life is progress and every good thing you do increases your spiritual growth while every evil thing you do or opportunity for the good lost, sets you back a step. Although you may well offend against others and you may offend against God, the greatest offense is against yourself because you have diminished what you might have been. If you commit an offense of any sort, the person who suffers irreparably is yourself because it is your soul that you have damaged. Therefore, any crime is a tragedy most of all for the person who commits it; of course, it's tragedy for the person against whom it is committed but that may be reparable if not in this world perhaps in the next. As the offender, you can never be as if you hadn't done it; you may repent, you may learn from it, and you may forgive yourself, and certainly if you repent the Lord will forgive you, but the real damage you've done is to yourself.

DC: Anne, why do you write?

AP: I love to, I have to, it's necessary to me. The other day somebody said to me, 'you shouldn't write so much, you are turning out too much,' and I spoke to my agent Nancy, and said, 'I don't know that I can help it.' Her reply: "you can't write less, it's like telling the birds not to sing."

DCC: As Carlos Fuentes has said, a story is like something burning in your hand. You must let it go. You told me that this is the first interview that you've ever done. Some writers like V.S. Naipaul think that interviews are wounding, they take a part of you away. Other writers like the Nobel Prize winner Saul Bellow says that interviews are like a thumb-print on his windpipe, yet the great poet and novelist James Dickey thinks that interviews are a great art form of our time. Do you find interviews both enjoyable and/or useful as both a writer and a reader?

AP: I would have said that an interview by a good interviewer, such as yourself, is a mirror and therefore it is very useful indeed. It will hopefully show you your best side and perhaps some of the flaws because if you don't see the flaws you can't do anything about them.

I find it enjoyable and extremely useful as a writer. I enjoy reading good interviews; if the creative process and the thought process and the beliefs of the writers are gone into, it gives an added dimension to their work. If I don't learn from this interview, I'm stupid.

DCC: Finally, are you comfortable with physical and/or psychological violence? Why do you think you write physical violence so well?

AP: I find physical violence relatively easy to write even if it distresses me horribly when I read it back. I don't know. It's something I haven't resolved. It's a dark side of me that I don't understand yet.

Interview with Dick Francis

Diana Cooper-Clark

DCC: The novelist, V.S. Naipaul, dislikes detective novels because he thinks they are merely puzzles. He feels they are for people other than himself. Clearly, he hasn't been reading detective novels lately because that's not true. He says that he agrees with Edmund Wilson that he doesn't care, "Who killed Roger Ackroyd." How would you respond to people who have this attitude toward the detective novel?

DF: They are wrong in thinking that way. Detective novels written by people like Desmond Bagley, Gavin Lyall and many others, depict life as it is led. I know they probably painted life a little bit red, but never mind, I like the stories not because they're so much detective novels but because they are adventure stories. I love to read about different things. Gavin Lyall writes about flying aeroplanes, a subject which I know a little about but I've learned a lot from him. Desmond Bagley's book called *Snow Tiger,* was about the mountains and the snow in New Zealand. I learned a lot about the island of New Zealand from that book and I thoroughly enjoyed it. My own books are called detective novels. I think that's wrong. I like to call them adventure stories but I usually have a main character who has to fight his way out of tight corners and this main character is learning things all along. If you remember *Reflex*, the main character learns a lot about the photographic world. He did know a little about it because he was brought up with photographers as a young child and then he had a lot to do with photographers, but within the context of the story, a certain man was killed and left his equipment to the main character. He then started experimenting and he learned so much. I'm hoping that people who read my books learn equally well. Another book I wrote, *Risk*, was about accountancy, and then *High Stakes* was about a chap who knew nothing about horses really but owned them. He also manufactured childrens' toys and I hope that my readers learn a little bit about both owning horses as novices and a little about toys from what I write about.

DCC: The puzzle is secondary?

DF: I think so.

DF: You mentioned that you see your novels more as adventure stories than mysteries. Julian Symons also said that he thought that you wrote adventure stories more so than mysteries. What would be the essential difference between the two?

DF: Mysteries are just what they are, mysteries, aren't they? Someone does something and the reader is doing his or her best to find out or solve the mystery as the reader goes along. I suppose there is a mystery in my stories sometimes but I like to think that people are learning something about the world in which the main character lives. In *Forfeit,* Ty Tyrone was a newspaper man. He was a similar sort of newspaper man to what I was at that time. I was working for a Sunday newspaper as was Ty and I tried to get over to the readers what that life was like; you go around interviewing people about their horses which are going to run in big races or about why a certain horse sometimes didn't win these big races. I also brought into that book quite a lot about poliomyelitis. Ty's wife, Elizabeth, had polio. Actually, Mary (my wife) and I know quite a bit about that because Mary had polio, thirty years ago now, and Mary's made a wonderful recovery which you've probably noticed. She's walking round alright, although her chest isn't very good in the cold weather. We've kept in touch with a lot of polio victims since those days and I try to get over to my readers the trials and tribulations of someone who suffered from the complaint. It seemed to go down alright because it was the book I got the Edgar Allan Poe award for in America. Lots of people loved that book, not only because of Ty's struggles carrying Elizabeth up and down the stairs and into the car, but also because they learned a lot about the newspaper world from this.

DCC: Perhaps "adventure" is as much a misnomer in many ways as "detective" novels because you are writing about people's daily lives, their tribulations, and the process of living that all novelists experience. Do you think that the categorization of novels into genres is a waste of time?

DF: I think so. I never liked the word 'genre' because it means that you're so directed up a certain channel or along certain lines and I try not to follow those lines. I branch out into all different ideas and different lines really. In my novel, *Nerve,* Rob Finn was determined to find out why the television and radio commentator went out of his way to talk people into losing their nerve. It was because he had lost his nerve and he felt jealous of those jockeys who'd made the grade, so he was determined to cool them down.

DCC: Somerset Maugham believed that "when the historians of literature come to discourse upon the fiction produced by the English-speaking people in the first half of the twentieth century, they will pass somewhat lightly over the compositions of the 'serious' novelists and turn their attention to the immense and varied achievement of the detective writers." That may be taking it a little too far but do you think that this is true?

DF: Oh, I think what you were saying is true. The crime novelist or adventure novelist does get to the readers because they're all stories in which you don't have to be thinking hard all the time. They're enjoyable to read and you can read them if you go to work everyday. You can read them on the train or you come home in the evening and the television is terrible so you go to bed and read, or sit up and read. The good novelist writes such that the reader imagines himself playing the part of the main character. And they picture themselves doing it and that's what they like, they think, "Ah, I could do that." I know myself when I write, I never ask any of my characters to do anything I wouldn't be prepared to do myself and a lot of them are doing things which I have done myself a long time ago, especially the ones who are riding.

DCC: G.K. Chesterton claimed that the detective story was "the earliest and only form of popular literautre in which is expressed some sense of the poetry of modern life." Is there something about the nature of detective literature that allows the writer to capture that sense of modern living? I think you capture that sense too.

DF: That's difficult. I think Chesterton is quite right there but I can't comment on it. I write because I enjoy writing. I want people to enjoy what I'm writing and I try to write so that they keep wanting to turn the pages over. I get no end of letters from people, "Oh, I've had a very restless night last night, I read your book all the way through, I couldn't put it down and I kept on till four o'clock in the morning," and then other readers say, "I read your book in 2½ to 3 hours" and in all the months it's taken me to write that book, it's gone in that short time. But it's a great thing for me, in a way, to hear it because it means they've been turning over those pages, can't wait to get to the end, and they can't put it down. I'm not a fast reader. If I'm reading a book and I like a certain passage, I go back and read that passage again. But a lot of people read my books quickly and it's a great compliment when they do.

DCC: Ross Macdonald wrote something that I think is very interesting. He said that "detective novels differ from some other kinds of novel, in having to have a rather hard structure built in logical coherence. But the structure will fail to satisfy the mind, writer's or reader's, unless the logic of imagination, tempered by feelings and rooted in the unconscious, is tied to it, often subverting it." Does the best detective novel subvert that logical structure? Should it be tied to feelings and the unconscious to make it a more esthetically satisfying experience?

DF: I suppose so, yes. I'm probably not one who paints my novels in that way. Mine have a little bit more action about them but when one does read a book like that, one can appreciate the time spent on getting those things over to the reader. All the exciting episodes in my stories come from the action episodes, when the main character's in a certain situation and he's got to get himself out of it. I do appreciate what we were talking about just now, the subversive side of it, yes.

DCC: You subvert the logic and the order?

DF: But probably I don't do that quite as much as some of them do.

DCC: In your autobiography, *The Sport of Queens,* you wrote that writing a novel proved to be the hardest, most *self-analyzing* task that you had ever attempted. We were just talking about Ross Macdonald and I think that he is one example of someone who has done a lot of this in his work. How is this self-analysis reflected in your novels?

DF: In most of my novels, the main character is either a horseman or someone very closely connected to the horse world. Most of the things I write about are with a horse background. I know the horse world pretty well, I've been in it some years and there are not many mistakes I make when I'm writing about that but then I write about other things. I write about photography, I write about flying, I write about accountancy and I write about televison interviewers. Well, those are the things which take up the most time, doing the research for those other things. I did it and my wife does it. I do hate to read any book, whether it's a horse book or flying book or a book about life in general, if there are mistakes. I am a stickler for accuracy when I'm writing and I do the research so thoroughly that I hope that when these books are read the reader can't find any mistakes.

DCC: Maybe, then, I didn't understand. When you said 'self-analyzing task,' I thought you meant your own psyche but you mean analyzing in terms of the subject. You see, self-analysis in North American jargon means the probing of your psyche.

DF: No, it's analyzing the subject which I'm writing about.

DCC: In a time when a number of mainstream novelists, such as John Cheever, Margaret Atwood and John Irving, all assiduously disavow any autobiographical relationship to their characters or that they speak for them, several detective novelists claim the opposite. Ruth Rendell, Jean Stubbs, Ross Macdonald, Janwillem van de Wetering, are just a few who acknowledge their detectives as alter-egos. Are your protagonists, in one form or other, reflections of yourself? Outside of the racing expertise?

DF: Yes, I think they are because all my stories are written in the first-person. The one I am working on at the moment, *Twice Shy*, is different. It's going to be written in two halves by two brothers and each brother is writing each half in the first-person. One is very much like my own family. One is a schoolmaster and my youngest boy's a schoolmaster, and the other one is a jockey, well, my eldest boy isn't a jockey but he did ride and he's a trainer now. I don't know how it will go down yet. I was going to write it in three parts and that's how I started off. I thought now I have three brothers all with a decade in between them, there's ten years between each brother. I told my publisher in London, Mrs. Michael Joseph, who unfortunately died about three weeks ago, very sad, but I told her that I was going to call it *Tom, Dick and Harry* and she said "yes, we'll use it, but I don't like that title." Well, after that, I sort of lost my enthusiasm a little bit and then the next meeting we had, I said "no, I think it's going to be too big a book, I'm going to do it in two halves. I don't think I could call it *Tom, Dick and Harry.*" And she suddenly came out with it straight away, "why don't you call it *Twice Shy?*"

DCC: And will the two brothers be reflections of you or your sons?

DF: They will be reflections of me, I think. But my younger son has already been a great help. He teaches physics, you see, and has quite a lot to do with computers and there is a computer coming into this story. In fact, I've bought a computer since I've been here. My wife and I have been working on it but we're getting away from some of the questions you were asking me, right?

DCC: A bit. To continue with this notion of 'self.' It has been suggested that one of the characteristics of a Dick Francis hero is the ability to transcend his physical limitations and to push himself beyond accepted boundaries of pain and endurance. Sid Halley is an obvious example. In *Odds Against,* Sid says, "Always from my earliest childhood, I had instinctively shied away from too much sympathy. I didn't want it. I distrusted it. It made me soft inside." Again, Sid, in *Whip Hand,* even though his character has evolved considerably from *Odds Against,* still embodies these characteristics. Are these qualities necessary for survival?

DF: I don't know whether they're necessary but they're a great help. Yes, I think probably my characters do push themselves. Life in the racing world, as a jockey, is a hard life, you know. You don't have only the race to complete and jumps to get over safely and to the winning post, you hope, but there are lots of other obstacles that stand in your way. You've only got to do something slightly wrong and the owners and trainers of that particular horse will say, "I don't think he rode that quite as well. We must get someone else." And you're all the time trying to prove your ability because you get no sympathy if you make a mistake. If you get hurt you get sympathy, but you get no sympathy if you make a mistake. No sympathy at all and you're all the time fighting against that. Also most of my main characters have got some other cross to bear, they've got a crippled wife or they've got a child which isn't quite the 'round penny,' as you might say. In *Knock Down,* the hero had a brother who was alcoholic. I try to give my main characters a cross to bear because I don't consider myself first and foremost a novelist. I've written twenty books but I find that giving them a cross to bear and writing about this cross or their other handicaps does help me to fill up the pages. It gets me from page 1 to page 250 or 300, but if I had to write like some of the other novelists who don't write about crimes, I don't think I could fill the book up.

DCC: Really? You are too modest. Your characters have often suffered wounds whether they are physical or psychological or both which they must endure. You've mentioned several of them; also there is Kelly Hughes, in *Enquiry,* whose wife is killed, Sid Halley's hand is crippled in a terrible accident, and many more. It's interesting to me that critics and scholars have assumed that the various afflictions and wounds that you give your characters have some deeper meaning, whereas, in fact, you've just said it's for very practical reasons.

DF: Yes, I think so. Also, I have tried at times to paint the problems that these injuries have upon a character. Jonah Dereham, in *Knock Down* had a recurring dislocated shoulder. Well, I've got a recurring dislocated shoulder and there is nothing more painful. I've broken a lot of bones but nothing has been as painful as when you have your shoulder out. It is agony, absolutely agony. My right one used to do it and when I was a jockey, I had that operated on, but it wasn't a very nice operation, I can tell you. It was very nasty and then in the later years of my riding the left one started dislocating and I didn't have that operated on because my days as a jockey were getting shorter. It's not necessary now because I usually have a pen and not a whip in my hand but I still put the shoulder out if I'm riding a horse now. I always ride with a strap on. If I have a fall or sometimes I'm trying to put on a damp mackintosh and if I shrug my shoulders, it'll go out, or it'll go out at night in bed if I'm asleep. So I always go to bed with my arm strapped in.

DCC: But what about the psychic pain because that's very real too in your books? Even though Sid is reduced to fear and a temporary loss of courage by Trevor Deansgate in *Whip Hand*, his stoicism does win out. Deansgate can't break him a second time and the last line of the book is his bitter question to Sid, "Isn't there anything that you're afraid of?" Why is it so important to *not* show fear and vulnerability to people, even those closest to him like Chico, Charles or Jenny? This is one of the reasons why Sid lost Jenny.

DF: It would go against the grain to show it. I'd hate to show fear myself for those things I write about. Mind you, I've got fear if a snake crawled into this room. That would frighten me but then I don't think there are many other things which should frighten me.

DCC: Don't you think that sometimes it's a form of creating a bond with people? Jenny tells Sid that he never ever lets her know when he needs her. Weakness can also be a greatness, in one sense.

DF: Yes, I suppose so, but Sid wouldn't show fear at all, would he? And that was his failing, I suppose. But that was how I drew him and I wasn't going to change him as I went along.

DCC: Why do you seldom use professional detectives but rather amateurs like Alan York in *Dead Cert?*

DF: I've got more respect for the amateur detective in real life than I have for the professional detective. The professional detective is tied to so many things which the establishment forces upon him. They never have the opportunity of showing their individuality. When they do try to show it, they are stamped upon and that's why the sort of chaps I write about are not detectives but they're investigators in their own right, aren't they? One professional investigator I had was Dave Cleveland, in *Slay-Ride,* who was the jockey club investigator who was asked to go to Norway. That is the only professional investigator that I think I've had. Sid becomes one in *Whip Hand* but he's sort of drifting that way in *Odds Against,* but it is forced upon him really.

DCC: Why have you never sustained one character throughout your novels? I don't agree with him but Otto Penzler has suggested that if the protagonists are not carried through, they are forgettable.

DF: Again, I don't consider myself a full-blown novelist and I think painting the character of the main character, does help me to fill the book up in the same way that drawing the cross that the main character has to bear does help me to fill the book up. This comes from my life as a *Sunday Express* newspaper man. If I put in an article, as I did to them every week, and there were one or two words in it which were unnecessary, the sub-editor would cross those out and it used to hurt me a lot when these words were cut out. By the end, hardly any words were cut out and therefore my books, I hope, are along those lines. There are very few wasted words in my books. They're all written for the story which I'm writing about. In fact, *Reader's Digest* published *Nerve* and it was their task to condense it, to take out all that which wasn't necessary. The girl who did it said that she had the hardest task ever condensing my books. There was nothing they could take out.

DCC: Inevitably, in a discussion of this kind, the question of good and evil arises. Good and evil seem to be more distinctly delineated in your novels than in those of many other contemporary detective novelists, such as P.D. James, Patricia Highsmith, Jean Stubbs. Elliot L. Gilbert observed that as early as Dickens's *Bleak House,* "Inspector Bucket is as much the creature of crime as he is its nemesis.... Bucket...succeeds in avenging the inhumanity of murder only by coldly perverting the human obligations of friendship and sympathy." Your protagonists, however, are persevering individualists, fighting against a universe that seems determined to reward evil and penalize good. The moral triumph is definite and much less ambiguous in your books than in many other contemporary writers.

DF: Yes, 'right' must come out in the end in my stories. In *Reflex,* the main character, Philip Nore, did something which none of my main characters had done before, he threw races, didn't he? None of my main characters have done anything like that but Philip Nore came out alright in the end. Also the photographer who had got killed was blackmailing but the proceeds from his blackmailing went toward the injured jockey's fund which I thought was alright. I do like 'right' to score.

DCC: Julian Symons has said that, "the detective story reduces the unruly shape of life to an ideal order." Marjorie Nicholson has added that, "The detective story is a revolt...from a smart and easy pessimism, which interprets men and the universe in terms of unmoral purposelessness, to a re-belief in a universe governed by cause and effect." Do you think that this is what your novels do?

DF: No, I don't think they do.

DCC: You've said right always does triumph but we know that in real life that is not always the case.

DF: Right does triumph in the end but right doesn't reign supreme all along. In *Reflex,* George Millace's blackmail was immoral order being restored.

DCC: Many writers have discussed the criminal as a mirror image, a double figure, to the detective. I'm sure you've heard that theory. Oedipus functions simultaneously as criminal and detective, hunter and hunted. I don't see that connection in your novels. Your detectives are quite distinct from the criminals.

DF: That is one of the reasons why I don't write about professional detectives or professional investigators because those professionals whom I know have minds very much like criminals, I find. I don't want my main characters to have a criminal mind because I'm writing in the first-person and I'm getting *my* feelings over to the reader as much as the main character. I haven't got any criminal leanings at all, I don't think.

DCC: I don't mean to imply that any of these other writers do. (both laugh) Eric Hobsbawm, a scholar, asserted that: "Modern civilization leaves blurred what is criminal, and hence our own picture is complicated by the relation between crime and social revolt." Again, I don't think your novels make this connection. That which is criminal is very clear.

DF: Yes, I can't recall any of my books which have any guns flying here, flying there. They are crimes against civilization more than against individuals. When I started *Enquiry*, the accused at *Jockey Club Enquiries* weren't allowed to be legally represented. Well, they were owners, trainers, jockeys. They were drawn up before the stewards and they had to answer their own defense in their own words, and it must be hell to be accused and stand there and try and explain your own feelings and reasons for doing this and doing that and it was. Well, it was because I was making so many enquiries and they knew what I was writing that the Jockey Club brought in a condition whereby the accused could be represented. Since that day, if an individual is called up in front of the stewards, they can be legally represented and I do think my book did a bit of good in that way. In all my stories, I have a moral duty to civilization. I try to improve the life of the main characters or of the people I'm writing about. I do try to write with a moral scene running through.

DCC: I wouldn't think then that you'd like Andre Gide's statement that he found Dashiell Hammett the best American writer because Hammett "never corrupted his art with morality."

DF: Yes, that's very well put. But I don't think I would agree.

DCC: You were talking about the fact that you don't have guns flying about in your books. But you are probably aware that some people have raised the point that your books have a degree of sadomasochism in them, and I'll give you some examples. Jacques Barzun and Wendell Hertig Taylor in *A Catalogue of Crime* stated that *"Nerve* and *Forfeit* abundantly show the infliction of pain here deprecated,"* and they started the piece by putting, "Note for masochists." Also in their note about *Flying Finish,* they say, "One of his (Francis's) good ones—that is, with the sadism kept to a minimum." Richard Freedman wrote about the "purgative sadism" in *Bonecrack,* whatever he means by that. Barry Bauska also felt that the sadism of the villain's revenge is especially prominent in your earlier books like *Nerve, Odds Against, Flying Finish.* What do you make of those responses?

DF: People write that my books are sadistic, but I don't know, I don't think they are all that much. It's life, you know. If you're in a competitive world, you've got to be positive in your movements and you've got to go to a few degrees to stop people beating you. You've got to beat them down in one way or another and I may write about it in rather severe terms but if you're not beating your opponent down physically, you're beating him down mentally. It's a difficult question to answer, I'm afraid.

DCC: Mickey Spillane, who has been attacked by many people for the gratuitous violence in his books, has recently said: "I have trouble writing about violence now. I just don't have that old antagonism anymore." The violence in your books doesn't seem to come from the antagonism that he felt within himself. The violence in your books comes from....

DF: From life in general.

DCC: Another thing that I find interesting in your books is the notion of living life on the edge. Alan York talks about the need for excitement, one can't be too secure; he says in *Dead cert*, "The speed of racing, the quick decision, the risks, these were what I badly needed to counteract the safeties of civilization. One can be too secure." And, of course, in *Whip Hand*, Jenny accuses Sid: "You can't live without danger, Sid. You're addicted." Do you think that life should be lived on the edge or do we live on the edge without wanting to?

DF: People in my world do, very much so. In the racing world, they live on the edge all the time, jockeys because of danger, and because one day you might be on top of the world, the next day you're laying out on a stretcher. Trainers, because they might be training lots of winners, then suddenly they get the virus in their stable and no horse can possibly win a race. People in the racing world are living on the edge all the time, and I've tried to portray this.

DCC: But I find as an interesting counterpoint to that your attraction to characters who are ordinary people. They have no particular flamboyance or flair, they are not larger-than-life heroes. In *Blood Sport*, Gene Hawkins says right away, "I look ordinary." In *Rat Race*, Matt Shore describes himself as being "as negative as wallpaper." In *Flying Finish*, Henry Grey describes himself: "A repressed, quiet, 'good' little boy I had been: and a quiet, withdrawn secretive man I had become. I was almost pathologically tidy and methodical, early for every appointment, controlled alike in behavior, handwriting and sex." In *Slay-Ride*, David Cleveland is also a seemingly forgettable person. In *Whip Hand*, Jenny tells Sid that, "I want... an ordinary man."

DF: It's difficult to keep explaining and portraying your own character in a book, isn't it? I don't want them to be autobiographical but a lot of them are inclined to be. I write about my own life and the world in which I live. It's difficult to write about a character who probably doesn't think the same way as I do but one has got to write about characters who don't think like I do, and it is difficult doing it.

DCC: In *Bonecrack*, you explore the nature of relationships between fathers and sons. In that novel you have three sets of fathers and sons, and some theorizing about Henry VIII's obsessive quest for male offspring. In *The Sport of Queens,* you write about your close relationship with your father. In *Odds Against*, Sid is the illegitimate child and his father is dead, but his father-in-law, Charles, is a surrogate father figure. Are you drawn to fathers and sons for any particular reason? Scholars love to pick up on things like this and I'd rather have you tell us whether we are heading down the proverbial garden path.

DF: No, I'm not drawn to father figures. In fact, I don't really like father figures but I do like elderly men who are modern in the way that they think. I don't like to talk to elderly men when all they can talk about is, "what life was like in my young days." I like elderly men to move with the times and if they do move with the times and they have got those years over their shoulders, they are very fine, good people to talk to.

DCC: The importance of doing something for the love of it, and not for money, is important in your writing too. In your autobiography, amateur steeplechase jockeys, like Lord Mildmay, rode for the love of the chase, not money. Presumably this is also important for your detectives. What is it that they must love?

DF: They love the competition and the *esprit de corps* which reign in the changing room at the racecourse. When people like Lord Mildmay were changing next to a little miner lad, the lad would probably respect Lord Mildmay but he would talk to him just like he would talk to someone in his own way of life, his own class, and Lord Mildmay would talk to him just like he was another Lord. Unfortunately, nowadays, the outsiders can't go in there. When I was a jockey, trainers could come in and sit down and talk to you when you were changing and maybe one or two owners as well, but no one's allowed in there now, except the jockey and the valets. And it's probably better because when one races at places like Aintree and Haydock Park which were the nearest places to Ireland, the waiting rooms were full of Irishmen. You couldn't hear yourself talk for "Be Jaysus" this and "Be Jaysus" that, going on. I think the present day jockeys miss the comradeship which was in the changing room when I was riding.

DCC: Novelists like Julian Symons and Ross Macdonald have written critically about the detective genre. Is there any reason why you have never responded critically?

DF: No, I don't wish to fall into that field at all. I don't think I've got any reason. I think a person who writes a novel or is earning his living from writing novels, which I am doing now, shouldn't criticize other people because you are there to be shot at yourself and if you've written one or two unkind words, I think these people are probably going to have a go at you too.

DCC: I don't mean critical in the negative sense. I mean critical in the sense of scholarship. You know Julian Symons' book *Bloody Murder* which was a look at the history and philosophy of the detective genre as Ross Macdonald has looked at it.

DF: Oh, I see. The only time I appeared in print in any newspapers was when I was writing about the racing scene all the time and I said what I'd liked and what I'd disliked in that, but I don't think I was too critical of my jockeys with whom I used to ride or trainers who I used to ride for. Because I wrote along those lines, I was made very much more welcome.

DCC: I take it from what you're saying that you are not really interested in reading academic, critical books about the novels that you're writing.

DF: No. I'm not a well-read person, I suppose. I don't read nearly enough books.

DCC: Would you like to?

DF: I haven't got the time.

DCC: No, you're writing them, that's why. (Both laugh.) Some of these critical theories are quite fascinating. I won't go into all the academic words like formalism and hermeneutics, they're too terrifying if you don't know anything about them and more so if you do. Nicholas Blake wrote: "Anthropologists in the next century will call attention to the pattern of the detective novel as highly formalized as that of a religious ritual with its initial necessary sin, the murder, its victim, its high priest, the criminal, who must in turn be destroyed by yet a higher power, the detective. He will conjecture and write with the devotee, identified both with the detective and the murderer, representing the light and dark sides of his own nature." That's one response. There are other scholars who explore the idea of the detective novel as fairy tale and myth. One scholar, Nadya Aisenburg, wrote that "The crime novel must accomplish for the adult what the fairy tale does for the child; it is a method of expressing and perhaps thereby banishing universal, libidinal and perennial fears and guilts." Do you think there's any point in responding to detective novels in these ways?

DF: I suppose the people who are writing about it and reading it think it is, but I don't, no.

DCC: From your point of view, you're not interested in searching for these profound connections and you don't necessarily want your novels read that way?

DF: No, I don't think so. I want people to read them and enjoy the story. I don't write them to get a message across. I write them for someone to pick up and have a good "yarn." I do think that's why a lot of readers are waiting for my next novel to come out. It shows that they enjoy my stories that way, that they're not being blinded by science.

DCC: But on the other hand, don't you think that the criteria by which we judge a good or great novel is also that it can be reread over and over again and deeper meaning is one of the reasons that the good story works so well? There are so many different things going on, it's not just a one-dimensional good "yarn."

DF: True. Although I say I like people to read my novels as a good yarn, I get a tremendous lot of letters from men and women who keep saying to me, "Whenever I want a good cheering up, I read one of your books again." It's a great thing when people read them and read them. It's a wonderful feeling, but I can't appreciate that—they must know what the story is!

DCC: You obviously have that great quality of appealing both to people who are not necessarily very well educated or great readers as well as to university professors and other writers. For instance, Amanda Cross, who is really Carolyn Heilbrun, is a professor of English at Columbia. She told me that you are one of her favorite authors. You have that eternal quality that all great story tellers have. You appeal to a whole spectrum of people.

DF: Yes, I like to think I do. I can't really explain why.

DCC: I'm astonished to hear you say that you don't think of yourself as a novelist.

DF: I still think of myself as a horseman.

DCC: Well, I see tremendous changes and growth as a writer. In your earlier books, the confrontations of good and evil were much more simplified than they are in your later novels. Also, the writing is better. Your sentences are surer, you have greater descriptive powers, the characterization becomes more and more complex and very interesting, the dialogue rings truer.

DF: No doubt my writing has improved because, well, the books wouldn't keep on selling if they hadn't, would they? And Mary often says to me (I worry a lot about the writing), "Well, you've only got to write one like you wrote the last and it'll do." "Well," I said, "no, I don't want to write one like I wrote the last. I want to improve on the last, providing I can go on improving, that's all I want." Touch wood, none of the books have been slayed by the critics. I've got a number of friends who are critics and they all say that they can't keep on saying, "This is the best Dick Francis." And it's music to one's ears. I don't want *Twice Shy* to be as good as *Reflex*. I want it to be better. And it's hard to achieve.

DCC: You have the heart of an artist, as well as a great jockey. In Anthony Boucher's review of *Nerve*, he wrote: "The author constructs his suspense so skillfully, builds his characters so firmly and, in short, writes so well that one's reaction is not, 'How can a great jockey write such a good novel?' but rather, 'How can such an excellent novelist know so much about steeplechasing?' "

DF: I find writing very hard work because it doesn't come easily to me, like riding or walking down the street. I have to think about every word and there is my number one critic, my editor (points to wife, Mary). She has been a great help. She has a university degree in French and she's read English as a subsidiary subject and anytime I'm lost for a word, I say to Mary, "Can you find words to suit the situation?" We discuss the plots, we write as a team really.

DCC: Why isn't her name on any of the books?

DF: Her name is on her own books, but she says the stories are not hers. Mary is where I get my English literature from. She reads my work after I've done it and she says, "Well, this would be much better if you put it round the other way.'